Sound for Picture

Film Sound Through the 1990s

2nd Edition

by Tom Kenny

236 Georgia Street, Suite 100
Vallejo, CA 94590

Library of Congress Catalog Card Number: 99-62535

Cover Design: Linda Gough
Book Design and Layout: Linda Gough
Publisher: Mike Lawson

MixBooks is an imprint of artistpro.com, LLC
236 Georgia Street, Suite 100
Vallejo, CA 94590
707-554-1935

Also from MixBooks

The AudioPro Home Recording Course, Volumes I, II and III
I Hate the Man Who Runs this Bar!
How to Make Money Scoring Soundtracks and Jingles
The Art of Mixing: A Visual Guide to Recording, Engineering, and Production
500 Songwriting Ideas (For Brave and Passionate People)
Music Publishing: The Real Road to Music Business Success, Rev. and Exp. 4th Ed.
How to Run a Recording Session
Mix Reference Disc, Deluxe Ed.
The Songwriters Guide to Collaboration, Rev. and Exp. 2nd Ed.
Critical Listening and Auditory Perception
Modular Digital Multitracks: The Power User's Guide Rev. Ed.
The Dictionary of Music Business Terms
Professional Microphone Techniques
Sound for Picture 2nd Ed.
Music Producers 2nd Ed.
Live Sound Reinforcement

Also from EMBooks

The Independent Working Musician
Making the Ultimate Demo 2nd Ed.
Making Music With Your Computer 2nd Ed.
Anatomy of a Home Studio
The EM Guide to the Roland VS-880

Printed in Auburn Hills, MI
ISBN 0-87288-724-3

Contents

v   Introduction

1   An Interview With Walter Murch

16   The Doors

26   Terminator 2: Judgment Day

35   Beauty and the Beast

44   Malcolm X

56   Jurassic Park

67   The Wrong Trousers

73   Star Trek: Generations

84   Batman Forever

95   Casino

103   Twister

116   The English Patient

128   The Lost Highway

139   Titanic

151   Snake Eyes

158   The Thin Red Line

172   Austin Powers 2: The Spy Who Shagged Me

182   Yellow Submarine

193   The Green Mile

208   Glossary of Terms

239   Appendix: Academy Award® Winners for Best Sound and Best Sound Effects Editing

Introduction

In early 1991, I was an associate editor at *Mix*, sitting at my desk, when I got a call from the late Paul Rothchild. He said, or rather screamed, from his car phone, "I hear *Mix* is doing a story on The Doors movie!"

"That's right," I answered, knowing just enough to know that he was the Doors' producer.

"And I hear you talked to Tod Maitland!" he yelled over traffic, referring to the production sound mixer on the film.

"Yes," I said. "I just finished editing it."

"Well you're missing the whole #%*@!&* story!" he screamed. "This is a 2 hour and 10 minute movie, and it's got 2 hours and 4 minutes of music! Doors music! From the original 4-tracks! That's the story!"

He was right. I stumbled as best I could and said, "What do you suggest we do, Mr. Rothchild?"

"I suggest you get a writer down here to Hollywood and I'll give you the story," he fired back. "I'll get the team together for you."

So I took down numbers for his car phone, home phone, work phone and office fax and promised to get right back to him. I ran upstairs into *Mix* co-founder and then-editor-in-chief David Schwartz's office and told him about the phone call. He didn't miss a beat and, to my eternal gratitude, said, "You want to go down and do it?"

Three days later, after a crash course in film sound from editor George Petersen and an overnight read of *Audio for Media*, I was on a plane to Los Angeles. I remember that it was pouring rain as I hcadcd into the Hollywood Hills, and the hotel staff had warned me about mudslides.

When I arrived at Rothchild's home, there at the table were Rothchild, Doors engineer Bruce Botnick, lead re-recording mixer Mike Minkler, supervising sound editor Wylie Stateman and Synclavier hitman Tim Claman. I didn't realize then how many Oscars and Grammys were in the room, and in retrospect, I'm glad that I didn't. But that group of five provided my real introduction to film sound. And they taught me about the passion some people can have for their art.

Still, that original Rothchild statement—"You're missing the whole story"—haunted me. Each film tells a story, and each film sound job has its own tale. For *The Doors*, it *was* about the music, while for *The Green Mile*, the "news" was in the location-based Foley. Sometimes the sound story is obvious: For *Jurassic Park*, you can't ignore the dinosaur vocals, and for *Titanic*, you must eventually address the iceberg. Sometimes it's subtle: In *Malcolm X*, there is tremendous voice-over and narration work; and in the *Thin Red Line*, a war movie, I found that the tracks were all about delicacy. Again, each film tells a story; sound is an integral part of the storytelling process.

A lot of the press in the '90s focused on the technological developments in film sound, and rightly so, because the decade saw the introduction of digital audio workstations and discrete, multichannel playback systems. But technology is merely a tool, and while I hope that the following stories highlight some of the great strides that have been made in making the craft *easier*, I also hope that they convey a sense of the incredible creativity that can be found in a good soundtrack.

We can easily divide the film sound universe into dialog, music and effects, but how those three are balanced, within each scene and within each film, is what the art is all about. The distant bell chime in *The English Patient*, for instance, is every bit as meaningful to the story as the 400 tracks of rushing winds and animal growls that go into *Twister*'s F5 tornado. Sometimes, as any sound designer will tell you, the sweetest sound of all is silence. I lead this book with an interview, not a film, because, quite frankly, nobody speaks more eloquently on the art of film sound than Walter Murch.

Sound for Picture: Film Sound Through the 1990s is a collection of some of the articles I've researched and written over the past decade for *Mix* magazine. I have had the rare privilege to sit in edit suites and dub stages with some of the real giants of the industry, and I would like to thank each and every editor and mixer who has given this journalist a piece of their time and insight into their art. I owe a special debt of thanks to Larry Blake, a sound editor, re-recording mixer and damn good writer, who has kept me honest over the years and provided a rare sense of clarity. Finally, I would like to thank the editors and artists of *Mix*, who have put up with everything from weeks of bad humming of "Break on Through" to my consistently late deadlines. Any errors, you can be sure, are my own.

With the advent of DVD and 5.1-channel playback systems in the home, the time has never been more appropriate to go back and *listen* to classic soundtracks. Use this book as a jumping-off point and learn to *hear* films. No doubt you will find the art.

Tom Kenny

CHAPTER 1

Walter Murch

The Search for Order in Sound and Picture

PHOTO: STEVE JENNINGS

When Walter Murch walked to the stage of the Shrine Auditorium in March 1997 and accepted his second Oscar of the evening for *The English Patient*, most of the billion people watching, even the ardent film fans, probably asked themselves, "Who is this man, and why haven't I heard of him before?" Good questions. His is not a household name, as are his peers and fellow Hollywood emigres Francis Coppola and George Lucas. But his was the rarest double in 69 years of the Academy Awards—Film Editing and Best Sound—and his contribution to the success of that film, and to many others, cannot be overstated.

Among producers and directors he has worked with, Murch is a co-conspirator—a friend who speaks the language of film and inspires confidence at every level of the filmmaking process, from dailies to final release. When he's standing at the Avid, the intensity of the frame is captured in his eyes. When he walks into a dub stage, his soft-spoken, gentle manner permeates the room and lends a sense of calm, a sense that everything will come out all right.

In many ways, his dual role as picture editor and re-recording mixer makes him an informal "director" of post-production. Nobody working today in post-production for major films can claim such an influence on the final product. Murch, in his typical humble, understated style, looks around and wonders why nobody else does it this way; it's just how he's worked since moving north to the San Francisco Bay Area in 1969 to join Coppola and Lucas in the formation of American Zoetrope (*nee* TransAmerica Sprocket Works) and the production of *The Rainpeople*.

This article appeared originally in the April 1998 issue of Mix.

The Rainpeople turned out to have a profound influence on the formation of a Bay Area film industry. Coppola had financing from Warner Bros., and Lucas was fresh off a Warner Bros. scholarship but was disenchanted, as many were, with the Hollywood decline of the mid-1960s. Coppola shot the film on a cross-country jaunt from New York to Nebraska, ending up in a storefront in Oglala for the last six weeks of filming. (Lucas lensed a "making of" documentary along the way.) The film was then edited in Los Angeles and brought to American Zoetrope for the mix.

"George and I had been finalists for the Warner Bros. scholarship in 1967," Murch recalls. "We were going in for our last interview, and we knew that one of us would make it and one of us would not. So we made kind of a blood pact that the one who got it—if something interesting happened as a result—would turn around and help the other guy. George got it, went to Warner Bros. and met Francis Coppola, who was the only other person with a beard making a film on the lot at the time. So Francis and George paired up, and Francis was as aware as anyone of this gradual decline in Hollywood and wanted to make films in a new way—an American version of the European way—so he wrote, got financing, and then directed a film called *The Rainpeople*, starring Shirley Knight and James Caan.

"At the end of shooting, George and Francis looked at each other and realized they had shot this feature film operating out of an old shoe store on the main street of Oglala, and if they could do that, there didn't seem to be any reason they needed to be in Hollywood," he continues. "So they drove from Nebraska back to Los Angeles via San Francisco. While here, they met John Korty, who was making independent films out of Stinson Beach [Marin County], and they thought, 'Well, if he can do it, we can do it.' Shortly after that, I got a call from George saying, 'Do you want to move up north to San Francisco?' So the three of us—George, Francis and myself—and our wives and families loaded up a truck with all this equipment and moved to San Francisco. Actually, it was my wife, Aggie, who drove the truck, while I slept in the passenger seat with our eight-month-old son, exhausted from preparing the tracks for the upcoming mix of *The Rainpeople*."

Lasting Impressions

Mix asked Walter Murch to participate in a film sound version of call-and-response, where we name the film and he says what he remembers from an audio point of view.

The Rainpeople My virgin film. It was the first film that I did sound on, and I did everything— recording, transferring, cutting, mixing. It was a one-man band. Many of the lessons that I was to learn later are present in that film embryonically.

The Godfather My first "Hollywood" film. Taking my personal way of doing things into an industrial environment. The expressionistic use of sound, but integrating it into the reality of the visual.

Godfather II Sheer size. Three hours and 20 minutes. A very broad palette. Lots of dynamics.

American Graffiti Theme and variation of world reverberance. The challenge of having almost two hours of continuous music in the background but making it seem to ebb and flow dramatically with the scenes.

The Conversation Clarity and Density. The first film where I also edited picture.

Apocalypse Now Density and Clarity. My first film in stereo. Striving for authenticity in both the exterior sounds of that war and the interior state of mind of the participants.

Crumb Simplicity.

The English Patient Sound as an emotional guide-track through the complexities of story.

Murch went on to co-write, sound edit and mix *THX-1138* with Lucas, then supervise the sound editing for *The Godfather* for Coppola, then mix *American Graffiti* with Lucas, followed by *The Conversation, Godfather II, Julia* and *Apocalypse Now* (for which he also won an Oscar for Best Sound). He has directed and co-written a film, *Return to Oz*, and has assisted on scripts including *The Black Stallion*. After 30 years in the business, his filmography (see sidebar) is not long, but the films he has worked on have had a profound influence on the shape of American cinema.

Mix sat down with Murch in early January 1998, in the screening theater at the Saul Zaentz Film Center in Berkeley, Calif., as he was preparing to view a friend's film. Despite his pioneering work in the use of automation and nonlinear editing, the conversation had very little to do with technology. His is a mind that centers on art, creativity and the workings of the human brain. In a sense, his lifelong mission has been to find order amid chaos.

Let's begin with a cliché question.
What was your first experience with film that had an influence?

Well, the first thing that struck me forcefully was the invention of the tape recorder and its dissemination as a consumer item, which started to take place in the early '50s. The father of a friend of mine owned one, so I wound up going over to his house endlessly, playing with this recorder. And that passion, which was a kind of delirious drunkenness with what the tape recorder could do—that it could capture an aspect of reality and instantly play that reality back, and that you could then reorder that reality by transposition, and that you could even do layerings of sound—was just intoxicating, and it occupied nearly the whole first half of my teenage years. So, my entry into the world of film is really through sound rather than image.

The moment that the whole idea of filmmaking hit me was when I was 15 and went to see *The Seventh Seal* [by Swedish director Ingmar Bergman]. I'd seen lots of movies before that, of course—the average number of films a kid growing up in New York City would see. But *The Seventh Seal* was the film where I suddenly understood the concept that *somebody made this film,* and that there was a series of decisions that could have been different if someone else had made the film. I really got a sense of a single person's interest and passions through watching that film, which in fact was true. This was Ingmar Bergman, after all.

Then I became interested in architecture and oceanography and art history and French literature, and those were the things I mainly pursued as an undergraduate. It was only later on in my college years that I started to get interested and see the actual possibilities of working in film, which was largely through having spent my junior year in Paris in 1963. This was when the New Wave, the Godard & Truffaut-style of filmmaking was at its peak. I came back buzzing with the idea of film, and then I found out that there were actually schools that you could go to to study film—graduate schools in film, which I found incredible. I applied to a number of them, and I got a scholarship at USC. Strangely enough, it was only when I got to school that I discovered the fact that films needed sound, and that somebody had to record it, and then you had to "cook it," in a sense, in post-production. And I saw immediately that this was exactly what I had been doing ten years earlier.

You occupy a rare position of being a film editor and re-recording mixer. How does your involvement with the picture influence the final soundtrack?

Well, it goes very deep with me. I've been doing this professionally since *The Conversation*, which we started shooting in 1972. But I was doing it previously in film school. It's a combination that appealed to me and appeared to be a natural thing to do at the time, and I've now been doing it so long that it seems second nature to me.

An illustration of one aspect of my approach is that when I'm first putting the images together—creating the first assembly of a film—I turn off all the sound, even for dialog scenes. What that does is focus me more intently on the visuals, because I'm reading them the way a deaf person does—I have to extract meaning, greater meaning, out of them because of a sensory deprivation. But also, paradoxically, I pay more attention to the sound because, although I've turned the speaker off, I'm still "hearing" sound; it's just that I'm hearing the sound in my imagination, the way it might finally be. I'm lip reading the dialog, imagining the music, imagining sound effects, I'm imagining all these other things that, were I to turn the bare production track back on, would all disappear, kind of like fairies frightened away by the voice of an ogre. So, at the very first moment that the film is acquiring its shape, it's already welcoming the influence of the final soundtrack.

It's interesting that when I watched you working on **The English Patient,**
*you said you prefer to mix to a slightly degraded image because you're going to
"fill in" with sound later, which is almost the reverse of what you're saying.*

You're right; it's exactly the opposite of how I begin the process. When you look at a sharp color image, the amount of detail in that image is so great that you really don't need very much sound to complete it, to fill up your perceptual breadbasket, so to speak. So by showing a black-and-white image, or by showing a video color image, or even the digitized Avid output, the image tells you that it's not complete. As a result, you pay more attention to the sound. Because the image is degraded, you tend to demand more of the sound. There's a nice symmetry to that process.

On the other hand, all the months I'm editing picture I'm adding sound little by little. I start out with the sound off—which gives this empty "imaginative" space for sound to move into. It's just the sound in my head at the beginning. Then I add the dialog, then later on key sound effects, and then eventually temp music and then finally the rough versions of the final music. And, of course, you can do mixes on the Avid: You can mix up to eight tracks as you cut the picture. Once you start to actually add the sound and music, it changes how you look at the picture, and the two become synergistically involved.

In **In the Blink of an Eye,** *your book on film editing, you place a high
importance on emotion. Can you talk to me a bit about the emotion of sound?*

I think the image of the eyes facing forward and the ears facing sideways is metaphorically indicative of how we confront visual reality as opposed to aural reality. The visual seems to be direct and confrontational: You look at what's in front of you, and what's in front is seen and apprehended with a measure of intellect and emotion. And it's seen all at once, in a single grasp—let's call that the front door. The visual material knocks on the front door, and when somebody knocks on the front door, you sort of adjust your clothing, go to the door, take a deep breath, say, "Who's there?" and open the door. Whatever meeting occurs will have an element of formality to it, because it's somebody who came to the front door.

"The Conversation"

Walter Murch began working on The Conversation *in the fall of 1972, and when it was released in the spring of 1974, it woke many people up to the power of sound in film—and not just because the main character was a sound recordist. We asked Murch to make sense of the impact of that film.*

It's a film that has an intensely singular point of view. Everything in the film is seen or experienced by Harry Caul [Gene Hackman]. You know he's a soundman, and the film never lets you off the hook, so after a while, you just begin to accept the fact that you, too, are a soundman and you, too, should consider that sound is important.

It interested me when the film came out and people started saying, "Boy, wonderful sound." I liked the sound, but I felt it was no different in approach to work I'd done on other films. I eventually traced it back, not surprisingly, to this subjectivity factor, but also to the fact that halfway through the film, people stop talking. There really is no dialog in the normal sense past the halfway point of the film. There are exclamations occasionally: "Hey, stop!" or, "We know what you're doing, Mr. Caul." Then, of course, the tape of the conversation is played over and over again, accompanied by the natural sounds of the world through which Harry Caul is moving. And I think the human mind is constituted such that when dialog is present, it's like having the full moon in the sky at night. You know the stars are there, but you don't really think about them as much because of the moon. On moonless nights, these smaller lights begin to acquire a fascination and an interest for you that they don't have when the moon is present. So when dialog is absent, and when the human mind is consequently not busy decoding language, it relaxes, and without knowing it, it says, in effect, "Hmm, where am I going to find meaning now that there is no dialog? I have to look for it at some other level." Well, the mind will find it at the level of sound effects because we put meaning there, in the sounds we chose and how we treated them. In other films, that meaning is still there, but the mind is blinded by the presence of dialog. It doesn't mean the sound effects aren't having their effect, though, it's just that it is a more subconscious effect.

Sound tends to come in the back door, or sometimes even sneak in through the windows or through the floorboards. Remember, the ears point out the side of your head and take in a 360° spherical field. And while you're busy answering the front door, sound is sneaking in the back door. It's in the house as much as anyone who came in through the front door, but you're not as aware of it, and so its presence is more of a conditional presence—it tends to condition the things you are consciously aware of. The strange thing is that you take the emotional treatment that sound is giving, and you allow that to actually change how you see the image: You see a different image when it has been emotionally conditioned by the sound. So sometimes you will swear that you actually saw something that never, ever happened on the screen or in the soundtrack, but is the unique combination of the two inside your head.

Also, for some reason that I don't fully understand, I am very emotionally moved by the space around a sound. I almost think that sometimes I am recording space with a sound in it, rather than sound in a space.

Your book also promotes the idea of restraint. Gary Rydstrom on Titanic said he wouldn't know what to do with 100 faders of effects. Could you speak to me about restraint and the number of tracks.

The thing, on a practical level, that terrifies somebody who works in sound is to be in the mix and for the director to say, "Let's eliminate everything except the dog collar." "Uh, we didn't do the dog collar." "Why not? Why didn't you do it?" "Well, because there's a big fight with garbage cans going on over there, and we thought nobody would ever hear the dog collar." "Well, dammit, who are you to say…?" So, the dog collar goes in "just in case," and you multiply that by a hundred and all of a sudden you have a hundred tracks. That's not the way I work. I willingly accept the risk of being humiliated because I don't have the dog collar—for the speed and conceptual clarity of going for the jugular. Now, if the director sees it and over-rules it, that's the director's prerogative.

Having all these tracks is the equivalent of a director of photography going in with a thousand lights for a single set thinking, "Hmm, the director might want flat light; on the other hand, he might want bright key light from the left, but then maybe bright key light from the right, and if we do that we need inkies for the eyes, and we need a wash back there," and all of a sudden you've lit the scene seven or eight different ways. You'd never shoot a film that way! But, strangely, sound is done that way. There's often a tremendous amount of overkill because we don't know what's going to be asked for.

Let's cover it in effects, let's cover it in Foley...

Right. And that was the Zoetrope dream at the beginning—the whole concept of what turned into the sound designer in the Zoetrope sense—which is a director of photography for sound. Somebody who took on the responsibility of "auralizing" the sound for the film and making definitive, creative decisions about it. Someone the director can talk to about the total sound of the film the way he talks to the director of photography about the look of the film. If you could establish this dialog and encourage directors to have a sense of sound that was as acute as their sense of picture, particularly at the script level, a lot of these multiple-track overkill problems would go away.

Yet you have the real luxury of being involved early, whereas the supervisor down in Hollywood is not getting that communication.

That's the other benefit of also being an editor—I have months and months to experiment and show things to the director and talk about sound. My heart aches for people who work the other way because they have to start from a dead stop. They have to come up to speed not having really any idea of what is going to happen. And the bad thing that happens is everything gets put in, and, as a result, you get a logjam of sound at the mix that frequently results in a kind of conceptual muddiness: all those dog collars. And this I think is related to some general criticisms of films being too loud. Because it is so dense, the ear can't make any sense out of it, so the director asks to increase the level. The mixers make it louder, and you quickly arrive at the threshold at which you can endure it, hoping for some kind of clarity to emerge from the loudness. But it's the clarity of the mallet on the head, and what an audience hears is noise. Because it's conceptually muddy, they can't begin to separate out what they're supposed to hear. And when they don't know what they're supposed to hear, their threshold of where loudness begins is much lower.

There is a rule of thumb I use which is never to give the audience more than two-and-a-half things to think about aurally at any one moment. Now, those moments can shift very quickly, but if you take a five-second section of sound and feed the audience more than two-and-a-half conceptual lines at the same time, they can't really separate them out. There's just no way to do it, and everything becomes self-canceling. As a result, they become annoyed with the sound and it appears "loud" even at lower levels. However, if they "understand" the sound, they can easily take 105 decibels, 110 decibels. But I don't even like to go that high; at the loudest points, I prefer to limit things to just nipping over 100 at most on a digital track. Dolby SR, with a maximum of 97, is just fine with me.

How do peaks and valleys—a phrase I hear often—fit into this?

If there are no valleys, then it doesn't matter how high the mountains actually are; they won't *seem* high. In every film, I try to find two or three places—and I often like them to be paradoxical places—where you can get absolute quiet, or as close to absolute quiet as possible. A good example of that is the Do Lung Bridge sequence in *Apocalypse*, where the character named Roach is brought over to kill a sniper. You can see all these explosions going on in the background, but gradually over the three or four minutes leading up to this moment, we've been taking the sound out. So that creates a valley, and it's interesting to me because you're in the middle of a battle, so how can there be a valley? My rationale is that we have evoked out of the darkness this human bat. A man whose hearing is so acute that he can echo-locate a voice to within a foot or two, and that's his skill so he doesn't even need to see. He can tell exactly and shoot the grenade right at that place and blow the person up, which is in fact what happens. At that moment, you are hearing the world the way Roach hears it: just the voice in the darkness. The other quiet moments in the film are just before the tiger jumps out of the jungle, and the approach to the Kurtz compound.

You can barely even hear the water on the boat.

The best sound is the sound inside somebody's head. What does it take to trigger that? That's the key to it all because those sounds will be unique to each person in the audience. They'll naturally be the most personal and the most high-fidelity of all the sounds.

Walter Murch Filmography

The Rainpeople	(1969, dir. Francis Coppola). Sound montage, re-recording mixer
THX-1138	(1971, dir. George Lucas). Co-screenwriter, film editor, sound montage, re-recording mixer
The Godfather	(1972, dir. Francis Coppola). Supervising sound editor
American Graffiti	(1973, dir. George Lucas). Sound montage and re-recording
The Godfather, Part II	(1974, dir. Francis Coppola). Sound montage and re-recording
The Conversation	(1974, dir. Francis Coppola). Film editor, sound montage, re-recording. Double winner at British Academy Awards, American Academy Award nomination for Best Sound.
Julia	(1977, dir. Fred Zinneman). Film editor. American, British Academy Award nominations
The Black Stallion	(1979, dir. Carroll Ballard). Uncredited screenplay collaboration
Apocalypse Now	(1979, dir. Francis Coppola). Film editor, re-recording mixer. American, British Academy Award nominations for Film Editing and Best Sound. Oscar for Best Sound
The Right Stuff	(1983, dir. Philip Kaufman). Documentary research and assembly
Return to Oz	(1985, dir. Walter Murch). Co-screenwriter, director
The Unbearable Lightness of Being	(1988, dir. Philip Kaufman). Film editor
Ghost	(1990, dir. Jerry Zucker). Film editor (Academy Award nomination), re-recording mixer
The Godfather, Part III	(1990, dir. Francis Coppola). Film editor (Academy Award nomination), re-recording mixer
The Godfather Trilogy	(1991, dir. Francis Coppola). Editor
House of Cards	(1992, dir. Michael Lessac). Film editor, re-recording mixer
Romeo Is Bleeding	(1994, dir. Peter Medak). Film editor, re-recording mixer
Crumb	(1994, dir. Terry Zweigoff). Re-recording mixer
First Knight	(1995, dir. Jerry Zucker). Film editor, re-recording mixer
The English Patient	(1996, dir. Anthony Minghella). Film editor, re-recording mixer. Academy Awards for Film Editing, Best Sound. British Academy Award for Film Editing
Touch of Evil	(1958, dir. Orson Welles). 1998 Editorial reconstruction and sound montages based on memos written by Welles

What is the relationship between creativity and technology?

People eat with knives and forks, they eat with chopsticks, and they eat with their hands. The real goal is getting the food into the mouth. Balzac wrote 80 great novels in 20 years with a quill pen. So from a certain aspect, technology is irrelevant. What is always relevant is what you want to say. If you have something to say, you will find a method irrespective of the technology. But I have to say there is a real excitement and surge of exploration that comes from an emerging technology which now makes easy something that you have been straining to accomplish. The "wow" factor.

In the early days, I was very interested in echo, in reverberant fields, but I couldn't get what I wanted out of the spring-loaded machines that were all we could afford. They just gave out a kind of metallic twang. So I would take the sounds that we had, the voices or the sound effects, put them in their cut form, transfer them onto a Nagra, and then take that Nagra out into an actual environment acoustically similar to what was in the movie. Then I would take another Nagra and turn both on at the same time and record from one to the other through the air. I would then take this new track and put it in sync with the original tracks. Then in the mix I would judiciously blend the two together. [Murch has referred to this process previously as "worldizing."]

I don't do that so much anymore. The digital technology is such that it's now better, certainly easier, than I can do manually. So in that sense, digital caught up with my ambitions and in some cases exceeded it. And more and more research is going on into this area. What I would like to be able to do is to go into an actual environment with a square-wave generator and "snap" that environment, record the snap and use the recording of that snap to create an algorithm in the digital processor to now re-create that sonic environment. Right now, we do it by taste and trial and error. We think, "Well, this room is kind of like a bathroom, but it's got some fabric, so let's start with a bathroom and reduce the high-frequency reverberation. Let's emphasize a peak at around 200 cycles, let's slightly reduce the decay time because of the fabric but add some kind of metallic spike some-where because of the ceilings and the porcelain fixtures." Now you just twiddle dials until something feels right.

*Over the course of your more than 30 years of filmmaking,
what technical developments have had the most impact on the
film mix or the film's sound?*

Apocalypse Now in 1979 was the industry's first multitrack, auto-mated mix. I think Dick Vorisek at Reeves Soundcraft was using automation in New York earlier for mono films, but this was the first automated multitrack mix. We had a tremendous amount of material for that film, so automation had a huge impact. Also, ten years earlier, the innovation of rock-and-roll (punch-in) recording, where you didn't have to do entire reels in one take. The Rainpeople had punch-in, but my experiences mixing before that had all been "one-take" mixes. Dolby—a huge influence in generally making stereo and "magnetic quality" sound easily available to us in theaters. The use of 24-track recorders synched to the film image. And now digital workstations that can feed the sound directly to the stage. And the Avid, with its facility to mix eight tracks as you edit the picture. It's amazing to think that I started before any of these things.

Automated boards were supposed to speed up everything, weren't they?

Automated boards, digital editing, use of the Nagra rather than magnetic film recorders, the use of "punch-in" re-recording—all of these things are initially sold on the basis of saving time because that's how these things have to be marketed. Somebody's going to be paying a lot a money for new technology and they have to have a reason to do it. Well, saving time is fine in theory, but in practice it usually doesn't work that way. What all these innovations do give you, though, is the ability to do more in the time available, and to defer critical decisions until a later point. If you're not careful about it, though, that deferment can precipitate a crisis because having too many deferred decisions is like not paying your taxes for ten years. Suddenly, the IRS is after you, and now you really have to pay up with a penalty. The dangers in deferring too many decisions come either because the decisions never get made—and in that case you just get this big "ball of noise" effect—or you have to make difficult and painful decisions that are the creative equivalent of being audited.

What about the digital release formats?
You mixed 6-channel 70mm for Apocalypse, correct?

There are differences between 70mm magnetic, Dolby Digital, DTS and SDDS, but they are primarily in the delivery systems. Creatively, the differences are minute, relatively speaking, between any of these systems. They are all basically discrete 5-channel (7-channel for SDDS) tracks with stereo surrounds and low-frequency reinforcement. That was the format we pioneered for *Apocalypse Now* and which has now become the standard for both theaters and home theaters, where it is called AVR3 on Laserdiscs or 5.1 on DVD. A good 70mm 6-track with split surrounds gave you the same experience—emotionally and technically—as you get today with digital systems. Prints were a lot more expensive, cumbersome and fragile, however, so the new systems are a definite improvement on that level.

Besides film, what are your passions today, and how do they
feed your creative instincts? You mentioned architecture earlier...

I think you will find a high percentage of filmmakers who are interested in architecture. Both are a mixture of art and business, where you have to build something complicated that's going to look great but also withstand the storms. And you have to collaborate with a large team of people and build for a price, and it has to integrate itself into the society as a whole and yet hopefully elevate the prevailing standards, as well. Architecture is an exterior medium, film is an interior medium: an architecture for the interior of the mind. The patterns of image and sound and story of a good film have to have a certain entertainment value, but ultimately they also last in the mind as sort of a template or matrix of how to organize reality. After you have seen a good film—a *good* film—you leave the theater with a better idea of how to make sense of the world, of a world that would otherwise be chaotic or unacceptable. But this is the same function as the arts have always had—painting, music, writing, etc. Architecture, too, of course.

My other passions are translating Italian poetry, and astronomy. Translation is transformative; and astronomy is the discovery of an underlying order in apparent chaos. Both good descriptions of the editorial process.

Have you found order in your life? Are you in a comfortable place?

I guess it's the appropriate blend of chaos and order. I have a big family, and I've been married for 33 years, and we live on a horse/berry/apple/chicken farm out in West Marin County.

The Music Is Your Special Friend

*Oliver Stone adjusting a
microphone for Val Kilmer*

SOUND ASSEMBLY FOR "THE DOORS"

The Doors is not a rock 'n' roll movie. Let's start there. It's a dramatic film that contains more than two hours of music—Doors music—as underscore, as score, as performance, as narrative. Press reviews have labeled it a film about excess or a film about the '60s, and in many ways it is. But Wylie Stateman, co-supervising sound editor, says it best: "It's the 1960s the way you would want to remember them in 1990, which is in full-blown stereo with vibrant energy."

The Doors is a rock 'n' roll movie. It's about energy and passion. To the sound team on *The Doors*, that passion was translated into music, effects and dialog tracks that breathed and punched the spirit of the time period, 1967-71, pivotal years in the development of rock 'n' roll.

*This article appeared originally
in the May 1991 issue of* Mix.

On a rainy night in Hollywood, the night before *The Doors* opened worldwide, a few key members of the sound crew assembled for a post-mortem rap in Paul Rothchild's home. Rothchild, the Doors' original producer and music supervisor on the film, was joined by Bruce Botnick, the Doors' engineer and music premix/pre-record engineer on the film. Also there was Stateman, Mike Minkler, lead re-recording mixer and co-supervising sound editor, and Tim Claman, digital music systems supervisor and NED PostPro operator. Absent was Budd Carr, executive music producer on the last five Oliver Stone films, who handled administration and coordination.

"As with any Oliver Stone film, it was a collaborative effort," Rothchild says. "Everybody makes suggestions into everybody else's domain, and the good ones stick and the bad ones go. Oliver needed human interaction, sometimes from 8,000 people [in a crowd scene] and sometimes from five people in a studio."

"This was a love groove," jokes Stateman, referring to the slogan that was taped to the console throughout the mix. "It was a labor far beyond anybody coming into a daily job."

The film itself is immense. Minkler, who has mixed more than 200 films, including five of the top ten most expensive films ever made, says "This was the most difficult film I've ever mixed and the most enjoyable film I've ever mixed. There's so much going on that you can't get it all in one shot. If people want to examine this film and watch it ten times, I think they'll be pretty damn satisfied that we hit all the marks."

Sound crew collaboration began early in pre-production when the decision was made to record the live footage to multitrack. That meant location mixer Tod Maitland could carry actors separately, wouldn't have to mix as much, and could open up space for ambience mics and onstage dialog. It also meant a hell of a lot of tracks at the final mix.

"Musical biographies have been done plenty of times in the past," Minkler says. "Everybody knows how to do it. You have a pre-record, you do a playback, and then guys go out there and lip-sync."

"And then you write this retrospective," Stateman interjects. "That is *not* this movie."

Pre-production began with the problem of how to handle the live performance vocals. Should Val Kilmer, the actor playing Jim Morrison, lip-sync to Morrison's vocals, lip-sync to his own pre-recorded vocals, or sing live on camera? The decision would determine the rest of the process.

IS IT LIVE, OR IS IT MORRISON?

Kilmer, meanwhile, had sent Stone a rough demo of himself doing Jim Morrison. Rothchild describes it as "an actor in a cheap wig, cheap makeup, cheap camera, cheap lighting— performing Jim Morrison—singing the role." Stone knew Kilmer could do Morrison physically, that he had the moves. So when Rothchild told him that Kilmer was 80 percent there on the voice, and that he could bring him up to 95 percent, Stone decided to test it.

Rothchild, Botnick and Kilmer went into Botnick's Hollywood Studio, Digital Magnetics, to create new demos for "Back Door Man" and "Texas Radio & the Big Beat." One day Stone dropped by with the surviving members of the Doors. "I'll never forget this," Rothchild says. "We put up 'Texas Radio,' and about halfway through, John Densmore [Doors drummer] turned to me and said, 'Is that Jim or is it Val?' And we cheered."

Stone still had to be convinced, however. Rothchild and Botnick took Nagra tapes of Kilmer lip-synching to Morrison, to himself and live, transferred them to PCM-1610 digital 2-track, and matched music and voice to picture. They then transferred to mag and locked to picture, stereo format. "It was a primitive way of doing it in relation to the way it was actually done [in the film]," Botnick says. "But the technique was the same to the end."

Stone immediately saw that you couldn't have the famous Morrison vocal coming out of Kilmer's mouth and still be convincing. So he opted for live vocals, which was the choice all along of the sound crew. Basically, when you see Kilmer, you hear Kilmer. Otherwise, it's Morrison. The resemblance is uncanny. The music is all original Doors, with a couple of brief exceptions.

Sound for Picture

One of the editing rooms at Soundelux. Pictured (l to r): Keith Klawitter, Wylie Stateman, Scott Gershin.

Rothchild's task then was to fill Kilmer in on the nuances and idiosyncrasies that made Morrison's vocals what they were. In that process, he says, "An equal amount of time was spent filling his cup with information on Jim's personality and psyche and motivations, so that when he hit the stage as a singer/actor, he wouldn't have to be relying so much on mimicking Jim as to digging inside of himself for the essence of Jim.

"The musician synchronization in this film is amazing," Rothchild adds. "The other three Doors actors had the impossible task of learning by rote the pre-recorded work of the Doors, which was anywhere from 20 to 25 years old. Even the Doors couldn't resynchronize themselves to it. Every single note had to be learned because Oliver likes to shoot in 360—you never know where the camera is going to be. Each actor had to be prepared to be playing the tune perfectly at all times."

Each of the actors had an instrument coach, and each was supplied with a nightly "stringer" cassette of the next day's sequences. It was basically a Music Minus One—his part on the right, the mix on the left. These were put out daily and had to be re-edited according to Stone's changes.

Months prior to the shoot, Rothchild and Botnick began designing a system for music playback and track assembly. They transferred the original Doors 4-track (first album) and 8-track masters carefully onto a Sony PCM-3324 digital 24-track. Then 24-track analog SR dubs were made with matching timecode, referenced at 60 Hz. Kilmer overdubs and vocal comps were added to the concert/song scenes, before transferring back to 3324 for pre-production and production editing.

For the set, Stone wanted to have every playback option available at any time, including the ability to use Morrison's or Kilmer's vocal track. "It occurred to us that we could use a Fostex 16-track," Botnick says, "and using a [TimeLine] Lynx synchronizer and the house composite sync generator, we could resolve the 16-track. We could provide playback in any magnitude of order because we had a mono composite mix. We had a separate drum track mix. We had separate bass, guitar, organ, Jim and Val.

"We could resolve the 16-track onstage, and the code would be transferred and jam-synched to an Otari 24-track with SR," he continues. "That 24-track had a print for every take of everything that was on the 16-track, plus everything live that was recorded. The analog 24-track was then resolved and transferred to mag for dailies." Dailies were handled by the staff at Soundelux, the editorial house that Stateman co-owns, doing combine-mixdown of six to eight selected takes, in stereo.

If a shoot was to be handled differently the next day, edits were done overnight on the 3324. "On rare occasions," Rothchild recalls, "Oliver would say, 'I want to throw out that entire verse' in the middle of shooting. At that point, it was, 'Get out the blade, cut the 16-track and pray.'"

"The Lynxes are smart enough that they rode right through the edits," Botnick adds. "What helped was the fact that since we were jam-synching brand new code onto 24-track, it was continuous code." While the resolution stayed constant, different music appeared at the same timecode number for different days of the shoot and different takes of the same song. It was all lined up in post-production.

For the live vocal sequences, it had to be absolutely quiet on the set. There was no playback on the set, no thundering rock 'n' roll for the audience. The actors/singers were set up with an earwig system, plastic flesh-colored inserts containing miniature, high-energy drivers for foldback. Pre-recorded playback was sent to beltpack receivers, each with volume control. "We had standard recording studio earphone technology happening on this huge shoot," Rothchild explains, "with different foldback to each performer."

Sound for Picture

Keyboards and guitar were not amplified, so keeping them quiet was no problem. Drums, however, had to be specially constructed. The snare, toms and kick were stuffed with foam rubber, and Zildjian supplied custom cymbals with top and bottom pieces of bronze, with compressed foam in the middle.

To cover the likelihood of the actor-drummer playing a passage that wasn't on the pre-recorded track, each of the drums was set up with a piezo transducer, which triggered samples that were recorded onto the 24-track. "We could then sample John Densmore's toms and snare and come back with a drum part that was played perfectly to the eye," Rothchild says. "Even if it was played badly, it would work in the film."

The audiences, meanwhile, had to be loud and wild and crazy, but while Kilmer was singing, they couldn't be fed music. Up until the camera rolled, the song would be cranked out to the audience. Then when the scene started, it was replaced by a 30 Hz tone called "Thumper." Essentially, Thumper was a hand-tapped click track (tapped into the 3324 by Rothchild's son Dan) that was filtered out in post-production. Since the music playback stopped just as the cameras began rolling, production mixer Tod Maitland was able to capture some of the finest audience tracks you'll hear. In many cases, the screams for "Light My Fire" and the like are the screams from the actual shoot, rather than group ADR.

THE MUSIC EDIT

After shooting was finished, all of the music elements—pre-recorded vocals (Kilmer's and Morrison's), production vocals and the original Doors tracks—were transferred D-to-D from the 3324 into a New England Digital PostPro. Archived and unre-leased material was loaded as well, including outtakes from the tour that produced the album *Absolutely Live*. The PostPro was locked to a KEM flatbed, both picture and music mag track, using the same setup as the film editors.

Rothchild, Tim Claman and music editor Carl Kaller then worked with the picture department, providing music for the temp dubs and making edits to fit selected takes. At the same time, they were comping production vocals that came in on 2-inch Dolby SR, synchronizing the actor/musicians and the vocals—basically assembling the premix.

"It was sort of like making a record of the live vocal perform-ances that we had to build," Claman says. "We were collecting tiny little pieces of words and phrases from as many as two or three dozen live takes from dailies. We were constantly stretching and compressing—very minute surgery to get the synchronization to work. We were trying to keep the energy of the live performance, but picking the best performances to match it."

"[Tim] would take every single edit that we made, an instrument at a time, and he'd move the edit point," says Rothchild, who made his first window edit (manually, with meticulous, jigsaw-shaped splices) on the Doors' first album back in 1967. "He'd find the cleanest, sweetest spot for every instrument in that edit."

The music premix was not without its challenges, one of which was to sonically match the Kilmer and Morrison vocals, often within the same song. "In the song 'The End,' we originally had Val's vocal from beginning to end," Rothchild explains. "The first two verses are outside and inside the cave. Then at one point you go through the Indian's eye and...Bam! You're onstage at the Whisky a Go Go with Val singing the Jim part. I watched it three times and said to Oliver, 'This doesn't work. If we're not looking at Val singing, we have to hear Jim.' It's the reverse of the other problem.

"But now we have a curious problem," he continues. "We have Jim's famous vocal 20 seconds away from Val's entrance onstage at the Whisky, in the same song. Fortunately, Val's performance is excellent. The original recording had a Sunset Sound live chamber on the take, so we couldn't take it off. We then had to match that echo to convince you psychologically that you're hearing the same person."

"On the original Jim vocal," Botnick adds, "it was an EMT 140 chamber with 15 ips slap—167 milliseconds. [On the film premix], we didn't have any EMTs, but we had these Lexicon 480Ls. And through fooling with EQ and adjusting the delays, we got it pretty much the same. It took a long time."

"But it was a very important point in the film," Rothchild cuts in. "At that moment, you sell the whole idea of Val's voice."

The PostPro was then taken into the Cary Grant Theatre on the Columbia lot, where all the music was mixed to three 6-track mag dubbers with SR, and back to the PostPro as well. "We basically had a master on the PostPro," Botnick says. "It had three tracks of our left-center-right, plus all the effects and reverb. We didn't marry them to our mix so that when we got to the dub stage, Michael could adjust it."

Claman was working completely with first-generation elements, and that's what was delivered to the re-recording stage at Skywalker Sound South for Minkler, Stateman and Greg Landaker to mix. Botnick also provided underscore 3-tracks, which he converted from 2-track Doors originals using a Bedini Audio BASE processor. That way, Minkler had the option of lowering the vocal level when dialog appeared onscreen.

OVER AT SOUNDELUX, SKYWALKER

While the PostPro was the workstation of choice for the disk-based music editing, any and all DAWs were used in the creation and manipulation of effects.

"Every piece of the latest, most sophisticated equipment was used on this film and exploited for its greatest attributes," Stateman says. "For the creation of transitional sounds and musical supporting sounds that had to be played along in tempo, we used the WaveFrame AudioFrame. We used the Synclavier 9600 for its abilities to sequence and task sounds out of RAM, where you need tremendous list management. And we used it for sound creation—camera flashes and some of the wind gusts that spin us in and out of sequences.

"For developing the editorial work on the crowd scenes, we used the AMS AudioFile for its brute force," he continues. "Take a sound that's going to be repeated 750 times in one scene, cut it, then take another sound to lay over the top or to sweeten that particular effect, run the list, spit it out to a 2-inch machine, Dolby SR."

Lexicon 480Ls were used for reverb and echo. Many of the effects had to be brought to their most mature point in the cutting room, long before the final mix. Sound editing was handled by Scott Gershin, Jay Richardson and Lon Bender at Soundelux.

The crowd scenes are memorable in this film, largely because they're very real. Sure, there is some sweetening to add bulk, but the ambience and noise Tod Maitland gathered on the sets was used extensively in the final mix.

"After the edits were final," Minkler says, "Wylie went into the 5-track stereo recordings of these crowds, which have a reflection of the vocal, reflection of the music, but mostly crowds. They had great balance between them. We used them for ambience on the music, as well. So when you see people in the audience, you feel them completely around you in 5-channel configuration—three in the front and two surround. You are in the middle of this concert."

Dialog editing took place at Soundelux and involved more than 2,000 hours of work. "There are lots of words in this picture," Minkler says. "We were up to 70 or 80 channels of dialog on a reel, instead of the conventional five, six, seven or eight."

ADR was handled at Skywalker Sound South's "Bundy" annex (formerly Lion's Gate), while Greg Orloff supervised the Foley from the new pit at the main facility.

The final mix began at Skywalker South in mid-December on the newly installed Otari Premiere console in Dub Stage 1. It was the first feature film to pass through the facility, which opened last October. It's a THX-certified monitoring environment, though KRK monitors were brought in for reference, as they were used throughout the project.

"We had two objectives [in the re-recording]," Minkler says. "One was to supplement the reality, and the other was to enhance the non-reality and tell a story with it. The reality part has to be good and accurate and dramatic and fit in so you believe it. The non-reality is a lot of guesswork.

"During 'The End,' for instance, the guys are all on acid and doing their thing, and we started introducing tons of sounds," he continues. "Paul started freaking out: 'What are you doing to my music?' Well, it was a palette. We came in with everything and then started weeding and wading and playing."

On the dub stage, the three-man re-recording team basically had the 6-track mag reels, the production analog 24-track, a Synclavier and an AudioFrame. They continued to seek and receive input from their colleagues. "It was literally like building a house with five or six or eight people all giving input on how that house should look," Minkler says.

"There are nine people talking in a scene and you have to hear every word," he continues. "And Paul wants to hear every lyric. And somebody else wants to hear every note of the bass. And somebody else wants to hear the guy talking in the background. We ended up where everybody was completely happy with the outcome, but oh, Manny, it made me old!"

The film was released in all major formats, with selected 6-channel Cinema Digital Sound prints sent throughout the country.

"There's a lot of pictures and a lot of years at this table tonight," Minkler says in summation. "We've all done gigantic projects as well as small ones, but certainly none of them have come up to this. Every foot of this film was rough. From dealing with the music on a file, dealing with the creativity of blending the dialog, effects and music together, premixing sound effects. Every single frame of every little element was difficult because we pushed ourselves. That was the spirit of this film."

"This film is a lot like this house," Rothchild adds. "This house is a state-of-the-art machine in an antique facade. This film is a technological breakthrough, a monster of energy, and you can't see the wires."

Terminator 2

Judgment Day

The camera pans across burned-out car bodies, charred carousel horses, a bent and fragile teeter-totter—a broken playground from the year 2029 A.D. A desolate wind is all you hear. Then CRUNCH! A robotic foot crushes a vacant human skull. Lasers, explosions, screams. Here comes *Terminator 2: Judgment Day.*

What hasn't been written about *T2*? A hundred million dollars to make, some claim, though it should bring in double that in domestic sales alone. It came together in just a shade over a year, from first rough draft to its July 3 release date. And we all know by now that Arnold Schwarzenegger received a private jet in lieu of $14 million salary. Would it surprise anyone at this point that the sound of the wind in the opening scene comes from the crack of an open door to the main mix room at Skywalker Sound, and the sound of the crushed skull is a pistachio being crunched by a metal plate?

The re-recording on *T2* began at Skywalker Sound, San Rafael, Calif., on May 23, and it ended on June 21. That's four weeks, from premix to final to 70mm CDS master. And this is a big movie. With big sound.

"We had every mix room in the facility going," says Gloria Borders, sound supervisor. "We re-recorded all the effects in the movie before the crew came on—all the motorcycles, guns, cars, semis—knowing that when the crew came on we were going to have four weeks to cut the thing, and it had to be ready to go."

Two weeks before the premix, the film was still 2 hours and 45 minutes long. Because of a clause in writer/director/producer James Cameron's contract, a week before the premix it was cut to 2 hours 15 minutes. "We had about 2,000 units built, ready to mix," Borders says, "and they cut 30 minutes. It meant going into every single unit to take out a foot, then another bit, then

This article appeared originally in the September 1991 issue of Mix.

The mix room at
Skywalker Sound

30 feet, then 50 feet. A lot of patchwork was done. We had 35 editors and assistants, and we worked nonstop. After we premixed it, we had very few picture changes, which is wonderful because then we could just go into the final, and that was where Gary Rydstrom took over and did a genius of a job."

Rydstrom, sound designer and re-recording mixer, would be the first to admit that he had plenty of help. Beside him at the SSL 5000 for the final sat Gary Summers for the music mix and Tom Johnson on dialog. All three credit the editors for delivering quality units under pressure. And through it all stood James Cameron, a hands-on director till the end.

"[Cameron's] approach to sound is hyperrealistic," Rydstrom says. "I wouldn't call it stylized, but everything is very big, and you can make it movie-sized. But he also likes it to be fairly authentic—realistic, but hyperrealistic. A testosterone, sort of macho approach to match what he's doing with the visuals.

"Your first thought when you see a lot of special effects is that sound's job is to not only do something as fantastical as the visual, but also to make it real. It's not competing with the special visual effect, because people perceive the visual and the sound differently. [Sound designer] Walter Murch had a way of putting it: 'The eyes are the front door, and the ears are the back door.'"

What is the sound of a nuclear holocaust coming in through the back door? Or a liquid metal Terminator walking through steel bars?

SOUND EFFECTS

The gathering of sound elements began unofficially in November 1990, when Rydstrom visited the steel mill set used for the climactic final sequence in the film. Production granted post-production two days of access to the mill, and two Skywalker recordists, armed with Sony 2000 R-DATs, came back with seven hours of metal and machines on tape.

"Most of what's in the film is ambience, like steam hisses, metal clanging, conveyor belts," Rydstrom explains. "The conveyor belt that Arnold comes up on in the end before shooting T-1000 is a conveyor belt from the steel mill. In the fight scene [between the two Terminators] you hear some of the sheet metal being dropped."

From November on, sounds were gathered, often from the field, and sometimes created in the studio. Video arcades, car crusher junkyards, and all the vehicles and guns were recorded to DAT. The sound for the motorcycle that Arnold drives comes from a Harley owned by a construction worker at Skywalker Ranch. People brought in dirt bikes, SWAT vans and all sorts of specific vehicles. Though production provided the actual motorcycles and semis from the film, they were used mainly for suspension squeaks and running over boards, not for engine sounds.

Sound for Picture

Production also provided many of the guns used in the film, including the hard-to-find Mini Gun that Arnold uses in the police shootout outside the Cyberdyne building. Three recordists went to the Stembridge shooting range outside of L.A., two with R-DATs and one with a Nagra (with Dolby A card). "I was thinking of combining the R-DAT version with the Nagra," Rydstrom says, "trying to get the snap of the digital sound. It usually has a nice transient snap to it, but sometimes doesn't have the full-body punch of the Nagra." The R-DATs were coupled with Sanken M-S mics; the Nagra had a Neumann on one channel, Schoeps on the other.

When you record a Mini Gun at full speed, Rydstrom says, it doesn't sound like a machine gun but a cannon. So, it was recorded at less than top speed, then speeded up in the mix, with a touch of EQ added and a thunderclap from the house library to sweeten the initial burst of sound.

"That was a fun scene to do," Rydstrom says. "The difficulty was that he is so in control of shooting this gun, that the destruction he creates has to be within reason. It has to be such that you don't believe a lot of cops are dying. So, we couldn't use ricochets, because standard Hollywood ricochets would imply that the bullets are flying out of control and killing somebody. And we couldn't use explosions on the cars, which look like they are exploding, because they weren't exploding. They were just being demolished to the point where they would collapse. It was tricky to just use hits on metal and glass breaks and suspension drops and ricochets that sounded like thuds."

The wind sounds, so ominous in the beginning of the film and so prominent in the desert scene, were often performed off of a Synclavier. "Some of that, I have to admit, is me going 'whooooo,'" Rydstrom notes. "Some of it is from the door to the mix room that I usually work in. By playing it on the Synclavier, you can put in as long a loop as you can afford to. You set the octave ratio on the keyboard so that it's not in usual steps—much smaller musical steps—then you just put long attacks and decays on the wind and ride the pitch wheel. Very often you can perform the wind while watching the picture."

Randy Thom, sound designer (standing), Gloria Borders, supervising sound editor (and now Skywalker's VP), Tom Johnson, re-recording mixer

The biggest sound design challenge, however, was the sound of the T-1000 Terminator moving into and out of liquid metal, the quality that makes him virtually indestructible. "It's not really liquid, because it doesn't look like mud," Rydstrom says. "It doesn't have any bubbles in it. It doesn't gurgle. It doesn't do anything visually except flow like mercury. But mercury doesn't make a sound. It's very silent."

So Rydstrom and Tom Myers, his assistant, developed a number of sound elements, sampled them into a Synclavier, and played them against picture to see what worked. When the T-1000 is just sort of flowing and transforming, that's Rydstrom spraying Dust-Off into a flour and water mixture, with a condom-sealed mic stuck in the goo. "It would make these huge goopy bubbles," he says. "And the moment when the bubble is forming, it has this sound that's similar to a cappucino maker, or a milk steamer. Funny enough, it had this metallic quality to it, so I believed it. And it also had sort of an evolving quality to it, so I believed it for transformation."

For the sound of bullets hitting T-1000, Rydstrom slammed an inverted glass into a bucket of yogurt, getting a hard edge to accompany the goop. The sound of T-1000 passing through steel bars is nothing more than dog food being slowly sucked out of a can. "A lot of that I would play backward or do something to," Rydstrom explains, "but those were the basic elements. What's amazing to me is the combination of Industrial Light & Magic using millions of dollars of high-tech digital equipment and computers to come up with the visuals, and meanwhile I'm inverting a dog food can."

Processing on the effects, as with the music and dialog, was pretty standard—Lexicon 224s and 480s, Quantec QRS XLs, and an AMS Harmonizer or two. Sometimes Rydstrom would feed the Lexicon back into itself, sometimes he would flip-flop it on the Synclavier for a truly reverse delay.

MUSIC

"I think the score in this movie works as sort of the driving element that holds parts of the mix together," Rydstrom says, "something that keeps driving the scene forward without telegraphing the suspense. Using score in that way has been used so much that it loses its impact. So we did other things to give dynamics to the scene. It's not traditional screeching violins leading up to a fight scene." Often it is just a soft "boom boom" from the percussion track, as when Arnold lands his Harley after a short, silent flight in the canal chase scene. And sometimes it's delicate guitar in the desert.

The soft yet militaristic score was composed by Brad Fiedel and mixed in the final by Gary Summers. Fiedel was on the tightest of tight schedules, still composing as the mix was taking place, sometimes delivering cues for the second half of a reel as the first was being finished. It wouldn't have been possible, according to Summers, without Fiedel's chain of three Fairlights.

"He did all the sampling and sequencing from the Fairlights," Summers says. "He would do that over to 24-track and mix down. Then he would deliver to me, per cue, two or three 3-tracks—basically a left-center-right mix of percussion, strings, and maybe some synths. He would separate out the different groups so that we could rebalance or whatever.

"[The score] was mixed very well by Brad," Summers adds. "I did very little to it, some EQ and reverb occasionally. I had a 224 and two Quantecs for the music, so I could filter it in as well as put it into rooms. I like the rooms on the Quantec—the small-room programs are great."

T2 was mixed in a THX monitoring environment, and no surround sound was laid on the masters. "Surround is what we call magic surround," Summers says. "The out-of-phase component will automatically go to surround. Now when I'm making the 70mm master, we have our 18 channels into the board—music, dialog and effects separate. I take the left-center-right of the music and I send that to left-center-right of the 70mm master. But I also feed it into the DS4, and I bring that up in the console and add it in as a discrete surround.

"We were mixing in a discrete, split-surround 70mm format," he continues, "and in the monitor mix I was listening to that magic surround component. I was hearing the whole time what was going to happen, although none was going down on tape. It's a little bit complicated, but it worked out real well, and it gave me free tracks on the recorder."

DIALOG AND FOLEY

According to Gloria Borders, around 70 percent of the dialog in the film and most of the breathing is ADR, which shouldn't surprise anyone since most of the movie takes place on the run. By all accounts, the looping performances were excellent, even those by Eddie Furlong (playing the 10-year old John Connor), whose voice grew deeper over the nine months of production.

"I actually had to pitch all of his loops up quite a bit," says dialog mixer Tom Johnson. "I ended up using the Lexicon 2400—a device used mainly by TV studios—which will actually speed up or slow down a tape machine, or whatever, and pitch it accordingly so you don't get a pitch change. Using the AMS or even the Lexicon 480 pitch programs, you get artifacts after 1 percent or so. I was having to pitch the kid between 3 percent and 4 percent."

ADR constantly had to be matched to production dialog within scenes, sometimes within sentences. In the hospital scene where Linda Hamilton watches herself revealing her nuclear holocaust dreams on a TV monitor, the first half is from production, on 1/4-inch and videotape, the second half ADR. Johnson matched them up, then futzed it in the final mix. "All I had to was match the natural room echo, which is easy if you get lucky. I used a Lexicon 480.

"I feel that it's important to retain as much of the natural sound of the production dialog as possible, smoothing the backgrounds out by using handles, or whatever," Johnson adds. "The editors give me handles on both sides of the line, and I just have to do a bunch of crossfades to make it sound like it was recorded by a microphone in one take. Then I smooth it out as much as possible, taking out weird tones with notch filters or really sharp parametric EQs.

"Rather than using noise gates, I'll clean the track up as much as possible with EQ," Johnson continues. "There is a device that Dolby makes, and I think they're finally building more of them, called the 430 *[Not in production yet, this piece is presently being beta tested—ed's note]*. It uses a Dolby SR card and some other stuff to create a sort of sophisticated noise gate. It allows you to clean backgrounds up, but it doesn't sound like a noise gate where it's pumping a lot."

Johnson also helped premix two reels of Foley, and it was the Foley team that had perhaps the least time of anybody.

Since it would have been a nightmare to conform all the Foley elements to picture changes during the week before the premix, it was decided to hold off on Foley recording. "We decided to gamble and record Foley as close to the final as possible," says Gloria Borders. "We learned to take that chance on *Godfather III*. The final mix for *T2* started on June 6, and I think we were done with the last reel of Foley on June 10."

Despite the rush, it is flawless Foley, performed by Dennie Thorpe and recorded by Christopher Boyes. "Most audiences have no idea that we replaced all the leather creaks on the Terminator's jacket," Rydstrom says, "and the buckle clinks, and the footsteps—all the incidental movements have been replaced.

"I think the shining moment for Foley in this movie is when Sarah is getting out of her straps in her hospital bed," Rydstrom continues. "She takes the paper clip, spits it out, it lands on the bed, she puts it in the buckle, she gets out of her strap, and she uses the paper clip to pick the lock of the door. The whole scene is nothing but Foley and music. And a lot of the tension is coming from focusing in on those little sounds from Foley—the paper clip into the tumblers of the lock."

Long after you leave *Terminator 2*, it's the small sounds, and the silences, that you remember more than the explosions. When Arnold shoots the frozen T-1000 in the steel mill, all background ambience fades out in the split second before the gun goes off. And when Arnold flies on the Harley, the engine, the music, everything cuts out until he lands.

"I learned on this film that silence works even for an extended period of time," Rydstrom says. "The biggest mixing challenge was making everything be loud, at least apparently loud, when a lot of the time you have loud things happening simultaneously and in a row. It's not always easy to make something huge. I love moments like when the Cyberdyne building blows up—when the big explosion of the building is preceded just by a long period of silence and the click of a detonator."

Beauty and the Beast

A Punchy Soundtrack for a Disney Classic

The songwriting team of the late Howard Ashman (l) and Alan Menken, with the orchestra behind the glass

It is difficult to get past picture and talk about sound for *Beauty and the Beast*. The animation is so rich, detailed and lively that you walk away wondering, "How do they do that? How do they paint a ballroom scene with such spatial textures? How do they so convincingly humanize a candelabra? Who dreamed up those colors?"

Then a little later you start humming the "Belle" song, throwing in an odd lyric or two. The memory of an operatic wardrobe brings a smile. And who can forget the snarls and growls of the wolves on the way to the Beast's castle? The animation, you realize, gives the picture life; the soundtrack gives the picture punch.

This article appeared originally in the January 1992 edition of Mix.

Beauty and the Beast, released Thanksgiving weekend 1991, is Walt Disney Pictures' 30th animated feature film, its fifth classic fairy tale adapted for the screen. The project spanned three-and-a-half years, requiring more than one million drawings—226,000 individually painted cels! As is typical in Hollywood these days, the sound engineers for the final mix were allowed four weeks.

Luckily, the rerecording team of Terry Porter, Mel Metcalfe and Dave Hudson—all Buena Vista Sound staffers with impressive sound portfolios—were handed premium elements. The score includes six original songs created by Oscar-winning composer Alan Menken (*The Little Mermaid*), with lyrics by the executive producer, the late Howard Ashman (to whom the film is dedicated). Effects were created by co-supervising sound editors Mark Mangini and Dave Stone of Weddington Productions, with assistance from John Pospisil. And voices? Some the best from stage and screen: Angela Lansbury, who plays Mrs. Potts and sings the title track, David Ogden-Stiers, Paige O'Hara, Richard White, Jesse Corti, Rex Everhart, Jo Anne Worley and…Robby Benson as the Beast.

VOICING THE BEAST

Robby Benson as the Beast? The same boyish voice from *One on One* and *Ice Castles*? Apparently, dozens of people auditioned for the part, and Benson sold the producer, directors and everyone else on the strength of his performance, blending the warmth of a human prince with the ferocity of an eight-foot monster. Still, the first question asked of Mangini in his initial interview was, "What would you do with the Beast's voice?"

"My suggestion was to re-voice him," Mangini remembers, "a more stentorian voice that we could grab onto with processing gear to deepen up. But they were sold on the performance, and their biggest concern was, 'What can we do to make this better?' I told them quite frankly that I had no clue. I was worried about it. I think I flunked my first interview.

"Actually, I knew then that I would add animal sounds in and around it," Mangini adds. "His performance was just spoken word, but he had to behave like a beast. He was animated to prowl and growl and roar. So we came up with a technique of cutting fore and aft of everything that he said with growls and purrs and things like that from tigers and camels. Then, of course, for sounds that stood in the clear like a big beast roar, it would be stand-alone, processed tiger mixed with camel mixed with bear—live animals, all sounds that I went out and recorded, getting in a pen with my Nagra or DAT.

"Most of the beast turned out to be camel," Mangini explains. "Camels seemed to be the animal that sounded most like Robby Benson, if that makes any sense. Occasionally, Robby would come into or go out of a line with a growl, trying to make the track as complete as possible when they recorded two years ago. When it was pitched down, some of that stuff sounded okay, and we thought of it as a bridge between Robby's voice, Robby's growl and an animal to finish it up. We figured if we could match that with the other material, we would have this seamless blend."

About six months before Mangini started adding in camels, however, lead mixer Terry Porter began experimenting with processing on the voice. According to Porter and others, the timbre just didn't match the visuals, so they brought it into pre-post for a little magic. The main processing tool ended up being a pitch shift program from an Eventide H3000 UltraHarmonizer.

"We had to address it line by line and shift him down depending on the delivery," Porter says. "I also found another program on the Eventide that created lower harmonics, which I could add to the voice to reinforce the low end. Besides dropping the voice, this created another part of the voice in the lower spectrum, which helped. I also used a limited-band dbx [120X] boom-box to again reinforce some of the low tones. For a voice, you could get it down way too low, so I had to cut off a lot of low frequencies and pick up a spectrum somewhere between 50 and 100 cycles. That one I used salt-and-pepper—just a little bit."

As expected, once Porter started harmonizing and dropping the voice down, intelligibility became a concern. "We were able to bring back some of the intelligibility with just pure equalization on a line-by-line basis," Porter explains, "making sure that we kept a nice clean top end with a little spike in the upper-mids to put some bite in his voice. When he's angry at the beginning of the movie, I'm using the tools a lot more—a lot stronger on the low end. And we do decrease that as the movie goes on."

Buena Vista Sound Goes Full-Service

Not many sound facilities can boast a 51-year history. Released in 1940, *Fantasia* was the first animated feature to come out of the Disney lot. Now, half a century later, *Fantasia* has been restored and released on video, bringing the process full-circle, with the remix handled in essentially the same building as the original.

In those 51 years, Walt Disney Studios has become much more than a producer of animated features, and Buena Vista Sound has become much more than an in-house sound department. Disney is a tremendously prolific producer of entertainment products. Most of the feature film work is still handled on the lot's soundstages, though much of the television sound work is sent off-site. Disney gets first crack at booking the stages, but it's now to the point where roughly 50% of Buena Vista Sound's business comes from outside clients.

To attract those clients, Buena Vista Sound now offers complete, full-service post-production facilities. "For us to be a full-service department," says Chris Carey, director of Buena Vista Sound, "the last area we needed to expand into was sound editorial—that is, the actual recording of sound effects, cutting them into sync with picture and preparing them for the dub stage. We have been hired for a Disney feature film called *Straight Talk*, which will be released this spring. That will be our first full post-production sound feature, where we will have done everything from the ADR, Foley, editing, sound effects recording, mixing and print master." Sound editorial will open with conventional film-style editing, though Carey expects to add electronic editing systems within the year.

The company has also acoustically redesigned a small, all-purpose, high-quality monitoring environment known as Room 5A, opening on January 1. It houses a Neotek Encore console, JBL monitoring and an Otari DTR-900 32-track digital recorder. Its genesis was to handle the archiving of the entire Disney sound catalog (see *Mix*, September 1990), transferring to digital multitrack. The archive department is now one year into the seven-year project.

But 5A has taken on so many roles that it might soon need a twin. It's being used to shoot stereo optical sound negatives, to ensure Disney quality right up to the final phase. It doubles as a mixdown room for foreign home video variant mastering, where dialog tracks are provided in up to 20 foreign languages and assembled into a print master for worldwide release. Finally, it serves as a listening room for new pieces of equipment—basic testing and experimentation are done here before equipment hits the dub stages.

Buena Vista Sound has also renovated and restored all sound facilities on the lot over the past three years. Stage A was renovated in 1989 and now offers video and 35mm film-based dubbing capability. A Harrison PP-1 console was installed, along with a custom THX monitoring environment (Electro-Voice components) and 33 Magna-Tech 1000 and 2000 Series dubbers linked with Otari 24-track analog and 32-track digital recorders.

Stage D, where *Beauty and the Beast* was mixed, also received a structural overhaul, mainly a shortening of the hall and complete rewiring of the building. Again, a PP-1 was installed, as were custom THX monitoring, 32 Magna-Tech reproducers, three 35mm recorders and three 32-track Otari digital machines.

Stage C now holds a Solid State Logic 5000 console, with many of the same machines as the other two dub stages. Stage B features a custom Larson Technology/Sound Workshop board and is used for ADR/Foley work. Stages A and B feature a JSK Engineering motion control system, allowing machine room operators to manipulate any combination of picture or sound elements from tape or film sources. Buena Vista Sound also holds a four-wall lease on two ADR/Foley stages from Rubber Dubbers in nearby Glendale, renamed Buena Vista East.

While the Beast's voice was by all accounts the most challenging sound design element, the film lends itself to all sorts of interesting effects and sound moments. The creepy forest that separates the town and castle is filled with plaintive baby cries and cat meows, slowed down to half- or quarter-speed, not to mention the wolf sounds, which are actually 90 percent pit bulls. The candelabra character, Lumiere, constantly waves his "arms," gesticulating with fire. Strangely enough, the fire sound is Foley, because it needed to be articulated to match the action. Foley artist John Roesch simply blew across a Sony ECM-50 lavalier mic, and with a little bit of highpassing to take off the rumble, it turned into fire. And just listen to the transformation from Beast to prince, the climactic moment when inner beauty reveals itself—it sparkles. Finally, much of the action takes place in a cavernous 18th century French castle, with all the ambiences that implies.

REVERB, REVERB, REVERB

Back when Mangini and Porter teamed up on *Star Trek IV*, Porter came up with a system for creating a separate reverb premix so that ambience wasn't locked to the dry dialog tracks. That way, if someone didn't like the feel later, it could just be dumped. But the reverb was textured to fit every scene, so if you needed it, it was there. No futzing in the final.

In this film, Porter and company were dealing with enormous rooms, intimate dinner table settings, courtyards in a storm…you name it. And, of course, the voices and lyrics had to be heard. "I try to mix a dimensional dialog," Porter says. "So often when you're trying to play perspective on dialog, the most common thing is to adjust levels. You want distance, you drop it way back. I find that in the real world—meaning, the audience reaction—dialog gets lost when you try dropping levels too much for perspective. I try to keep basic levels the same and give dimension with echos, delays and slap echos. I alter levels a little bit, but not as much as you normally would."

Porter makes extensive use of his Quantec Room Simulator (accesssed via the Macintosh) and writes programs into a Lexicon 480. He also uses a Lexicon 200, the Eventide H3000 and even an old 949 for the delays. He often combines, layers and blends into a single machine.

"Most of the reverbs that come out of a single machine are really nice," he says. "But in stereo it's nice to spread them out left-center-right-surround with multiple reverbs and characteristics, all within one reverb. Normal reverberation in the real world has a lot of different reflection times and distances and contours, depending on more than the pieces of equipment that I have. On some of the big shots, I would probably have ten different channels of reverb spread out into the different speakers, with different delays, contouring, reverb times—to make one reverb."

One scene, in particular, stands out. It's Mangini's favorite sound moment, though he had nothing to do with it. Gaston, the rival for Belle's affection, has stormed the castle to kill the Beast. They are outdoors, in a second-story courtyard, with thunder, lightning and rain cascading all around. Gaston yells for the Beast to show himself, and his voice beomes an eerie, operatic tenor, bouncing off the walls, so that for a moment, you ask, "Is he inside or outside?" Porter reveals that it was more than a slap delay:

"That's a combination. I used both Eventides to get four separate delays, and then sent each of those through my 480 and Quantec to pick up reverbs on the delays. And I used the 200 to pick up a real thin reverb on the dry voice. On the 480 you can get secondary delays within the reverb. So the main component is the delay, but with each delay there are secondary delays with reverb on them. Definitively, with the effects and music in the scene, you hear the slap. But a dry slap wouldn't sound right. The combination smooths the slaps out and elongates them.

"Again, that one is sent out left-center-right-surround, with a very large delay reverb in the surrounds so that it trails out behind you with each delivery of the line. That always helps to keep the focus on the screen. I find that when I go into surrounds with reverb, it's best to keep the delay quite a bit away from the front screen. The last thing you want is to start hearing—especially if you're in the back of the theater—something in the surrounds preceding the front screen. Very distracting. You don't notice it if it's a far enough delay behind the screen. It just becomes part of the ambience."

"He's one of the few mixers who loves tasty, unique reverbs in every scene," Mangini says of Porter. "He not only loves to ride reverbs, he loves to work those delays and ride them through a scene. He loves to ride EQ as a character turns. In animation, you record the voice on-mic, up-front. But Terry will put that sort of live recording quality back into it—you know, if somebody turns off-mic, he'll roll off a little top, roll off a little bottom. The character turns back on-mic and he puts that curve back into it. He gives it a live action feel, which creates that verisimilitude you need to help sell something that's such an artifice, which is a cartoon."

Actually, cartoon is a no-no word on the Disney lot, and this animated film feels nothing like Saturday morning. Part of that is because most of the animated characters in *Beauty* are human-based—no anthropomorphic dogs here (though there are anthopomorphized tea pots and dinnerware). And also, studio head Jeffrey Katzenberg wants to move away from previous Disney projects, which called for very few effects, and toward a live-action soundtrack. The seam that holds the two eras together is the traditional Disney music. And in *Beauty*, the music is stunning.

Beauty and the Beast is wall-to-wall music. You never really get away from it—six songs and a beautiful, melodic, pastoral underscore. The songs were recorded in New York City with a 65-piece orchestra (mostly from the New York Philharmonic) at BMG's Studio A, mixed by Mike Farrow; the underscore was recorded on the Radford stage at the Sony lot (formerly the MGM lot) in Culver City, Calif., mixed by John Richards at Evergreen in Burbank. Overseeing the 18-month process was music editor Kathleen Bennett.

"This film is the music," Bennett says, "and I know I say that from a biased viewpoint, but it truly is built around the songs. They are integral to the story."

All songs were recorded well in advance of final picture, as storyboards and pencil tests were coming together. The orchestra came in first and recorded to a Mitsubishi 32-track digital machine. Vocalists came in for overdubs. When the songs called for a choir, such as the opening number, "Belle," or "The Mob Song," a 24-track vocal slave was added for appropriate size. The 16-voice choir was doubled and sometimes tripled when action called for the whole town to sing. Then everything was remixed to 24-track analog with Dolby SR.

"On the 24-track, we had three channels of left-center-right orchestra, with all the vocals separate," Bennett explains. "Because the process was so long, many times over the past year the people in editorial had to pull mag from that 24-track. So we tried to mix it into a configuration that was going to be useful for any purpose.

"Another one of my jobs," she continues, "was to provide editorial/animation staff with a variable click tempo for what's known as beat readings. That's how they determine where a particular action should take place. Part of where I got that information was the 24-track. We recorded all of the songs free-time, so after we recorded I had to build a variable click track for all the songs. It also helped in case we wanted to go back in later and sweeten a particular character movement with harp gliss or a horn blat on the orchestra track. We did this extensively on *Little Mermaid,* and this is where I learned to do it right, I think. On

Mermaid I was provided with a final vocal track, laid against a scratch synth and piano track. I had to build a variable click track that we recorded the orchestra against. We then had final orchestra with final vocal, but it was like putting the cart before the horse."

All transfers were made on the Disney lot, and Bennett arranged for song tracks to be delivered to editorial in various formats—single-stripe, full-coat, whatever—to fit all potential purposes. Editorial then took the tracks and cut rough animation to fit the music tracks, in individual units.

"We had very little trouble in the final dub, just a little EQ," Bennett says, a sentiment echoed by music mixer Mel Metcalfe. "And you'd never know that [the score and underscore] were recorded not only in two different places, but at two different times with two different orchestras and two different mixers."

"You go out whistling those songs and singing the lyrics," adds Terry Porter. "And the whole feeling under the songs—with the input of Mark and our effects mixer, Dave Hudson—of keeping a live action sound always underneath it, is absolutely wonderful. There are no egos here. If music handles a moment just right, Dave is more than happy to pull the effects out. And if an effect is playing a moment right, Mel will make sure that he pulls the music back in the right spot. In animation, you can get away with not playing a real effect if the music is stinging something, where it just doesn't feel right in live action. That's what I love about animation: There are no rules."

"You have to look for the abstraction of the action as opposed to taking it literally," Mangini interjects. "That's true in all animated material because it's this make-believe world where you can do anything. Of course, it's a natural playground for sound nuts."

CHAPTER 5

Malcolm X

Director Spike Lee

Malcolm X is out! And *Malcolm X* is big! Step back from the controversy for a minute. Forget about Amiri Baraka and the various claims on who can best represent Malcolm X to the world. Forget about flag-burning and rights to the Rodney King video. Forget about corporate budgets and the call to skip work and school. Look at this film. Listen to this film.

Spike Lee has pieced together a one-of-a-kind project, certainly his most ambitious to date. The storyline, adapted by Arnold Perl from a 20-year-old script by James Baldwin, predates Malcolm's birth and continues after his death. Location shoots ranged from the streets of Harlem to the Egyptian desert to the slums of Soweto to the Holy City of Mecca (the first Western film crew allowed in, we are told). And it's beautifully shot by cinematographer Ernest Dickerson and edited by Barry Brown, with that bold visual style we've come to associate with Spike.

This article appeared originally in the December 1992 edition of Mix.

"It's not a totally personal film," Spike says while watching over the final mix, "because Malcolm X was somebody who lived and breathed. But I think that was the challenge, to make it a personal film and at the same time respect that it is somebody's life. I can't just do anything I want with it. Still, anybody who has seen my work and looks at this film will be able to tell that I did it."

By the same token, anybody who has listened to Spike's work will notice similarities in *X*. The core sound team has been together since *Do the Right Thing* (1989), through *Mo' Better Blues* (1990) and *Jungle Fever* (1991): re-recording mixer Tom Fleischman, supervising sound editor Skip Lievsay and music supervisor Alex Steyermark. (Lievsay and Fleischman also work together for a number of other East Coast directors, among them Scorsese, Demme and Sayles.) The final mix took place over 12 weeks in Studio D of Sound One, New York City. Fleischman, mixing only his second discrete 6-track film, sat solo behind the 60-input Neve with Necam 96 automation.

This is New York, and unlike L.A., where three people sit down for the final, a single re-recording mixer is the norm. Fleischman, who looks considerably younger than his 42 years, moves like a large cat up and down the board, intensely focused on the screen. Behind him or beside him sit Skip, Spike and Alex, with various ears walking in and out of the room. Phones ring silently and constantly. There are no decisions by committee—Spike definitely has final call on whether a particular sound stays or goes or is altered—though there is considerable decision-making by consensus.

X wasn't a particularly difficult film to edit or mix, and it didn't involve any particular revolutions in soundtrack creation. By all accounts, the biggest difficulties had to do with the sheer size and scope of the project. The film is more than three hours long and it's chock full of dialog, music and Foley, which means a helluva lot of material to sort through. As more than one person commented, it was like working on two movies.

The film is 20 reels long, but the mixing process remains the same: Start with the dialog predub and mix it down to two 6-tracks, one being production dialog, the other ADR and group ADR. That takes four weeks, which Fleischman admits is a luxurious schedule. Then start on effects, mixed down to three 6-tracks, while monitoring the dialog. Play those back against Foley, which is mixed down to another two 6-tracks, and when

The BMG Connection: Score, Foley and Group ADR

Two blocks away from Sound One, on the fourth floor of 1133 Sixth Avenue, stands BMG Recording Studios, still referred to by many as RCA. Walking by on the street, you'd never guess that some of the finest ensemble recordings anywhere are laid down on tape here. Broadway show albums, the New York Philharmonic, Hollywood scores for everything from *Beauty and the Beast* to *Consenting Adults*, Placido Domingo, Garrison Keillor, Wynton Marsalis—BMG has seen them all. It's safe to say that *X* could have been done without BMG, but it's also safe to say that it wouldn't have been the same *X*.

It's the big room at BMG, Studio A, that attracts artists and composers. Designed by Alan Stephens, Studio A opened in 1969 with a three-section ceiling that can be raised from 25 to 40 feet. It holds up to 150 pieces on the floor, with an additional 50 voices capable of fitting on the stage off to the right. For *X*, the smaller ensembles and the big band jazz numbers were recorded on floor 10 in Studio C. Studio A was used for the 65-piece orchestral cues and some of the group ADR and Foley dance sessions.

"This was unique for us because we approached the score as a multi-track recording and live mix date at the same time," says James P. Nichols, BMG engineer and scoring engineer for *X*. "We have 48-track analog SR, with another 24-track mix machine. The mics come up in mic position and you bus them; then you bus them and monitor in another position; then you in turn bus to your mix machine. Since we have in-line faders on the Neve VR60, we monitor the mix machine on the monitoring position. So you have microphone-bus, monitor-bus, monitor. And the monitor is then sent to the surrounds."

All the recordings were miked similarly, with the discrete 6-track format in mind. Five mics captured the room: three Neumann TLM50s out front and two outriggers. KM140s were used as close-mics on individual instruments (87s on percussion), laid down to the 48-track for possible sweetening later. According to re-recording mixer Tom Fleischman, they weren't needed.

"It was excellently recorded," Fleischman says. "Very beautifully done. To my way of thinking, [a live mix] is the best way to do it if you have a composer and engineer who can keep an eye and ear on making sure the orchestra stays in balance. If one section is playing louder or softer than they should, then you have to sweeten that section with the spot mics. We didn't have to do that. They were diligent about keeping the orchestra in balance, and it worked out very well."

The same mic configuration was used on the Boys Choir of Harlem overdubs (with some additional close U67s mixed into the five channels) and the Terence Blanchard and Branford Marsalis overdubs, just as it was used on the big band, jazz trio and solo piano sessions. It was altered slightly—two mics held the front, two in the middle, and two in the rear—for the group ADR sessions, when Denzel delivered his lines from a podium to a live audience, complete with audience response. Men were on the left, women on the right, just as actual Muslim rallies were at the time.

Perhaps the most authentic and stimulating group session involved the Fruit of Islam, the security force, if you will, of Louis Farrakhan's Harlem chapter of the Nation of Islam. Spike wanted authenticity for the Black Muslim rallies of the early '60s, so who better than the Nation? According to everyone involved, their responses to the speeches onscreen were genuine and loud. Right on cue with little or no prompting. As they were leaving, Nichols got an added treat.

"As the people were filtering out, the brothers from the Nation started going through their march cadences, their mathematics for the day. We had the microphones on them and we got it all. It was just like armed services march cadences, about 20 minutes of marching around the room. It was incredible."

Finally, there are a number of dance hall scenes in the movie, including a huge Roseland Ballroom scene early on with Malcolm doing the Lindyhop. A choreographer and about 18 dancers were brought into Studio C for Foley. Another 25 people surrounded them for crowd effects, just as you see it on screen. Distant room mics were used to capture the thumps, and Shure SM57s captured the steps.

"You find a group that's going pretty good, that's got the right rhythm," Nichols explains. "Then you mike them about knee-high, three feet away. Just like recording Broadway tap dancing. My assistants were Major Little and Sandy Palmer; couldn't have done it without them."

Big hits, little hits, all kinds of hits have been recorded at this incarnation of BMG over the past 23 years (RCA Studios have been around in one form or another since the Camden, N.J., days in 1901). The sad truth, however, is that the studios are being shut down on March 31, 1993. BMG International is moving the New York operation to smaller quarters on West 45th, where administrative offices and tape mastering rooms will soon be moved. Apparently, BMG was willing to keep the studios open, but the landlord wants to sell all 12 floors of Sixth Avenue real estate as a package. Once those walls are touched by a new owner (provided it's not a studio owner), the unique sound is gone forever.

New big rooms will open up in and around Manhattan to fill the void and meet the demand. But when the last of the music stands is loaded on the elevator and taken down to the truck, a chunk of New York recording history is gone forever.

the three predubs are finished, bring in music for the final. On average, Fleischman can get through a double-reel a day (about 20 minutes of film) once the predubs are finished. For *X*, a single reel takes a day and a half. The final print master eventually goes out on three 6-track full-coat stems.

"This is the third time we've done 70mm but the first time we've done a discrete mix," says Lievsay. "We went out of our way to have as much as possible in the 6-track format. The music, sound effects and voice-over are very special-sounding and unusual. We didn't break any new ground, but I think taken together they make for a very lush soundtrack."

Lush is the perfect word to describe the soundtrack and the picture. Too often we associate "good" sound with big, explosive, attention-grabbing effects, when the reality is that the best tracks are usually the ones we don't notice. *X* certainly has big sound, and Spike likes it loud, but in no way is the sound distracting. Creative? Yes. Up front? Certainly. But you will remember Denzel Washington's oratory long after you've forgotten the sound of the Molotov cocktail crashing through Malcolm's window.

DIALOG, ADR AND VOICE-OVER

"Dialog is king," Fleischman says. "If you don't hear the dialog, you don't get the story. The hardest scenes to mix are never the big action scenes—those kind always mix themselves. You just open up what you have and it's a matter of balance. The most difficult, tedious work in any film is a small, intimate scene between two people, particularly if there is no music.

"For example, there's a scene between Malcolm and his wife talking in a room, just the two of them," he continues. "Then the camera pans across the room and there's some dolly motor noise in the track, along with some clothing rustles. When the dialog editors prepared it, they removed as much of the dolly noise as they could and replaced it with clean room tone. The problem was that where those sections were lifted out and replaced, the clothing rustle suddenly popped up. So every time there was a splice, you could hear the clothing pop. Nothing was covering it satisfactorily, and we got to the final before we solved it by adding a little bit of rain."

If that represents the puzzle-solving tedium of film mixing, then the "fun" must come in scenes where there are rapid cuts from live-action, wide-screen 35mm to a grainy, black-and-white, 16mm image. Usually the switch takes place when the press is surrounding Malcolm, offering the illusion of a documentary perspective, circa 1965.

"We squeeze down Denzel's [Washington, who plays Malcolm X] lines, equalize them and filter them," Fleischman explains. "And we keep it in the center. When we cut back to live action, we used the production track, full-bandwidth, and added some reverb in the sides and surrounds to open it up. It's quite effective, but there again, it's just a matter of experimenting. If you use too much reverb, it sounds canned. You have to find something that fits the image.

"There's another interesting sequence in the film in terms of panning," Fleischman adds, stressing that he normally does not like to pan dialog. "[Denzel] is standing on a stoop, and Bobby Seale is up on a ladder, and Al Sharpton is up on a ladder, and they're all giving speeches at the same time on this street corner. The camera pans off Malcolm, moves in a 360-degree circle, and eventually winds up back on him. Unfortunately, the voices of Bobby Seale and Al Sharpton were not separated in the recording, so they're locked. But [Denzel's] voice actually moves from center to left to left-surround to right-surround to right and back to center. I really won't know whether that works until I see the film all together in a theater this weekend. I have my doubts."

Dialog tracks came in on 1/4-inch and were cut on Moviolas by Kevin Lee, Magdaline Volaitis and Philip Stockton at C5 Inc., Lievsay's home-base editorial house that he owns with three partners. ADR (and there was a lot of it) was recorded mainly in Sound One's Studio K by Dave Baldwin: Six-hundred main character lines; small lines; crowd sessions at BMG (see sidebar); and voice-over. Roughly 50 percent of the film dialog was ADR, according to Lievsay.

"The actors were extremely good loopers," Lievsay says. "I boomed a lot of the looping myself, and we tried to guess where the boom mic was in the sync recording, the idea being to pick up the ADR microphones in a similar place to match better. And it does. That's a pretty good technique that we're starting to use more and more. Also, that way I have something to do besides sit in the session and say, 'Faster, slower. Non-sync, in-sync.'"

Voice-over tends to work best in film when it somehow stands apart from the action and does not act as a storytelling device. The voice-over in *X*, Denzel Washington reading passages from *The Autobiography of Malcolm X* over picture, works for precisely that reason. It also works because it sounds different. It sounds rich and full. It has presence.

Lievsay came up with the idea of recording the voice-over in multimic stereo in the big room at BMG Studios. Denzel spoke from a podium with a Neumann U87 out front, a lavalier on his lapel, and a pair of Schoeps cardioids left and right. When the omnidirectional Neumann picked up too much of the room, it was filtered down and backfilled with the lavalier, which also brought a sort of "chesty resonance" to the tracks, a "mechanical proximity," Lievsay says.

"By doing it multimic, we can take advantage of the three speakers up front [in the theater] instead of just one," he adds. "The voice-over can then be separated and be perceived [by the audience] to be different. Also, you can make it much louder. You can have voice-over over dialog and maintain the separation. You can have voice-over, music and effects all playing together at a louder volume. You can play with perspectives, like music playing out one side and effects the other. It basically multiplies the number of options by three."

"We wanted to make sure that there was a dramatic quality difference between the voice-over and the sync dialog," Fleischman adds, offering a mixer's view. "You try to find a balance between the two center mics—the 87 and the lavalier—then balance that with whatever you're using from the left-right Schoeps pair. We then treated it with the SPL Vitalizer, a psychoacoustic equalizer. It synthesizes upper and lower harmonics, sort of like a [dbx 120] boom box except that it also works on the high end. It brings a lot more presence to the upper end of the spectrum and a very deep low end so that the voice sounds full."

X is about dialog and words; it is not a big showcase for sound effects. Authentic backgrounds were constructed in stereo, using period cars (from recordings done for the Coen Brothers' *Miller's Crossing*) and non-distinct traffic sounds, accompanied by authentic sirens when necessary. Some motorcycle sounds in the JFK sequence came from work done on *Cool World*. All effects were culled from DAT and CD libraries at C5, then applied creatively.

Anybody can make a building blow up, but not everybody can construct a sinister telephone ring or an increasingly menacing flash bulb sound. Lievsay, who won a Golden Reel for sound effects editing on the Coen Brothers' *Barton Fink*, likes to put elements up there for the mix. If the director doesn't like an effect, it's gone, just as Spike vetoed a gunshot sound that accompanied a telephone slam in Reel 18. Creative use of sound involves risk, and it involves hearing things that sometimes aren't seen on the screen. If it works in the final, great. If it doesn't, move on. The flash bulb sound, cliche as it seems, works.

"There were a lot of elements that Spike encouraged us to tie together with the flash bulb sound," Lievsay says. "There's the idea that fame can be a bad thing politically. Cinematically, the flash bulb has been used for dramatic impact, and that goes through many different films, like *Raging Bull* with its famous flash sounds used as a cinematic device more than a political statement. With *Malcolm X* it is used throughout the film as the marking of the passage of time and the evolution of Malcolm's character."

Simply put, in the beginning of the film the flashes are innocent; by the end they become distant gunshots. Fleischman calls it a "flash motif." Other threads of association are more subtle. A tiny bullet-by from the JFK motorcade sequence, mixed from left-front to right-rear, reappears later in the film accompanying a swish-pan camera move at one of Malcolm's final press conferences.

Most of the Foley—thousands of cues—was recorded at C5 directly into one of two NED PostPros. "This way we can record and edit without having to do all the transfers," Lievsay explains. "The labor becomes more intensely associated with editing and very little else. Once it's edited, we can transfer to mag—4-track with SR—to bring to the mixing stage. The recording process is pretty streamlined. It's faster; it's suitably cheaper, all things considered; and as a system-wide approach to Foley, it's certainly equal to doing it on film."

As with ADR, Foley is miked from a distance, with EV RE27s handling the metallic sounds, Sanken stereo mics for group effects, and Schoeps cardioids for footsteps and the like.

"Most stuff is miked from a distance, so whenever possible we use the room to add in natural ambience," Lievsay says. "We've gone completely around on this. It's difficult to edit when you have other artifacts like reverb, because if you need to link up with something, the decay cuts off. However, for the amount of time that's spent equalizing and adding reverb in the Foley premix, we find that we end up with much better product if the reverb is built-in.

"The more you imitate what's happening in the production, the better it sounds and the more logical it sounds, and therefore the easier it is to mix. This is not any news. This is the way it's done in California, although it's not typically the way it's done in New York."

MUSIC

Anybody who has read the *Autobiography* knows that Malcolm loved music, mostly big band jazz. And anybody who's watched Spike Lee's films knows that Spike loves music, all kinds of jazz and everything else. Bring their tastes together, add the emotion of Terence Blanchard's original score, and you have a source soundtrack that's sure to go platinum and a score soundtrack that's sure to gain high critical praise. (The source music soundtrack will be released by Quincy Jones' Qwest Records; the score will be released on Spike's new 40 Acres and a Mule Musicworks label.)

The score, recorded over three-and-a-half weeks at BMG (see sidebar) and ranging from solo piano to initimate jazz trio to 65-piece orchestra, is gorgeous and epic. It's 65 minutes of "Malcolm's Theme," "Betty's Theme," and numerous variations, with Branford Marsalis adding sax overdubs, Blanchard himself on trumpet, and the Harlem Boys Choir lending vocals.

Despite his realtively sophisticated sense of and use of score, Spike revels in the use of source music to help tell his story. Score works its way in subtly, through the back door to the brain. Source hits you over the head and makes you dance (like Public Enemy's "Fight the Power" from *Do the Right Thing*). It can also make you cry. The *X* credits include Count Basie, Lionel Hampton, Duke Ellington, Hoagy Carmichael, Ray Charles, Ella Fitzgerald, Billie Holiday, the Ink Spots, Jr. Walker & the All Stars, Aretha Franklin, Sam Cooke, and on and on. Spike picks the music. Spike picks the cues.

"When I hear a song that I really love, I always make a mental note to use it in a film one day. I don't know what film or scene, but eventually I will get it into a movie. This is a perfect example of that, 'A Change Is Gonna Come," he says, pointing to the screen. The camera cuts between people converging on the Audubon Ballroom on the day of Malcolm's assassination, February 21, 1965. Sam Cooke's vocals and a beautiful song lead them in. It is perhaps the biggest moment of Spike's biggest film.

Source music comes from various sources, but it's all 2-track masters. The mixer's job is to make each cut sound in line with the rest of the film, to make it as big and wide as the orchestra and as small as the piano or solo trumpet. Because most of the music in the film is seen emanating from a source—i.e., a jukebox, car radio, band on stage—Fleischman first narrowed the image musically by filtering it and squeezing it down to mono-center. Then reverb is added to fill it up theatrically, both left-right and in the surrounds. Once Foley dance steps, clapping and effects are added, as in the Lionel Hampton "Flying Home" ballroom scene, it's suddenly a full house.

"That recording was made back in the '40s," Fleischman says. "It was originally a mono recording, but I guess they had some kind of stereo synthesis on it. We treated it with the 480 [and the Vitalizer], using some variations on the set hall programs—one for the left-right, one for the surrounds. That's probably the biggest source cue in the film. The scene was shot to playback with a live orchestra, and if you listen closely you can tell. Spike didn't want to sweeten it at all; he wanted to use the original recording. It's a great piece of music, and I can understand the director not wanting to screw around with it."

One final musical note. Initial screenings of the film had a hard-hitting Public Enemy song over the end credits, which followed a beautiful film-montage accompanied by gorgeous score and Ossie Davis overdubbing the eulogy. Apparently, some people thought the contrast was too jarring. Phone calls were made, and Aretha Franklin agreed to record "Someday We'll All Be Free." On Friday, September 18, she was in the studio. On Monday afternoon, producer Arif Mardin walked into Sound One with the 4-track masters and a DAT backup under his arm. By Friday, Aretha was singing over the end credits, with Blanchard on horn. Who says there's no real drama in a final mix?

Though relatively trouble-free, the final was not without its problems. Some forgotten sounds had to be grabbed, a clock had to be slowed down by removing every other tick, and the effects predub had to be gone through twice. It seems that on Reel 17, Fleischman and Lievsay discovered an effect out of phase. An oscilloscope was brought in, and sure enough, as much as 50 percent of the effects were out of phase. Live and learn. Back to Reel 1.

Still, for most of the people who worked on X, the relief felt at the end of a long and tiring process will soon be replaced by the realization that they were part of something grand. Spike has said that he was born to direct this picture. Denzel has said he was born to do this part. One person I talked to even divided his professional career into Before Malcolm and After Malcolm.

"I learned something about the business," Lievsay says in summation. "I learned that there is a difference between movies like this and other pictures. I probably will never work on another picture quite like this. It was very refreshing, especially in these cynical times.

"You know, I was coming back from Los Angeles and Ossie Davis was on the plane," he continues. "Ossie was a friend of Malcolm X's and he delivered the eulogy at Malcolm's funeral. We have Ossie reading the eulogy in the film. I asked him on the plane if it was the same eulogy, and he said it was. There's something interesting there. It's powerful."

CHAPTER 6

Welcome to Jurassic Park

At the SSL 5000 in Mix E, Skywalker Sound, are (l to r) Christopher Boyes, Gary Summers, Gary Rydstrom, and Richard Hymns. Not pictured: Shawn Murphy.

SOUND DESIGN FOR STEVEN SPIELBERG'S DINOSAUR EPIC

Without giving away the opening, you're going to hear these dinosaurs before you see them. Whether it's the lilting melody of brachiosaurus, the vicious attack of velociraptor, or the earth-shaking footsteps of T Rex, it could be argued that sound offers the first real encounter with these warm-blooded, birdlike reptiles at the center of Steven Spielberg's much-anticipated *Jurassic Park*.

Based on the best-selling novel by Michael Crichton, who also wrote the screenplay, *Jurassic Park* is a weekend tale of an amusement park gone bad. Genetically engineered dinosaurs, the living heart of the world's most ambitious theme park, have begun to act unpredictably, so a team of specialists is sent to Isla Nebular for an assessment. None of them has yet seen a dinosaur. What follows is a two-hour, 14-reel roller-coaster ride that is sure to be the box office splash of the summer.

This article appeared originally in the July 1993 edition of Mix.

"You don't see the dinosaurs as well as you hear them for the first part of the movie," explains sound designer Gary Rydstrom from his mix room at Skywalker Sound, Marin County, Calif., "which is an interesting way to introduce their character. Spielberg and Crichton were very clever in setting up primal, scary situations where you can't really see what's going on, but you can hear it.

"In the case of the raptor, my first idea of its breathing was to have these reptilian, hiss-like, high-pitched breaths," he says. "But that didn't work so well, especially for scenes in which you don't see it, because you have no sense of size. If you just hear this little hissing, you think a snake is coming at you. So we went to these more horse-like breaths and snorts, which have a resonance, a resonant cavity that from breathing alone gives you a sense of size: It's much bigger. In this movie, we had to take into account not only how a particular sound matched the picture, but how it would stand on its own. Same with T Rex. You hear him roaring in the woods before you see him."

The dinosaur sounds—the hisses, breaths, screams, clicks, roars and grunts, referred to as vocalizations—were created over a six-week period in the summer of 1992. Rydstrom researched and worked up a library of interesting vocal effects, most recorded new by himself and assistant Christopher Boyes. He traded videomatics of works-in-progress with Industrial Light & Magic as they built the visual effects; sometimes sound led picture, as with the brachiasaurus' fluid head movement above the trees, and often picture dictated sound, as Rydstrom admits, "There were lots of cases where I had interesting sounds, but they didn't match visually." Either way, the animators had dinosaur vocals to draw to, much as you record the voice of Kathleen Turner before finalizing Jessica Rabbit.

But the question remains: How does Gary Rydstrom know what a dinosaur sounds like? "The first reference I think has to be other movies," he says, "because there's a certain expectation for what standard dinosaurs, like a Tyrannosaur, should sound like. If I had him sound like a big, squawking parrot, no one would buy it. With the other dinosaurs, it really came from how they moved, which is what [model makers] Phil Tippett and Stan Winston and all the people at ILM were trying to come up with. They all looked like lizards, but there seemed to be a lot of personality in movement. Would it walk like a bird? Would it run like a horse?"

DTS Digital Audio Playback on Jurassic Park

About 1,000 theaters were expected to be equipped with a special CD-ROM-based digital sound playback system in time for the release of *Jurassic Park*. According to Terry Beard, president of Digital Theater Systems (Westlake Village, Calif.), two replay formats are offered: DTS Stereo for 2-channel, matrix-encoded releases, with an additional subwoofer channel; and DTS-6, a 6-channel configuration offering LCR, split surrounds and subwoofer.

According to *Jurassic Park* sound designer and re-recording mixer Gary Rydstrom, mixing for the new format is no different than mixing for 70mm split-surround. "In the room format, you're listening to left-center-right and left-surround, right-surround," he says. "You have essentially a 5-track mix plus a boom channel, so it's six discrete channels. No matrixing or anything like that. The difference between this and standard 70mm Dolby is that there is some matrixing that Dolby does with 70mm where the low-end information on the split-surrounds is actually contained on a mono-surround channel. We're going to have a hard time when we finally come around to mastering this film for a traditional film optical, as opposed to what we're used to listening to, which is 20 dB of headroom and discrete channels, and really deep low end and everything else. There's so much of it that we're going to have to squeeze onto the regular optical track. It's frustrating. This movie in partiuclar really needs that low end and that dynamic range if it's to be articulate. I mean, the essence of the Tyrannosaurus vocal is that it's subharmonic, and it shakes your chest. That's the kind of thing that you would lose going to see this in a theater with a traditional sound system as opposed to the 6-track sound system."

A special time code stripe added to a conventional stereo optical print provides frame-accurate synchronization to DTS decoder units, which connect to the CD-ROM drives. According to Beard, extensive tests have shown that the extra time code stripe is transparent to all but the most misaligned projectors, insuring compatibility of the optical print with conventional systems.

Audio data compression on the CD-ROM discs is provided by Audio Processing Technology's APT-X 100 codecs. The data is received via SCSI and processed by the DTS/DTS-6 decoder units. Outputs from the decoder units plug into a movie house's existing cinema processor. No special conversions are required to replay DTS films.

The 2-channel system requires a single CD-ROM drive and DTS decoder; the 6-channel version utilizes two interlocked drives (which use the new double-speed Toshiba 3401B mechanisms) and a DTS-6 decoder that is capable of playing back 3-1/2 hours of multichannel audio. DTS is offering the two systems to theaters at an introductory price of $2,500 and $3,500, respectively. Beard expects to see 2,000 DTS-equipped movie houses by the end of the year, and 5,000 by the end of 1994. *Jurassic Park* is the first of a new generation of releases from Universal that will take advantage of this new technology, which Beard expects to compete favorably with the competing Dolby and Sony systems.

—*Paul Potyen*

Actually, the first step was hunting and gathering. Rydstrom and Boyes, especially Boyes, spent hours in the field chasing down unique animal sounds and recording them to a Sony 2000 DAT machine. An individual dinosaur may be made up of 25 to 30 different animal sounds, with four to six playing at any one time. For example, a T Rex inhale may include lions and seals and dolphins, while the exhale might be whale blow-holes and elephants. "I never create something from nothing," Rydstrom says, "because I don't do synthesis. Everything comes from sounds in the real world."

In this case, the real word ranged from a macaw farm to a cattle ranch to a "retired lion farm" to Marine World. "At Marine World [in Vallejo, Calif.] the trainer had me stand to the side by a box," Boyes explains, "and one by one these sea lions marched right up and went through a repertoire of about 50 sounds—the most amazing, bizarre sounds. Each one was completely unlike the others. They each did a solo performance into the mic, and they were better behaved than most people I've recorded in ADR. We also did dolphins, killer whales, baby elephants and mating tortoises."

The lions from Marine World weren't so successful because they mostly traveled in groups, so Boyes went to Ron Whitfield's "Big Cat" park to record an unusual territorial lion bark he had heard about. A geese hiss, used as part of the raptor's agitated breathing, came from an angry goose. And the sound of a herd of dinosaurs fleeing T Rex, what Rydstrom refers to as his "wild west" scene, came from a mini-cattle roundup on a Marin County ranch.

A whole story could be written on the raw material that went into creating the dinosaur vocals and movements. One of the more-interesting situations involved the owner of a reptile shop who came out to the Foley stages at Skywalker Ranch with animals in tow. "He brought everything from monitor lizards and iguanas to bull snakes and a 20-foot, 180-pound python," Boyes says. "From the larger reptiles we got these sort of crinkly, weird skin movement sounds. We ended up Foleying a lot of the movement, but there it was. We also got incredible hisses, including one from a rattlesnake that I believe plays with the dilaphosaurs, flanged."

Boyes could be considered an all-purpose recordist, as he also recorded the vehicle sounds, the rain and handled all the Foley. Rydstrom, he says, likes to have one person involved with the effects all the way through to the final. He uses the Sony DAT in the field, with Sanken mics for general-purpose situations and the Neumann KMR-81 for a close perspective and tighter matrix.

"I try to saturate—I would say saturate the tape, but I guess it's 'use up as many digits as possible' on the DAT—because I find that the harder you hit it, the better it sounds," Boyes explains. "Obviously, you don't have as much forgiveness working with DAT as you do with analog, because if you distort it, it basically becomes a non-usable sound. But I find that in almost every case you should go for maximum signal on the DAT because it becomes much heavier and sweeter."

Counting all the effects, not just the dinosaurs, Boyes, Rydstrom and supervising sound editor Richard Hymns ended up with 50 one-hour DATs to sort through. For the dinos, Rydstrom then set about creating and combining on the Synclavier by sampling the sounds and developing a massive library—everything from 50 different isolated horse breaths to screaming birds and elephants.

"I would then start playing with combinations, literally playing," Rydstrom says. "It's very easy on the Synclavier to instantly combine stuff, play it backward, play it at a different pitch, and start seeing that maybe if you add an alligator growl with an elephant trumpet and a camel, maybe that would be interesting. It's like cooking.

"You choose the ones you like and spread them out on the keyboard," he adds. "There are four levels on the keys of the Synclavier, and usually at no given time is a dinosaur made up of more than four animals. A lot of times I put things together with the idea of having something with low end, mid frequencies and high frequencies. Or something with a strong attack and something with an interesting middle. I spent most of last summer finding these combinations, naming them, then storing them for future use. It was a very accessible library that was easy to edit with and easy to perform once picture came in.

Visual effects supervisor Dennis Muren at his Silicon Graphics workstation.

"The most time-consuming dinosaur was the velociraptor because these vocals come out of the creatures' intelligence and personality," he continues. "T Rex's personality is pretty much hunt-and-kill, so it pretty much roars and sniffs. The raptor hunts in packs and has communication skills, so there has to be intelligence in its voice as well as scariness. Breathing is one animal, screams are made up of geese and dolphins. There's a penguin, an African crane, sea otters. The guttural clicking is a friend of mine, Dietrich, so there's some human stuff in there, too. The reason it's made up of 25 animals is that it does so many things. It would have been great to go out in the real world and find an animal that was 'the raptor,' but no animal is ever that interesting."

While the rest of the film was edited conventionally on mag, the dinosaur vocals were edited and premixed in the Synclavier, mainly to avoid the massive tape library that would have been needed for all the variations on mouth movements and breathing. "It's very easy with digital editing to choose the pace of breathing that leads into the next roar," Rydstrom says. "You have 'roar-inhale-exhale-inhale-roar,' so it fits like a jigsaw puzzle. Sometimes you type in the time code number and have it happen at a precise time. And sometimes you perform it on the keyboard until you get a performance you like. Then I would skip dumping it to mag by just premixing it. And once I got a section I liked, I would mix it—pan it, add echo and mix it right there, because my room is both an editorial room and a full-fledged mix stage."

The editing and mixing of the dinosaur vocals took place from February to April while the editors worked on the rest of the units. But before that, in early January, Rydstrom, Hymns and ADR editor Laurel Ladovitch flew to Los Angeles for a meeting with Spielberg and a first look at the whole film. They sat at the KEM for an intense six-hour session, looking at basically a locked picture, *sans* many of the computer-generated images, and listening to the A track. They had a breakdown of each reel by scene description, and they furiously took notes—all the Foley, dialog, effects and ADR questions answered at once. It was, Hymns says, a grueling day.

They returned to Skywalker with a dupe of the film and ran it through the KEM the following day, at a much slower pace. Rydstrom and Hymns took more notes and further defined their duties, deciding on Foley moments vs. effects moments and the like. They then split up and broke down the bigger categories into details and timings. Hymns spent the rest of January gathering specific material in tandem with Boyes, mainly focusing on jeeps, rain and ambiences.

When it's raining in the film, rain is the ambience. The sound team was lucky in that right when they began gathering sounds, California ended its seven-year drought and it rained for a month straight. Some nights Boyes slept with his DAT by the bed and a long mic cable, essentially waking up to press "record." He also recorded rain on a number of different surfaces.

"Since there are rain sequences that go on for a long time," Rydstrom says, "we tried to vary the types of rain so that it isn't 20 minutes of pink noise. I learned on *A River Runs Through It* that anything with water and rain becomes difficult. It eats up the high frequencies, and it's difficult to mix. So the key to making it interesting, to propel it forward and make it all work, is to be constantly changing it—from perspective cuts, or as you move to different locations, to have rain on wood, rain on cars, rain on pavement, rain on vegetation, rain on puddles."

"One of the first things we did once the effects editors came on in February was sit down with the four of them at an editing station and play the available ambiences one by one," Hymns explains. "I know that no editor is going to listen to 100 backgrounds for the first scene. They listen to them, hear the one they like and move on. We wanted to use all of them. We didn't want the same ambience turning up in several different places, or the same ambience at all. As much as possible, we wanted the editors to pick up a new ambience for every scene and make combinations, laying as many as six or seven in a given scene instead of one."

These are jungle ambiences primarily (though the park's master control room also is prominent in the picture), and they came from all over the world—Sri Lanka, Indonesia, Costa Rica, Hawaii. According to Hymns, this is where you begin building the tension that made the book a page-turning, one-day read.

Sound Designer Gary Rydstrom

"In some scenes you start off with this little pretty thing, and you know it's going to get bad," Hymns says. "So you just creep one [ambience] down and introduce another that has something else in it. It could be a raspy frog, or it could be a nighttime insect thing with a little electronic weirdness to it. If you just gradually take the birds out, the tension is already there."

Rydstrom agrees: "But the trick in making things quiet," he points out, "doesn't mean that you don't play any sounds at all. When things are quiet in a movie, it means that you're hearing details you wouldn't normally hear. If you're trying to build tension out in the woods before a dinosaur shows up, you have everything get really quiet, then you hear leaves hitting the electric fence, or you hear certain birds, or you hear animals way in the distance, or you hear winds whipping around. It's sort of a hyperawareness, like a drug state. Suddenly everything is incredibly sharp and detailed, but low-level. Those moments are tense."

And those scenes are difficult to design. As most designers, editors and mixers will attest, it's not the big car-chase, shoot-em-up scenes that are difficult—they play themselves. But when there are only a few sounds and everything is exposed, the effects have to be spot-on. For example, there's a scene where raptors are stalking children through a kitchen in the dark. The raptor footsteps and their guttural, clicking vocalizations are all Foley, masterfully performed by Dennie Thorpe. And the children's breathing stands out as an element of terror.

"I had to place myself in the head of the dinosaur for that scene," Rydstrom explains. "It was my job to want to kill the children—which is certainly not where the audience's head will be—only because I had to come up with the vocalizations. But the sound of the actors breathing is just as effective, if not more, than anything I could come up with. I wish I could design that. The kids in this movie are really good screamers, and there's nothing more horrific than a screaming child. I can come up with the best dinosaur sound in the world, and it can scare the pants off you, but the sound of a screaming child is going to be more effective."

Most of the screams were recorded at Skywalker, and according to Hymns, they made up the bulk of the ADR work. Despite the fact that most of the scenes take place outdoors, there were only 500 to 600 ADR lines. By contrast, *Backdraft* required 2,600 lines.

Jurassic is not a dialog-heavy movie, granted, and the production mix was delivered on DAT, with all the transfers taking place in-house. Ron Judkins recorded on location to the Fostex PD-2 time code machine and simultaneously to an analog Nagra. The Nagra reels were left in L.A. with Michael Kahn, the picture editor, so that he could work with last-minute changes.

When the editors came on in February, all the units were on the racks ready to cut. Premixing began the last week of March and lasted about three weeks. The only real time crunch came in the final, and that was made easier thanks to the already-complete dinosaur vocals and the rather extensive work on the premixes.

"Instead of having all the effects on one premix, we have them on four, sometimes five, 6-tracks," Hymns explains. "It sounds crazy, but we generally put ambience on A, ambience-related things such as individual birds or rain on D, my vehicle sounds on B, and the crashes and whatnot on C. The dialog will then be on two premixes, split into LCR, and the Foley will be on another.

"We found that even though we're using a little more stock," he continues, "we can avoid going back to the units. The biggest nightmare for me is to try to keep a hundred units of effects in-sync with an ever-changing picture. I can pull up a few individual units in an emergency, but I don't keep the whole hundred in-sync any more, and I haven't for a long time. This way, if Steven says, 'The crickets are too loud,' they are on their own. If he says, 'The crash is too loud,' it's on its own. If he wants to hear more of the gear shift, it's on its own. Nothing is mixed together. That's the most important thing."

The premixes were finished on Friday, April 16, the same day Shawn Murphy flew up from Los Angeles with the music to join Rydstrom and Gary Summers behind the SSL 5000 for the final. Murphy recorded the John Williams orchestral score on the MGM (now Sony) stage in Culver City, essentially making a live 5-channel submix that served as his premix. There was some interaction with the composer as the score was being developed, but for all intents and purposes, the final was the first time that the Skywalker team heard the music.

"This is a traditional and beautiful-sounding score," Rydstrom says, "and it creates a sense of awe that matches the classic beauty of the scenes. There's a certain majesty to it, and another part is very scary. It has to cover a broad range of emotions. Typically, music and effects people are in an unstated competition on individual scenes, but I've come to realize over the years that a good film score just makes everything I do sound that much better. And this is a very good film score."

Six days after starting the "first final," Rydstrom, Summers and Amblin Entertainment associate producer for post-production Colin Wilson flew to Paris with the complete film, minus a few visuals that were still coming in from Industrial Light & Magic. Spielberg flew in from Poland, where he was filming *Schindler's List*, and they met in a dub stage for a run-through. Spielberg talked into a dictaphone as the reels ran, noting changes.

It went amazingly well, Rydstrom says, and Spielberg's notes were very specific: taking music out or moving it to some other point; this effect should be replaced by something more like this effect later on; this T Rex vocal is really great, see if you can use it in this other scene. They flew back the next morning and checked off the changes one by one. Because they knew in advance that it would be a tight mix schedule, Skywalker installed Neve Flying Faders automation on the SSL specifically for this film. Fixes were made back in the original premixes, and the automation saved a great deal of time in translating the changes to the second final. Two weeks later the group flew back to Paris with the "final final," complete with final picture. Ten days after that, on May 18, the first print master was sent to the lab.

By all accounts, it was an unbelievably smooth post-production process, mainly because there were minimal picture changes following the initial January KEM screening in L.A. Everything was on-time and under-budget, and the editors even got to eat lunch. As Rydstrom says, "This really feels like a film made by people who have been doing it long enough and know their craft well enough that it's really efficient. Obviously these are people who know how to make a movie, from pre-production, through production, and into post."

More than one person has said that this movie will do for computer-generated visuals what *Star Wars* did for the photo-chemical, special effects process. And many people will judge this film on how "realistic" the dinosaurs appear on screen, not realizing, at least consciously, that sound contributes to the equation.

"I know what film sound people mean when they say that their job is 'to not be heard,'" Hymns says in summary, "and I agree with that to a point. But there's also a time when you want to be heard. I think when you have a visual of a dinosaur onscreen that lives, and is really there, your sound has to be equally astounding. Otherwise, people are going to stop and think about it. You don't want them questioning how this was done until they're out in the car and say, 'Wait a second, these things don't live. How did they do that?' You don't want that going on during the movie. I think the sound has to be balls-to-the-wall to match the visuals, and certainly for the dinosaurs that's the case."

It's the Wrong Trousers, Gromit!

Director/animator Nick Park

Move over California Raisins. Wallace and Gromit, a fifty-something inventor who enjoys a bit of the gorgonzola and his faithful, silent dog, are the new international claymation superstars. They may not have their own action figures or TV commercials…yet., but then the Raisins don't have an Academy Award.

Wallace and Gromit are the plasticine stars of director/animator Nick Park's 1994 Oscar-winning *The Wrong Trousers*, a 26-minute action-adventure short that took 15 months to shoot—frame by painstaking frame. It's the story of Wallace the tinkerer, who's created a pair of programmable techno-trousers to take Gromit out for "walkies." When money gets tight, Wallace decides to take in a lodger to help pay the rent.

This article appeared originally in the June 1994 issue of Mix.

The lodger turns out to be Feathers McGraw, a mysterious penguin who assumes Gromit's place of favor with Wallace while plotting a diamond heist with the aid of the techno-trousers. The film weaves in and out of elaborate indoor and outdoor sets, culminating in a wild chase scene, complete with gunfire, on a toy train that runs through the main floor of the Wallace and Gromit residence.

"*The Wrong Trousers* sort of aspires to be a feature film on every level—in terms of the sound, the visuals, the story, the plot, the characters, the lighting," says Park, who began working on his first major claymation film, *A Grand Day Out,* as a graduation project in 1985 while at the National Film and Television School. He finished it after signing on to the staff of England's acclaimed Aardman Animations, owned by Peter Lord (an Academy Award nominee himself) and David Sproxton, who produced *The Wrong Trousers.*

The Wrong Trousers marks the second appearance of Wallace and Gromit. They were introduced in *A Grand Day Out,* which was nominated for a 1990 Academy Award in Best Animated Short Film but lost to Park's other nomination, *Creature Comforts.* Three films, three nominations, two wins.

The lighting and staging of *The Wrong Trousers* combine the most elaborate aspects of film noir feature film production with the intimacy and detail of theatrical stage presentations. And the audio tracks are every bit as full and rich as a Hollywood feature, from the padded Foley footsteps of the penguin (animated primarily by Steve Box) to the dramatic Bernard Hermann-esque score.

THEATRICAL SCORE

The soundtrack, particularly the score, is effective because it is straight—few cartoon effects, no huge tympani-roll music selections. "The score is almost one you could have in a live-action thriller," says composer Julian Nott. "We made no concessions to the fact that all the characters are made out of plasticine, and no attempt to ridicule any of the characters because they are fake. The score uses Hermann-esque musical conventions from a Hitchcock thriller, rather that the conventions of a Tom and

Jerry film. I feel the value of this is that a comic absurdity is created—the audience starts to accept Wallace, Gromit and the Penguin as real characters, with real human idiosyncrasies, when at the same time they realize this is absolutely illogical, creating a comic tension."

Nott has worked with Park since their days together at the National Film and Television School. His composing setup is simple, as it is mainly used to provide temp music and demos for the director and to produce ideas for later orchestration. Nott relies on Mac-based Notator Logic synched with Opcode Studio 3 to a VHS deck, with LTC timecode on one of the audio channels. His keyboard of choice is the E-mu Proteus 2 Orchestral, with sounds coming from an E-mu Proformance. If he blends acoustic sounds with synth sounds, he generally uses a Korg WRV Wavestation, which, he says, "provides good atmospheric sounds—perfect for film scores."

The orchestral sessions for *The Wrong Trousers* took place at Abbey Road 1 in London to take advantage of the large room. "British films these days rarely can afford full-size orchestras," Nott says. "So I find that the large halls tend to make the sound 'bigger,' even though we could often fit the orchestra into much smaller studios." The score was recorded to 24-track with Dolby SR, then mixed down to SR-encoded 4-track 35mm film (LCRS).

BUT FIRST, THE DIALOG

As with most animated projects, the dialog tracks—the voice of British actor Peter Sallis as Wallace—were recorded prior to production, with only a few off-camera lines placed in post to achieve story continuity. The Sallis tracks were edited and layed in by picture editor Helen Gerrard on 35mm, then premixed by dubbing editor (the Stateside equivalent would be supervising sound editor) Adrian Rhodes to 35mm SR-encoded 4-track, panned and positioned as necessary. For a claymation feature, the lip sync is remarkable.

"After recording the dialog on its own," Park explains, "we break down the track and transfer it to 35 mag. Then we put it on the flatbed, and an editor goes through to mark the track phonetically by syllables. That is then copied onto a dope sheet, and that tells us exactly how many frames it takes to say each sound—basically the animator's guide to getting good lip sync."

In light of Park's distinctive animation style, it's interesting that the actors' voices, whether in *Creature Comforts* or the two Wallace and Gromit pictures, help to shape it. "I've found that the voices dictate to me the modeling," Park says. "They suggest to me the various extremes and the movement, and the different kinds of intonations and accents that the character has. For example, Peter Sallis' voice helped to establish my style—the wide mouth, close eyes—especially the way he says things like 'chhheeese.' Maybe it's just a very British way of saying things. I knew Peter from the TV, from a show he's been on for 20 years called *Last of the Summer Wine*. I never really considered anyone else."

SOUND EFFECTS AND THE MIX

Audio post took place at Interact Sound Limited, a private editing and dubbing facility in London's West End. Rhodes supervised and cut most of the effects, music and dialog, then sat in with Aad Wirtz for the final mix to 2-track Dolby Stereo. Bill Morgan recorded many of the original sounds, both in the studio and on location (toy train and garbage can rattle, to name a couple).

Approximately 70 percent of the effects in *The Wrong Trousers* are original to DAT; the other 30 percent came from Interact's in-house DAT/disc library. Effects were processed—pitch-shifted, reversed, flanged, looped, etc.—using a Casio FZ-1 MIDI keyboard sampler in combination with the Spectral Synthesis Audio Engine, a 16-bit, 256-track PC-based hard disk system. Interact has three systems set up in three edit suites. Editing took place on the Spectral, and two 6-track effects premixes were made direct from the Spectral system onto SR mag. Interact houses Perfectone mag dubbers.

By the end of the tracklay, Rhodes had created more than 14 hours of sound effects with more than 10,000 edits—for a half-hour film. But the most interesting and challenging sound design element was unquestionably the techno-trousers. Wallace presents them to Gromit on the dog's birthday, accompanied by an ominous, menacing score and the creak, squeak and clank of a mechanical contraption with a mind of its own.

"The sound for each step goes something like: 'Shhtump-der-weewip-dikadika-ptschhhhhhh!" Rhodes says. "The plan was to imply an internal mechanism made up of ratchets, cogs, knee-lifting electric motors and pneumatic gas struts. Then we added a turbo-drive motor for high speeds and a vacuuming sucker pod for wall and ceiling walking. In the Foley sessions, Jack Stew provided the surface impact with the aid of a circa-1950 metal bread bin and whatever else he could find.

"The hissy air-rush sounds were mostly me hissing into a Sennheiser 416," he continues. "Then we forwarded and reversed it, combined with the gas strut of a car trunk. A sink plunger and me slurping and kissing pulled the techno-trousers against the walls and ceilings. The electric motor element came from the rewind motor on an SLR camera, which we bent on the keyboard's pitch wheel. Rapid creaks were usually from slower ratchety sounds that were heavily sped up. In fact, many of the sounds were created by human mouth—a versatile instrument!

"Once the basic design of the trouser sounds was agreed on with Nick, I laid them up on the Spectral Multitrack page, synching, editing and overlapping them to make one homogenous sound. By the end of this process, the ingredients were spread over 12 virtual tracks. Internal premixes of these to two tracks made things more manageable, but at the same time enabled me to keep the original ingredients intact in the hard drive library for future use."

One final note: Listen for the Foley effects, especially the penguin's footsteps as he plots the heist, which is Rhodes' favorite Foley moment. Foley walker Jack Stew found the perfect slap for webbed feet, Rhodes says; add a little bit of Lexicon 480L "alley" reverb and presto! It would have been quicker and cheaper to do all the Foley electronically, but they opted to record directly to 6-track SR-encoded mag and transfer into the Spectral for editing.

"I like the kind of realism that the sounds have, and the earthiness," Park says. "Because the animation to me is more earthy—it's there and it's 3-D, rather than the sort of Tom and Jerry whoooop! There is a slight bit of that, but it's a fine balance. You just tweak all the buttons in the mix. In a way,

I find that the effects are as important as the animation. When I do the animation, I always imagine what sound they will make. Just like the music. I don't find that any element is more important than another. It's just a matter of finding the right balance in all of it, and all of it is serving the film."

Currently, *The Wrong Trousers* is touring the country on the animation festival circuit, garnering rave reviews from the *New York Times, Los Angeles Times* and countless other news agencies. Wouldn't it be nice if Hollywood would wake up and put the nominees for Best Animated Short Film at the head of summer releases, turning the movie-going experience into something you can't get at home. Then again, something as well produced as *The Wrong Trousers* might just blow away the feature presentation.

CHAPTER 8

Star Trek
Generations

From the first television show in 1966 to the debut of a new cast of characters on film, a 30-year lineage of sound is richly layered into the tracks of the latest Trek extravaganza.

Star Trek is a Paramount Pictures franchise. More than three decades ago, the unassuming original show hit the networks without a hint as to its longevity in syndication or its popularity among those who came to be known as Trekkies. It's a rare network television show that is able to work its way into the vernacular without sounding dated.

In 1980, *Star Trek: The Motion Picture* was released, and although the story seemed a little slow over the course of two-plus hours, its technical achievements in visual and audio effects were widely hailed. In fact, the sound effects credits on the original film read like a Who's Who of today's top Hollywood sound professionals: Alan Howarth, Frank Serafine, Joel Goldsmith and Francesco Lupica were the four synth artists charged with sound effects creation. Supervising sound editor Richard Anderson led an effects team that included Cece Hall, George Watters, Alan Murray, Steven Flick and Colin Waddy, among others. Mark

This article appeared originally in the January 1995 issue of Mix.

Mangini supervised the ADR; Kevin O'Connell was the recordist. The three-month final mix (Bill Varney, Steve Maslow and Greg Landaker behind the Quad Eight console) took place at the Goldwyn Sound facility, now Stage D on the Warner Hollywood lot. Robert Wise directed; Jeffrey Katzenberg was an associate producer. Plenty of Academy Awards there.

Five more features followed in the '80s, and the TV show was updated in 1986 to *Star Trek The Next Generation*, which quickly attracted a new following during its six-year run. It even spawned a spinoff, *Deep Space Nine*, and the promise of a third series.

Jump cut to 1994 and Studio 1 at Todd-AO Studios for the final mix on *Star Trek: Generations*. Old meets new. Television meets film. Kirk meets Picard. For the fans of the techno-hip *STNG*, it's the first chance to see and *hear* Picard, Geordi, Data, Number 1 and crew bumped up to 35 mm. For fans of the original, it's perhaps a last chance to see Kirk, Scottie and Chekhov in their aging glory. For Paramount, the past 30 years have now come full-circle, and it has yielded a gold mine.

The Star Trek lineage, however, carries with it a huge sense of responsibility—to the shows, to the films, to its late creator, Gene Roddenberry, to the special effects team and, perhaps most of all, to the Trekkies. ADR supervisor Becky Sullivan said that for the Klingon group walla sessions, they had to have a Klingon dictionary (!) on hand to make sure the language was accurate; if not, they would surely hear about it.

Over the past seven years, supervising sound editor Jim Wolvington has carried his fair share of the responsibility. His background is in musique concrete, and his training took place at the University of Utah, where David Offsky was his mentor. He has been cutting digitally since his days on the Soundstream system in the late '70s and early '80s. He listens to "difficult" music.

As supervising sound editor for *STNG*, he and the crew at Paramount won Emmys for sound their first four years (the year before that, Wolvington won for *Max Headroom*). Rather than completely reinventing Star Trek audio, however, continuity and evolution of sound were always considered extremely important.

For example, the producers of *STNG* wanted to update the very recognizable sound of the Enterprise transporter to make it sound more high-tech and intense. But the producer of the original show wanted the original sound. In the end, Wolvington says, Roddenberry stepped in and suggested using the original, but adding a sense of mystery. So Wolvington took the root musical chord and applied a series of tri-tones, performed on the Synclavier.

By the time *Generations* rolled around seven years later, however, Wolvington felt that some of the sounds had grown tired and needed to be updated with some high-end sparkle to match the new opticals. The original television show door openings and closings were used as a base element, updated with a more percussive head, reversed air gun and sneaker squeak for the rubber-seal effect. Many of the backgrounds—bridge, sick bay, etc.—created for the original motion picture were used straight ("We still use Alan Howarth's generic rumble for the Enterprise B," Wolvington says), while others were modified by adding low end to give the ships a sense of size and to take advantage of the subwoofer channel on the digital film sound formats.

Wolvington had access to all of the Star Trek features, and he made use of some of the effects. "The term sound designer is very popular these days, and I've certainly 'designed' a number of effects over the years and on this picture," Wolvington says. "But I feel it would be inappropriate for me to take the title because I'm making use of sounds created by Alan [Howarth], Frank [Serafine], Doug [Grindstaff], Mark [Mangini], Richard [Anderson]. There's a long history here, and I don't want it perceived that I'm taking credit for all this."

TELEVISION MEETS FILM

Wolvington freely acknowledges that he probably wasn't very many people's first choice to be supervising sound editor. Despite the awards, despite the obvious techno-creative bent in his resume, he's a "TV guy." And the big-budget studio pictures aren't usually considered a training ground for first-time feature supervisors. But the producers of the TV show—executive producer Rick Berman and producer Peter Lauritson—who are also the producers of the movie, insisted on Wolvington.

Remembering 1979

Only four people worked on all six of the previous Star Trek films: William Shatner, Leonard Nimoy, effects editor/supervisor George Watters and sound designer Alan Howarth. Shatner is the only one left on the seventh film, but for the acute listener, Howarth can be heard throughout, as can Frank Serafine, Joel Goldsmith and "The Beam" (a percussion instrument consisting of piano wires strung across a large wood beam) of Francesco Lupica.

As mentioned in the main story, the audio crew on *Star Trek The Motion Picture* (1979) would have to be considered one of the finest ever assembled. It was an enormous talent pool, right through the final and what many consider the finest mix team of its era (Bill Varney, dialog; Steve Maslow, music; Greg Landaker, effects).

"The were walking through the halls of Paramount looking for people who knew synthesizers," Howarth recalls. "Frank [Serafine] had something of a reputation from over at Disney, Joel Goldsmith's dad was doing the score and said his son knew synths, Francesco had the Beam, and a biker friend of mine who was working in sound transfer told Richard [Anderson] that he should listen to his friend Al. I had just come off of three years as the keyboard tech for Joseph Zawinul of Weather Report. So Richard calls me up and asks me to bring in an audition tape of what the Starship Enterprise might sound like. So I did, and I got the job."

That basic Enterprise sound, in one way or another, has appeared in every *Star Trek* film since, including *Generations*. Howarth created the definitive Enterprise rumble from the white noise generator on his Sequential Circuits Prophet 10. Then he added two channels of a blower/exhaust fan from the Lockheed plant, two channels of industrial machinery from the Rye Canyon site (huge silo-like devices with fans) and two channels from the Room 11 (at Paramount) air conditioner. "There always seemed to be some sort of ventilator effect," Howarth says.

The four stereo pairs were recorded to a TEAC 8-track modified for 0 to 60 ips continuous varispeed, which Howarth would "diddle" for acceleration/deceleration and different rooms. "That was my sampler," he says. His mixer was a Sony 8x2 suitcase; all the equipment was -10 dBu. The backgrounds were very difficult to cut on Moviolas, he recalls, because it would "pop" whenever there was a cut. Consequently, there were "a lot of diagonal splices." (On *Star Trek IV*, Howarth transferred his entire library to the Synclavier, the only unit at the time with glide [portamento], and he cut the elements himself.)

Despite the producers' desire for synth-like, electronic effects, the talk in 1979 also centered around an organic track. "The Bridge background of the '60s was electronic music with sonar beeps," Howarth explains. "And our challenge was to take these musical instruments and make sound effects—without having them sound like a series of filters and oscillators. They wanted the tracks to be organic, to be more emotional and appealing.

"So, something like the ship's lasers, or phasers, was a difficult effect because it has to be pleasing, which we normally associate with high end, and it has to be full-bandwidth—it has to have that low end to give it size. It just so happened that we got two days of an electrical storm in Southern California, which is unusual itself, and we recorded some very good lightning, which worked as phasers."

There was also an early discussion about the "sound of space," an important point because technically, there is no sound in space. But it's a film, and you have to have something, so Howarth rolled the TEAC 8-track at 60 ips in "record," physically knocked on a couple of spring reverbs for that "bwoinggg," and played it back at 3.75 ips, creating a "crawl" that served as a background.

Generally speaking, from the feature film point of view, television sound is formula sound, all directed to the center and designed for a single 2-inch speaker. From the television point of view, the feature film world is somewhat staid—steeped in traditional methods of working and slow to adopt new technologies and techniques. Not to mention, the film post-production cycle is considered luxurious compared to TV.

The two worlds came together on the Todd-AO dub stage in a rather synergistic fashion, as would be expected among professionals. After all, these are some of the best people working in television sound paired with an ace re-recording team led by dialog mixer and Todd-AO president Chris Jenkins, along with music mixer Mark Smith and effects mixer Adam Jenkins. There were no overt signs of film vs. TV competition, though there was the occasional tongue-in-cheek comment about wanting music big, prefaced by, "Well, I'm a TV guy, but now that I have the chance…"

On the stage, you could almost sense the TV crowd's excitement at having five discrete channels and a subwoofer to play with (the film is being released in Dolby SR•D and DTS). Even though *STNG* is mixed in surround, the move to film obviously allows everything to play bigger, with more attention to detail and more precise spatial placement. But, Wolvington warns, in a big special-effects film such as *Generations*, the subwoofer channel needs to be used judiciously.

"There was plenty of debate over use of the subwoofer," he says. "Either it's perfect or it makes your chest cavity shake. And you have to be careful because you don't really get any tonal differentiation—an explosion can end up sounding like a warp-by because you don't really get the definition; it's more of a rumble. We had a slight problem in reel 2, when the Enterprise shakes so much that we had trouble changing the quality of the sound. We didn't want it to wash out." On the other hand, the subwoofer does help to "sell" the various spacecraft by giving them size and dimension.

Another big advantage of working on film, Wolvington says, is that when you get three to four months to work on a project, you can add a tremendous amount of detail, especially in terms of Foley. On a typical TV show, you may get a one-day Foley session, consisting mostly of footsteps, door slams and obvious effects. On a big-budget film, you may get two weeks or more to add leather creaks, paper rustles, metal clangs and the like.

EFFECTS AND BACKGROUNDS

If it's big effects you want, reels 8 and 9—the climactic battle scene—went out to 66 channels on the ADM console, with a couple of 6-track stems coming off of Tascam DA-88s. Four DA-88s were brought to the stage, primarily to lay in hard effects to accompany the opticals, but they also doubled as extra playback machines on effects-heavy reels.

As mentioned before, the effects involve so many layers and come from so many sources that it's difficult to say just what is what and where it came from. Many of the hard effects were duplicated in Foley, then combined. Others were designed by Howarth, Serafine and others years ago, then augmented. One of Wolvington's proudest accomplishments is the sound of the mysterious Nexus energy wave, a "character" in its own right, which was a combination of more than 30 elements, including slowed-down arc sounds, distorted sparks and a few animal cries.

In the battle scene, the Klingons, along with arch-villain Dr. Soren (played by Malcolm McDowell), force the Enterprise to crash into a planet that looks remarkably like Earth. "The crash goes on for so long, and is loud for so long, that it's difficult to sustain the excitement," Wolvington says. "The ship begins its

Workstations, We Got Workstations

"This is the first time a TV crew has been bumped up to a feature, and this is the first Star Trek to be digitally cut," says Cece Hall, one of the original effects editors on *Star Trek The Motion Picture* and now executive sound director at Paramount. "We edited here at Paramount using all different types of workstations, and we brought DA-88s to the stage. (Paramount was also an early investor in the ASC Virtual Recorder, which allows editors to have random-access video on the audio workstation platform of their choice.)

Effects: Cut by Jim Wolvington on a basic Synclavier setup (20 MB RAM, 32 voices), locked to 3/4-inch video. Sounds cataloged on 1.2-gigabyte magneto-optical drives, performed on the Synclavier, then laid back to 24 tracks of Tascam DA-88. Four DA-88s on the stage to pop in hard effects.

Wolvington: "The Synclavier allows me to audition effects and resample back into poly-memory without having to go to DAT or something else. That way you can get the layers. But you can also go too far..."

Foley: Recorded at Paramount, supervised by Pam Bentkowski. Walkers were Ken Dufva and David Lee Fin. Cut on Avid AudioVisions.

Dialog and Backgrounds: Supervised by Joey Ippolito. Cut on TimeLine StudioFrames (two for BGs, four for dialog), 8-channel systems with the most recent software. Laid back to 2-inch, 24-track. ADR cut on mag.

Ippolito: "I wouldn't say that the workstations have shortened our schedule that much—the craft still takes the same amount of time, maybe less. But we're able to audition so many more options now. The real plus is the ability to sample takes and match instantaneously—to make fills. There are no more transfers and no making of loops."

Music: Composed by Dennis McCarthy. Recorded and mixed by Bobby Fernandez. Music editor Stephen Rowe. Some of the cues were edited on the Doremi Labs DAWN system, then dumped back to mag.

descent at 100 feet [of film]. It hits the planet at 200 feet and slides along the planet surface up to about 400 feet. But the music cuts out when it hits the planet, so effects have to carry the scene for about 200 feet [about 2 minutes 15 seconds]. I'm sure it will be played loud when we mix on Saturday.

"For the ship beginning to break up, I started where just about any sound editor would start—recording dry ice on bare metal, which gives this annoying moaning, groaning, wrenching metallic sound," he continues. "Then I added some earthquake rumble for a gritty, earthy feel, maybe a car skid through gravel, tree cracks, explosions. The idea is to introduce variety to sustain interest."

"High-tech is boring," adds effects mixer Adam Jenkins. "And I don't mean that high-tech sounds are a bad thing. They're just boring over time, and fatiguing on the brain, which is why we would consistently pull back on the telemetry tracks [the computer noises and electronic sounds that accompany high-tech-looking equipment]. Otherwise, it would begin to sound like a phone is ringing through the entire scene." At one point, Data opens a cabinet in his room by pushing a series of buttons, which is accompanied by a "boodle-oop," followed by a "whooshp." Executive producer Berman asked the mixers to bring down the button sounds and bring up the door-open. "Can you imagine anything more annoying in the 23rd century than if every time you pushed a button, it went 'boodle-oop?'" Berman asks.

It might be surprising to just about anybody outside the audio post community that the most-mentioned term to describe the effects on *Generations* was "organic." Editors used natural sounds—bird chirps, vocal effects, wind noises—all, of course, processed and combined with other sounds.

Organic sounds also can be found layered in the backgrounds, which are perhaps more critical in the Star Trek series than in most action films, since most of the action takes place on the same ship. If the backgrounds don't vary enough, there is the real risk of sounding too homogenous. Of course, sick bay will sound different from the Bridge, which will sound different from the more intimate confines of Whoopi Goldberg's quarters or Captain Picard's stateroom.

Sometimes the Enterprise interior backgrounds fill five or six channels on the mix, sometimes more. At the root of each is the generic Enterprise rumble-generator sound developed by Alan Howarth for the first film. ("You feel naked if you take it out," Wolvington says.) Then tones are modulated for the Bridge, organic wind sounds are added for other rooms, and "tonal color and vocal air," according to Adam Jenkins, are added throughout—whatever it takes to avoid a smooth hum.

At one point, Chris Jenkins suggested using the joystick panner and spinning the pulsing-throbbing element of one background around the room manually, a technique he says he picked up from watching the quad laserdisc version of *Blade Runner* a few nights earlier.

"The Klingon ships were fun," Adam Jenkins says. "They are not high-tech—at least they don't look high-tech. They're older and clunkier, so we wanted the backgrounds to be more wrenching and 'wronking,' and creaking and stalling. If we muted all the other tracks and took away picture, you would know immediately that this is a Klingon ship."

MUSIC

The Star Trek television shows and films are filled with music, and not just those highly recognizable transition scenes when the Enterprise is zipping off to another part of the galaxy and the theme kicks in. There are big strings, big choirs and very big swells—in *Generations*, about 75 minutes out of roughly two hours.

Dennis McCarthy, who scored *STNG* for the past seven years, scored *Generations*, too. The sessions, which involved anywhere from 35- to 95-piece orchestras, depending on the cue, took place at Paramount Stage M, recorded and mixed by Bobby Fernandez on the Neve VR60 Legend Series, to 48-track. Norman Dlugatch was the engineer, Paul Wurtheimer seconded, and Dominic Gonzales served as stage manager.

The score was mixed directly to mag, five channels—left, center, right and stereo synth. A haunting, eerie 24-voice choir was mixed to 3-channel mag. It was a tight, four-day schedule according to music editor Stephen Rowe, who is also music editor on the *STNG* spinoff *Deep Space Nine*. That was when we talked in mid-October. A call to the stage on November 4, less than two weeks before the worldwide release, revealed that they were doing "one more session," to accompany final picture, which had come in the day before. Tight schedule.

At the final mix, Mark Smith, a Canadian whose music background has led him from Robbie Robertson in Toronto to stints with Toto, to "just about every studio in the world," would listen to cues and set levels on a couple of passes before the dialog and effects re-recording mixers sat down for each reel. When effects and dialog came in, he would balance against effects, slip sync at times, bring the choir up when needed, and, in one case, "make the Whoopi [Goldberg] cue more ominous."

I'm a music mixer," he says, "I will treat [the scoring mixers'] music as it should be treated, as is appropriate to the scene. I've been known to mix music on the stage before, but that wasn't necessary on this film."

DIALOG

These are not talkie movies, admittedly. And the locations are often noisy, which usually makes for a problematic production track. Lead mixer Chris Jenkins says that, by and large, the production was cleanly recorded and well-edited, but he was puzzled by instances "when you expect it to be clean, such as on sets, it was sometimes noisy, and when you expect it to be noisy, it was very clean."

Roughly 50 percent of the lines were replaced in ADR, supervised by Becky Sullivan and cut on mag. Joey Ippolito supervised the dialog editing at Paramount and was a jack-of-all-trades problem-solver on the stage.

The biggest challenge in the mix seemed to be getting dialog to cut through big music, variable backgrounds and big effects, which often competed inn the same frequencies. But, as in every film, there were dozens of details to be worked out. Sometimes Jenkins had to remove sibilance, such as when Malcolm McDowell uttered the word "prosthesis." (Producer Berman said to Jenkins: "Chris, I hear you're the king of T's. How are you with S's."); another time he had to change "Robert" to *Robert* (the French pronunciation) by editing the "t," when no alternate lines from Picard were usable.

When *Mix* visited Stage 1 at Todd-AO in mid-October, the pace was relaxed and the troops were working "regular" days. Because the producers decided to alter the ending slightly, footage was being shot near Las Vegas, and reels 11 and 12 were being held up. Although the first six reels were being print mastered, they still had the premixes for the big effects reels to come, ADR sessions were being scheduled for the following Monday, some opticals had yet to arrive and a scoring session was set for the first of November. The release date was fixed for November 18.

But that's nothing new. Apparently, on the original Star Trek movie, they finished the mix on reel 1 an hour before the grand opening screening at the Academy Theater, and director Robert Wise literally took the reel and drove hell-bent across Hollywood.

The first six reels of *Generations* were being print mastered in DTS and Dolby SR•D on October 20. The mix team was gearing up for the final push on the second half of the film. Longer days were anticipated, but then that's expected in the world of modern movie-making.

The Bat Is Back

SOUND CREATION FOR BATMAN FOREVER

The third time is definitely a charm. In this age of formulaic, unoriginal, easy-money, Roman numeral Hollywood sequels, *Batman Forever* strikes a fresh and vibrant chord. All-new cast, all-new crew, a new director (Joel Schumacher), new producer (Peter MacGregor-Scott) and a new sound editorial team—SoundStorm out of Burbank. Warner Bros. is banking on a huge summertime hit, and from the vantage point of temp mix #2 in late April, they've nailed it.

The premise and plot of the film are comic-book simple. Former Wayne Enterprises employee Mr. E. Nigma (Jim Carrey) is intent on destroying Bruce Wayne (Val Kilmer). He develops The Box, which allows him to suck the brain waves out of Gotham City residents and brings about his transformation into the Riddler. Harvey Two-Face (Tommy Lee Jones), meanwhile, breaks out of Arkham Asylum and sets out to destroy Batman, who put him away and permanently disfigured his visage. When the brains-and-muscle team discovers that Wayne and Batman are one and the same…well, that's why we pay $7 a head on Saturday night.

Of course there's much more to the 2 hour, 10-minute roller-coaster ride around Gotham City. Through a series of flashbacks (which posed their own sound design challenges), and the help of Dr. Chase Meridian, Wayne confronts his parents' death and his origins as Batman. The astounding number of visual effects—276 opticals, including the Bat Car, Bat Wing, Bat Boat and Bat-a-rang—and huge, dark-yet-lush stylized sets provide a backdrop that pays as much homage to comic-strip creator Bob Kane as they do Tim Burton, creator of *Batman I* and *II*. At the same time, they scream with originality.

This article appeared originally in the July 1995 issue of Mix.

Bruce Stambler, co-supervising sound editor on Batman Forever.

"This is the most effects-heavy film I've ever seen, both visually and from an audio perspective," says co-supervising sound editor Bruce Stambler. "The only thing I could equate it to would be the last two reels of *Aliens*, where Sigourney is chasing down the monster. We've done a number of action films now [*Under Siege, The Fugitive, Clear and Present Danger*], and we try hard to create a soundtrack that doesn't kill the audience. The key is peaks and valleys, and I think we succeed in this film."

"This film is just so much bigger than I expected," adds John Leveque, Stambler's co-supervisor since *Under Siege*. "I've done pictures with special effects, but not like this. This is way beyond the norm. My first thought when we began in November was, 'How are we going to get this done?' I thought that when we did *The Fugitive* we had the tightest post-production schedule in the history of A-films. But this was even tighter, and there's more to it."

Although Stambler and Leveque began in November, and sound designer Lance Bowman came on in January, the editorial crew didn't start cutting until April 3. The first temp mix began two weeks later, the second temp a week after that. The final began on May 17, for a June 16 release. Fortunately, it's a crack team that has worked together before, and in assigning sequences and reels, an editor's strengths were taken into account: Richard Yawn on explosions and ballistics, Glenn Hoskinson on vehicles, Jay Nierenberg on the flashbacks, etc. From the bottom up, the editorial team raved about the amount of freedom and creative input they were allowed by the supervisors.

"The pressure that we're under with these incredibly tight schedules demands organization and selection," Stambler says. "Our philosophy is such that we don't overdo the Foley, we don't over-pull elements, we don't try to come up with too much, and we ask that our editors be decisive. We try to have as much finished as possible for the first temp mix, with fine-tuning from that point on, and we don't believe in flooding the dub stage with a lot of alternates. There's no such thing as poor prep, and there's absolutely no room for error in this environment. If a sound's not there at the stage, it ain't gonna be there."

ORIGINAL RECORDING TO BATDAT

As Leveque says, audio post is an interdependent, step-by-step process, where the final mix relies on the quality of original recordings, the editor's selections, the transfers and everything in between. If it falls apart at any point, he says, there's no way to recover. Still, you have to begin somewhere, so he and Stambler began, naturally, in bat caves. Because North American bats lie dormant all winter, they flew to Puerto Rico.

"The first cave we went to was huge, easily the size of two football fields," Stambler recalls. "The bats would come down one of two legs of a 'Y' each night and spiral out of the opening to go feed on insects—23,000 pounds a night, our guide said. So we got there at dusk, and John and I flipped a coin to see who would go inside and who would wait at the opening. I won, and I picked inside. I go into one of the legs of the Y, and it's damp, hot and pitch, pitch black. The guide had said that there's no way to tell when they would start moving or which side they would come out of, but that I would certainly know it when it happened. Well, I wait four-and-a-half hours with my [Fostex] PD-2 DAT, testing levels and the like—nothing. I'm about ready to leave when this strange whoosh started to come from the cavern—not really like a wind, but this unearthly sensation that was more like an energy wave, with high-pitched chattering and wing flaps. I'm up and ready in a second. Then it turns out they flew out the other tunnel. I still got some good sounds, and John got some great stuff at the entrance, but I was disappointed.

The Bat Crew

"This film, with this schedule, couldn't have been done on mag," says co-supervising sound editor Bruce Stambler. "And it couldn't have been done without this crew."

Sound Editing/Mixing

Supervising Sound Editors: Bruce Stambler, John Leveque

Sound Design: Lance Brown, Frank Kniest, Roland Thai

Sound Effects Editors: Don Warner, Jay Nierenberg, Richard Yawn, Bernard Weiser, Kim Secrist, Glenn Hoskinson, Steve Mann

Supervising Foley Editor: Shawn Sykora

Foley Editors: Michael Dressel, Jim Likowski, Steve Richardson

Supervising Dialog Editor: Becky Sullivan

Supervising ADR Editor: Fred Stafford

Dialog Editors: Kimberly Voigt, Sukey Fontelieu, Tony Milch

ADR Editor: Zack Davis

Assistant Sound Editors: Lance Laurienzo, Steven Gerrior, Jeff Cranford, Marc Deschaine, Chris Rouse

Transfer: Gary Blufer, Kelly Cabral

Operations: Gordon Ecker, Blake Marion, John Fanaris, Deryk Morgan, Dawn Kratofil

Foley Artists: John Roesch, Hilda Hodges

Foley Recordists: Mary Jo Lang, Carolyn Tapp

Composer: Elliot Goldenthal

Scoring Engineer: Steve McLaughlin

Music Editors: Zigmund Gron, Chris Brooks

Re-recording Mixers: Donald O. Mitchell, Michael Herbick, Frank Montano

Picture Editing

Film Editor: Dennis Virkler

First Assistant Film Editor: Mark Stevens

Film Editing Assistants: Dawn King, Adam Boone, Gina Zappalo, Jonathan Alvord, Kerry Kerwin, Melissa Kent, Judd Nealon

"So we take the two-hour drive back to our hotel, and there's a message waiting from our guide, saying, 'Be ready for pickup at 1 tomorrow. We're going to the Cave of the Snakes.' Well, I'm not an outdoors-type guy, and I'm not real crazy about snakes. But we're there, so we do it.

"It's called Cave of the Snakes because these boa constrictors hang on trees outside the entrance and feed on the bats as they fly out each night. We go in, and there's about eight inches of guano on the floor. I shine my flashlight down, and it's wall-to-wall cockroaches. I shine the light on the wall, and about every five feet there's a tarantula bigger than my hand. It's 110 degrees and wet. I slipped a couple of times and fell, with my equipment. But the PD-2 was durable as hell, and we got some great bat sounds."

The bat cave ambience is augmented in the film by waves crashing on rock and other elements, for a varied, organic feel to counteract the high-tech gadgetry. Wing flaps and screeches are used throughout the flashbacks and bat-cave scenes.

Because the look and feel of the film is not based in reality, in-house effects libraries just wouldn't work. About 99 percent of the film is original recordings, according to Stambler, and they "shot" sound in locations as diverse as the Mojave Desert (all types of vehicles and motorcycles for the big car chase, as well as rocket launches for sweetening), an air show in Oklahoma City (to record the Bud Light mini-jet), the Pomona Fairplex raceway (for dragster engines and wheel squeals) and Rocket Dyne in Canoga Park, where they make engines for the Space Shuttle.

"I've never heard or felt anything like those engines," Stambler says. "We set up a couple of hundred yards away when they tested one, and it wasn't so much the roar, which was deafening, as it was the low-frequency rush that just passed through my body. I felt nauseated by the end of the day, and I'm not even sure we'll get to use it for the Bat Car because it's just too big. But we got some great liquid and pipe sounds, too, because they pump thousands of gallons of water a second under these engines to absorb the heat, and they have a whole manufacturing system set up."

Finally, one of the goals for the audio tracks was to add a bit of light-heartedness to what can sometimes seem rather scary scenes or situations. It is, after all, a PG-13 movie, and the tone is not as dark as the first two Batman films. In one scene, for example, the Riddler dances around, dropping toy-like hand grenades. "We thought, 'Oh, no, there's ten more explosions,'" Stambler says. "Fortunately, they looked like toys, so we recorded a rather unique comic library on a Foley stage one day, where we scooped up a bunch of my son Bobby's little wind-up toys—those things that flip when they're wound up. Then we augment that and add some boings for when the bombs hit the floor. It takes the edge off the explosions and makes them hysterical. We did it more or less as an experiment, but Joel [Schumacher] was ecstatic."

"We thought we'd try something a little beyond the visual," adds Leveque. "But that's what a temp is for, to experiment. It's easy to pull back, but it's hard to push the envelope at that point."

SOUND DESIGN

For *Batman Forever*, SoundStorm set up its first-ever sound design station, based around the Fostex Foundation and the E-mu IV, and helmed by Lance Brown. SoundStorm is the only Hollywood editorial house to make such a large commitment to the Fostex workstation, having purchased eight systems, with plans to add up to 18 more, probably the scaled-down RE for brute editing. All of the editors raved about the unit, for everything from its tactile feel, to its ability to make changes, to the fact that there's no mouse and no maneuvering through windows. It was, they say, built for film sound editors, and their input was instrumental in the unit's development. Most of the 2000s are used simply for editing. Brown's is the only station at this point with full mix capabilities and the just-released TimeFlex time compression/expansion option.

"The credits will be kind of odd in this movie," Brown says. "Really, the whole crew is doing the sound design, with Bruce and John providing the overall vision. Everyone is encouraged to put their creative input into the sound job, and the editors are just as much a creative influence as the people selecting the sounds, myself included. It's not just what we pull."

Like everyone else associated with the project, Brown was overwhelmed by the amount of material that would be required and the unique bits of gadgetry, and effects that had no precedent. His principal assignments were the Bat Car, the Box and the giant (16-foot wingspan) bat, which, in a near hallucinatory fashion, is crucial to the flashback scenes.

The core sound of the Bat Car is made up of about 20 elements, reaching as many as 60 depending on the visual. A bunch of vehicles, including fire engines and dragsters were used, with the root element being an 800-horsepower Buick Grand National with turbo whine that Stambler found through *Car Craft* magazine ("0 to 130 miles an hour in 10.3 seconds," says Stambler, who owns a Grand National himself).

"The Bat Car seemed to come together pretty easily, actually," Brown says. "The trick is to make it constantly varied and avoid monotony. For all the approaches and pass-bys, it's the Buick Grand National, sweetened with some dragsters and other elements. Then, at the point it passes and you move to the rear, we took some of the elements from the Rocket Dyne sessions, augmented with some real rockets, jet roars and fire sweetener. It gives you a sense that the car is more complex by varying the sound as you move around. We could easily just leave it a big roar, but that wouldn't be very interesting.

"The interior of the Bat Car actually comes from Bruce and John's rental car in Puerto Rico, as they drove over this sort of unique grading," he adds. "I put that in the E-IV and totally twisted it, then added the electronic stuff—little servos and beeps and motors."

The Box, the Riddler's mind-reading device, was a combination of lightning, electrical devices and synth-generated sounds, more like James Bond specialty items, or laboratories, according to Brown.

The flashback sequences, in which Bruce Wayne confronts the death of his parents and his birth as Batman, were perhaps the most challenging scenes to design. Brown worked them up in conjunction with editor Jay Nierenberg.

"You have to start with what's there on the screen as you transition from the present to the past," Nierenberg explains. "In one scene, for example, he's at the hearth and there's a clock on the mantle, so we use some fire and clicks to spin in and out. But by and large, we tried to work with some elements that may be peripheral and stayed away from the more standard stuff, such as lightning cracks on an ugly, stormy day. There's another scene where we have the young Bruce Wayne walking through the church at his parents' wake, and we decided to go with wooden coffin creaks and coffin slams and metal screeches—things that might pass through a young boy's head in a situation like that.

"We also spent a lot of time on flashback ambience," he continues, "working with essentially five different intensities. In each flashback, it worked out that there were several points to escalate the intensity, from lowest pitch to highest pitch. It worked in the cave, in the church, and then we add specific designed effects on top. The key is to keep it interesting over time."

"The flashbacks are some of the hardest scenes," adds Leveque, "because you have what is a traditionally scary moment for a little boy whose parents get killed. Then there's a bat cave and a bat that attacks him. It's frightening, especially in terms of how flashbacks are put together. But we don't want it to be frightening; we want it to be haunting, and we want it to be evocative—at the same time powerful but not scary. This is a PG movie, and we want to take the audience someplace they've never been before, without alienating them. Haunting is more difficult than scary. It's the same thing with fun. To make a movie fun is very difficult. Putting cartoon effects to every head hit is easy, but it wouldn't mean anything in this context."

ADR, FOLEY AND SCORE

"It's a shame we had to ADR this guy," says producer Peter MacGregor-Scott, pointing to Jim Carrey on the screen. "His performance is phenomenal, and then he pulled it off again in the studio. He's unbelievable." Carrey ad-libbed many of the lines on the set, then duplicated the energy, rhythm and performance on the ADR stage. Not an easy task. Even at the temp mix, it was difficult to pick out which lines were replaced.

But then, depending on who you talk to, anywhere from two-thirds to 90 percent of the film is ADR—somewhere in the neighborhood of 2,500 lines, according to dialog supervisor Becky Sullivan, who worked in tandem with ADR supervisor Fred Stafford. The reason for the large number of lines, they say, was mainly due to the nature of the sets, which were lit extensively and filled with smoke machines, wind machines and other noise-generating devices. Also, some were constructed at Long Beach's Spruce Goose facility, which is cavernous, echo-y and right near a shipping port.

With more than 48 features to her credit over the past ten years, Sullivan serves as a part-time coach, psychologist and technician to actors. She also faced an incredibly tight schedule and had to coordinate with talent that was literally all over the planet working on other projects. Carrey ("the most prepared actor I've worked with," Sullivan says) in San Antonio and Charlotte, N.C., Nicole Kidman by phone patch in London, Chris O'Donnell in Chicago, Tommy Lee Jones and Val Kilmer, thankfully, in L.A.

"My first job is to listen to every single DAT, even from the takes that weren't printed, and try to save the production track," Sullivan says. "Then, since I've been working with Bruce and John for about seven years now, I try to think of effects and how scenes will play as a whole. For example, we have a scene where Jim Carrey is in his apartment-lab typing at the keyboard, so we put in a playful hum as he punches away.

"We also recorded a lot of group ADR," she continues, "especially for the big circus scenes. In a situation like that, you don't need the crowd roar—we have plenty of crowds in effects. You want what I call 'free and clears,' pieces that peek through the walla. For instance, we might have somebody yell, 'There's Harvey Two-Face!' followed by a pause, then somebody yells, 'He's a murderer!' followed by somebody yelling, 'Run!' You need interesting spikes in the group, or else it just turns to mush.

"I also really appreciated the director, Joel, because he allowed me some freedom, sought my advice, and in one case incorporated an idea I had. For one of the flashbacks, where the young Bruce Wayne is at the wake, I thought it would work well within the effects if exaggerated breathing was prominent. Then the older Bruce Wayne breathing becomes a transitional element, and it works emotionally. In another case, some light ADR sobbing is used as an effect. So you always have to think of the movie as a whole."

The SoundStorm philosophy seems to be that Foley should not be overdone. It should be used for footsteps, clothing rustles and the like—the more traditional Foley moments—but not for every door slam. Stambler's feeling is that with the 6-channel digital film formats, Foley should be used to augment and work with well-recorded and well-edited effects. They hired first-call Foley walkers John Roesch and Hilda Hodges, and gave them the rubber bat suit to play with for a week.

Elliot Goldenthal composed the sometimes tender, sometimes heroic, always dynamic score, which was recorded in early May at the Sony stage in Culver City by engineer Steve McLaughlin. The mixdown from 48-track digital took place at The Chapel.

Music for the final mix was played back directly from a portable 8-channel Pro Tools II system, controlled by music editors Zigmund Gron and Chris Brooks. Timecode from the board was fed to the Opcode Studio 1, then the LITC code was sent to the Power PC. All of the cues, some of which were final for the temp mix, resided on 2.4-gigabyte hard drives, which could be popped out and worked on in the background while the dub continued.

Re-recording mixers Donald "Papa-san" O'Mitchell, Michael "Mikey" Herbick and Frank "fill-in-the-blank" Montano— perhaps the finest team never to win an Oscar—handled both the temp mixes and the final at Warner Bros. Studio Facilities' relatively new Dub Stage 2. Part of the recent facilitywide upgrade, Stage 2 sports a custom hybrid SSL 8000/5000 board and custom, in-house designed, three-way monitoring system (JBLs for the highs, Community for the mids and Turbosound LE for the lows).

"If this crew doesn't win the Oscar, I'm getting out of the business," said a half-joking MacGregor-Scott, a former sound editor whose energy and style are infectious. "We thought we might get it on *The Fugitive,* but we settled for the British Academy Award. And this is even better. I keep saying that some day, in a pinch, I'm going to release a temp mix. They're that good."

Despite the incredible pressure of the tight post schedule, not to mention the pressure of a big, big film, the mood at SoundStorm with a month to go was completely relaxed. Yes, 16-hour days were the norm, and yes, the ulcers may have been churning away on the inside. But they had all the confidence and precision of an Indianapolis 500 pit crew—everybody dependent on everybody else, and hey, they've been in the big race before. It is not a large crew, as far as big pictures go. But it's solid. And enormously creative. Count on them for a fourth straight Oscar nomination.

Casino

THE SOUNDTRACK FOR MARTIN SCORSESE'S TAKE ON VEGAS

GoodFellas with Vegas glitz. That was the early line on *Casino*. And although that assessment works in terms of the film's style and feel, it is not at all fair to the story or its director, Martin Scorsese. Whereas *GoodFellas* established a more insular world, Casino is grand in scale, depicting a uniquely American human and cultural tragedy across a "paradise in the desert" backdrop. The Tangiers is the hottest hotel on the Strip, the characters become bigger than their surroundings, and the immensity, the vast landscape of the desert, is a constant reminder of the world outside the glamor and the scams. Nothing about this film is small, including the soundtrack.

Actually, the soundtrack, while dense and full, is not necessarily that big. Most of the casino scenes, shot on location in a working resort, The Riviera, are loaded with voice-over, dialog, group ADR, backgrounds and effects. And of course, on top of that is the ever-present, Scorsese-selected (along with music consultant and friend Robbie Robertson) source music, more than 100 cues from the '70s and '80s weaving in and out of the montages and underneath the drama. As in *GoodFellas*, there is no score.

"The way Casino works is that there's sort of a hierarchy to the mix," explains supervising sound editor Skip Lievsay of C5 Inc. in New York. "We had voice-over at the pinnacle, and that was recorded 3-track, with mics center-left-right, so that it was not only the biggest voice in the picture, but literally bigger than anything else. Then music and dialog sort of play tag as the next most predominant sounds. And then whenever it was appropriate for picture, we had a background or sound effect. It was actually very uncluttered, where we took away as much unnecessary information as possible. We try to work that way, so that what you're left with is the essence of the track."

This article appeared originally in the January 1996 issue of Mix.

Martin Scorsese and Sharon Stone on the set

THE PROCESS

The pared-back tracks work amazingly well in balancing the busy nature of the casino floor shots with the intimate moments between Ace Rothstein (Robert De Niro) and Ginger McKenna (Sharon Stone). But while the sound design and mix for the film are solid, Lievsay is the first to admit that there is nothing revolutionary in the tracks. What most interested him this go-around with Scorsese (Lievsay has supervised all his films from *After Hours* through *Age of Innocence*) was the process by which the soundtrack came together. Perhaps the most exciting change brought on by the technical advances in sound for film is that there are no more established rules for putting together effects, music and dialog elements for a re-recording session. In Hollywood, each studio lot, each independent sound editing house, has experimented with more efficient and creative ways to bring first-generation digital elements to the stage. They've been doing the same thing in New York.

Scorsese and his longtime film editor, Thelma Schoonmaker, cut picture on a LightWorks system, often to the temp music tracks. The sound editing took place at C5, mostly on the Sonic Solutions system (Foley was edited on an Avid AudioVision), and the elements were brought 23 blocks up Broadway to the mix on the newly remodeled Stage F at Sound One, on a 60-input Neve VSP with Flying Faders. Because picture was not locked, a system was developed to allow for constantly updated, rapid changes on the final mix. In many ways, Lievsay, says, they rocketed ahead technologically, and in other ways, he admits, they took two steps back. But for *this* picture, the process worked.

Dialog and some ADR were premixed at 21 reels, though the picture was eventually cut to 19 reels. While Schoonmaker and Scorsese went in and made picture changes on the sixth floor of the Brill Building, where Sound One is located, re-recording mixer Tom Fleischman began on effects premixes in Stage F, on the seventh floor. As soon as the film editors had reels ready, Fleischman switched over to finaling, and Lievsay and Reilly Steele took over effects premixing on Stage B, on the eighth floor.

Sound for Picture

"We tend to make our premixes very small and compact, with very few elements," Lievsay says. "All of our premixes for *Casino* were spread across a 48-track, only because we had a lot of voice-over and group ADR. So the premixed dialog, ADR and voice-over are on 1 to 24, and then eight channels each of backgrounds, effects and Foley were premixed separately from the Tascam DA-88s, then brought in on tracks 25-up of the 48-track for the final. Music, which wasn't premixed because it was all source cues, was played back directly off the Sonic on the stage. We try to build our predubs with as much flair as possible, making them sound how we think the movie should sound. We can always go back and make fixes."

Because the LightWorks does not currently output change notes for the audio tracks, picture edits from the premix version to the final had to be rebalanced by eye and ear. "They took their premixes from the 3324 and dumped them back into the Sonic," Lievsay explains. "We then shipped Exabytes [Sonic backup drives] down to C5, and they took the new video, as well as the new guide track, and put that in the Sonic, too. We then re-synched the premixes to the new version and did whatever fixes were necessary. The conformed premixes were taken on Exabyte back up to Sound One, and those were restored to a Sonic and dumped digitally back to the 3324. So the premixes never actually lost a generation. They stayed digital all the way.

"The final step of that conformation," Lievsay continues, "was that Tom would put up the premix, which had already been conformed and restored back to the 3324, and wherever there were gaps, the editors would take notes for whether it was new track or a fix. so if you couldn't jump in with a fix, he could always remix from the Sonic, and that's how he was able to patch up the 3324s without having to copy from machine to machine. It was elaborate, but it's the only way we could get it done. There was a tremendous amount of legwork by my crew and the people at Sound One, but even with no change notes, we could turn reels around completely within a couple of days."

Although Scorsese generally allows for six to eight weeks of mixing, a luxurious schedule in today's climate, he also turns in long movies. *Casino* is 19 reels and comes in at 2 hours, 50 minutes. Because picture was edited and voice-over was added or altered right up until the end, the entire film, from temp to premix to final, was mixed out of order.

"[Mixing out of order] affects the way I work in two ways," says Fleischman, who first worked with Scorsese on temp dubs for *Raging Bull*, then finaled *King of Comedy* and everything thereafter. "Logistically, it's difficult to keep levels and processing consistent. For example, in *Casino*, on the voice-over I started with reel 4, then went to reel 9, then reel 14, then back to reel 2. If you start in reel 1 and go through the film in order, you achieve that particular type of equalization or whatever type of processing you're using, and keep it consistent throughout the film. By the time I got to the final reel of dialog, I had found it. But then when we finished and played it all through, there was a big difference between reel 3, which was one of the last reels we mixed, and reel 4, which was the first reel. Things were fairly inconsistent, and levels were all over the place.

"Then the second problem is, stylistically, you try to achieve a build in the way things are put together and balanced," he continues. "Generally, I've found that that sort of naturally happens as you go along. It was very difficult to do that on this film because there was no way to really know what came before. You don't know where you were, so you don't know where you're going."

The first time the sound team saw the film front to back was at the first printmaster, which was where Fleischman adjusted overall levels and made the tracks consistent. The trick was in developing a system to keep the effects, dialog and music stems updated so that when adjustments were made after the printmaster, they didn't have to go in and redo the corrections as well. The premixes were played back from a single 48-track DASH machine; the stems were on tracks 1 to 24 of a second 48-track, and the printmaster was made to tracks 25 to 30.

"Before we were working in digital," Fleischman says, "when we recorded all our predubs to 6-track mag, it was a pain to go in and change a premix because you had to take down the stems from the recorder, take the premix off the playback machine, and put them up on the recorder, put all the elements up for that premix and make the correction. In doing the mix to digital tape, all our premixes—all the dialog, ADR, effects, Foley, backgrounds—were on one 48-track DASH machine, which we're able to record on. A lot had to be added after the predub—we were flying in effects at the final, new Foley. So I would just punch into the premix, which was running on another recorder—I was playing back from it most of the time, but if I needed to take something apart or add to it, I had that capability without taking anything down, without changing the console configuration. I just took whatever element I needed, put it in an unused fader, and added it into the premix, and that would follow through into the stem. We used that extensively. We got the idea on *Clockers*, but we made use of it on *Casino*. There were so many go-backs, so many things added, because we had predubbed it before it was locked.

"The stems were on the first 24 tracks of the 48-track tape," he continues, "and we made the printmaster on 25 to 30 of the same tape. We had made a clone first of the stems, and as I was making adjustments to the overall levels in the printmaster, I would punch into the channels that contained the stems and make the same adjustments. So when we finished that print-master, all the levels in the original stems matched, which saved us a good number of headaches later on, when we knew we'd have to go back to touch those stems up. To have to go into those and try to make those corrections [from the premix] would have been way too time-consuming."

The most challenging scenes to mix, according to Fleischman, were the expository montage sequences at the beginning of the film, which were heavy on voice-over, dialog and music, all of them tightly woven into the visual. To make those work, however, he had to first find the "voice" that would pop through the relatively dense audio action.

Robert De Niro as Ace provides most of the VO, with a few segments from Joe Pesci. Most of the sessions were recorded 3-track, with a Neumann U87 in the center and a pair of Schoeps cardioids on each side (a few of the Pesci takes were mono, sent via DolbyFax from a last-minute session in L.A., so Fleischman used stereo synthesis to match it).

"Using multiple mics to make the voice-over bigger was Skip's idea, and we've done it on other films," Fleischman says. [See *Malcolm X*, p. 44] "But it's difficult for me as a mixer to deal with because every time the actor moves his head, the image shifts a little bit. On *Casino*, there were so many sessions in so many different rooms that it got to be very difficult to deal with. Basically I just tried to keep it consistent and clean. I wanted it to sound fuller, with more chest and more of the low-frequency portion of the voice, which you wouldn't normally pick up in a production dialog track.

"I didn't do much processing to the voice-over," he adds. "I gated it, a little bit of compression, some EQ just to even it out and beef up the low end and achieve as full-range a voice as I could get. I did play the side mics considerably lower than the center mic. The U87 in the center had a much fuller sound. In the analog version [release format], I essentially made it mono because the three mics were leaking into the surrounds. But in the digital version, it's spread all across the front."

WEAVING MUSIC IN AND OUT

"This mix was a lot like *GoodFellas* in that something was always leading the track—voice-over, dialog or music, not so much effects," Fleischman says. "It's all very tightly woven, and it's dense. It's wall-to-wall music, pretty much. We were careful about trying to make the music so it wasn't distracting, but it was difficult because nearly all the music has vocals. And Marty might have one syllable that he wants to hear."

Like *GoodFellas, Casino* has no traditional score. There are 98 tracked cues from CD or records, according to music editor Bobby Mackston, occupying 2 hours, 7 minutes of the nearly three-hour film. (In one reel, music starts at 12 feet and goes from cue to cue to cue right to the end of the reel.) Apparently, music consultant Robbie Robertson assembled a huge list of potential cues from the period, and Scorsese integrated his choices into the temp track.

First the cuts were transferred from CD or record or DAT with timecode. Those were loaded into the LightWorks, where Scorsese would often edit to music. From the cut track, a timecode discontinuity list was generated, and Mackston would then go in and reassemble in the Sonic Solutions system. Final tweaks and positionings were often made on the stage, where a full Sonic system contained all the music on hard drives for playback. Still, Scorsese has a strong sense of where he wants music to play in the final, and much of that is determined in the picture edit. It doesn't matter to him that he just cut 12 seconds from the first half of a scene, Mackston says, he still wants the cymbal crash, or that one particular word, to fall at a specific point. So the music edit becomes a process of building bridges.

"He's very specific about where he wants certain sequences or specific hits, to be against that image," Mackston says. "For the Stones song 'Can't You Hear Me Knockin,'" he cut picture to the way the song plays out. Then he makes cuts where he wants to make the cuts, without really worrying about what that does to the guide track. But he still wants the drum to hit and he still wants the lyric on this image. So you have to find ways to bridge all that.

"And that's where the workstations are invaluable," adds Mackston, an Avid aficionado till he was cajoled into editing on the Sonic for this film. "We're able to do time compression and expansion, or if we come across a spot where the intonation was slightly off, we could pitch it up to match. And with the Sonic, there's this crossfade window that gave us a lot of flexibility to be creative. Most systems are just linear—it's fade in and fade out. But here we were able to go from live to studio versions of Stones songs in a very full manner. Also, there was a lot of material that came from older sources—one that came off a 45—that had inherent byproducts of that technology. Using the Sonic, I could go in and clean up the pops and snaps."

(In case you were wondering, Mackston didn't just jump in on Sonic and start editing. It is, after all, a rather deep architecture. Lievsay lent him an ace assistant, Todd Milner, and Mackston says, "Todd's the best. He was with me day and night, all the way through, and he did all the loading. I told him that if he ever left town, I'd give him a job. I'd never worked on the Sonic before, and he was there to tell me what buttons to push.")

The fact that it was all 2-track source material made the edit slightly more challenging, as it wasn't always easy to find appropriate in and out points once the original material had been modified. "Score is different in that it's been created and timed specifically to images and emotional content," Mackston says. "Someone looked at it, spotted it, they know where the dialog is, they know where they have to be out. With track cues, you have an element that may have the feel you want for the scene, but it needs to be sculpted to fit the action. You're kind of scoring it by finding the right places to make an edit work. Obviously, if there are picture changes with score, you have to modify it to fit, but it's already been scored for emotional content and length, so it's just a matter of determining where to make it fit the cut. I find cutting track music much more challenging."

You know music is going to play a large role in a Scorsese sound-track, but you also know that picture is paramount, perhaps more so than for any American director working today. The camera, and the edit, determine what's important in the track—the close-up of the dice hitting the table or a swish-pan from a dealer to the player making the bet. "These are not effects-heavy pictures," Lievsay says. "You can tell what sounds need to be emphasized, and he almost never uses a close-up without a discrete, distinct sound. So you know for some of those close-ups you need something big. He's doing the same thing with picture that we're doing with audio, where you have the big scene, then he zooms in for a close-up on a certain word. The idea is that you're in a big environment and can still be pulled in for something very intimate. That's really the best way to get the most mileage out of a track."

Twister

The Twister *mix crew in front of the Otari Premiere on Universal Stage 3. From left, executive music producer Bud Carr, dialog/lead re-recording mixer Steve Maslow, director Jan De Bont, film editor Michael Kahn, effects re-recording mixer Gregg Landaker, music re-recording mixer Kevin O'Connell, supervising sound editor Stephen Hunter Flick, music editor Zig Gron.*

This article appeared originally in the July 1996 issue of Mix.

Twister, the most talked about, hotly anticipated visual effects film since dinosaurs roamed the screen, is not your typical summertime action-adventure fare. There are no gun battles, no explosions, no squealing car chases or exploding planes, no aliens or orbiting spacecraft. Reduced to simple terms, *Twister* is man against nature, and in that respect it re-creates a style of tension and fear not seen on this scale since *Jaws* made a splash on a July weekend in 1975.

The comparisons in the previous paragraph will not be lost on filmgoers. The Warner Bros. release is an Amblin Entertainment production, and Steven Spielberg served as one of the executive producers. There is even a little Indiana Jones thrown in, as the unassuming, ragtag collection of storm-chasers take on heroic qualities in their race against a well-funded but sinister corporate group to better understand and predict tornados. The twist is director Jan De Bont, who established a more heightened sense of immediacy in his main character: the computer-generated series of tornados.

De Bont, a director of photography whose credits go back to *The Fourth Man* and include such action flicks as *Die Hard, Robocop, The Hunt for Red October* and *Basic Instinct*, made his directing debut last summer with *Speed*. Visual effects certainly played a large role in the success of *Speed*, but as event-specific film-making magic, not as a main character. In the same way that De Bont and the visual effects team at Industrial Light & Magic had to create a different identity and quality for each of the five twisters that roar through the film, the audio post-production crew had to establish different voices.

"Each tornado has its own character..." says dialog re-recording mixer Steve Maslow over lunch at Moe's in Hollywood, "...and whether they're a watery, high-frequency tornado, or ground-pounding, earth-shattering twisters, they all sound different," interjects Maslow's partner in crime for more than a decade now, effects re-recording mixer Gregg Landaker. "We didn't want to reveal all our cards right off the bat in reel 1 or reel 3. We knew we had to get to this 'finger of God' destruction, the last one, the F5, so we couldn't design it so big that it made the F5 seem small in comparison. With the winds and low-frequencies that Kevin [O'Connell, music re-recording mixer and 'helper guy'] and I had in hand, we built the characters up to the large one, the payoff."

An individual tornado's intensity is measured on the Fujita scale, from 1 to 5. *Twister* deals with F3s and F5s, and when you stop to consider the number of audio elements that went into any one reel, especially the climactic F5 in reel 11, it's somewhat surprising that the film didn't turn into a wall of sound. More than 600 DA-88 tapes worth of effects were delivered to the mix team at Universal's Stage 3; reel 11 contained 15 predubs just for the tornado; three 16-channel Pro Tools 3 systems—for effects, ADR and music—handled changes at the mix, with a fourth offline in a cutting room (effects units were duplicated on 1-gig Iomega Jaz drives for easy loading); some of the twisters were made up of as many as 250 tracks; and the recordists in the machine room—Brion Paccassi, Brad Biggart and Kevin Brooks—who have done monstrous pictures, including *Waterworld* less than a year ago, said it was three times as many elements as any film they'd seen. But you know what? It won't even be the loudest film out this summer. And that achievement can be credited to both tasteful editing and a delicately balanced mix.

"We didn't start with a script, we started with a visual effects test," explains supervising sound editor Stephen Hunter Flick, who won an Oscar last year for *Speed*. "That was March 1995, and it was spectacular. So I went in with Gregg and Steve for a couple of hours, and we did a 4-channel mix that subsequently ended up in the trailer and TV campaigns. The reason it's important to talk about the trailer campaign is that we weren't able to do any temp dubs on this picture because the [computer-generated] opticals were due in late January—very close to our mix time. So the trailers allowed me to play with the sounds of the tornados and develop concepts that would be approved by the studio, and they allowed me to go into the mix with a point of view. By the time we did the second trailer, we had essentially acquired the dragon characteristic of the tornado, which is prevalent all the way through.

"I think of pictures, in terms of soundtracks, as mythological," Flick continues. "What kind of fable or story are we telling? To me, fairy tales are dark and gripping pieces that move our subconscious. But we don't have any sort of European folklore of leprechauns and elves and fairies. We basically have man against nature. We have the literature of the new world. We have Whitman and Jack London and Hemingway and modern writers dealing with man living on the face of this Earth, with realistic issues of weather and natural disasters driving the drama in our lives. Look at earthquakes, look at tornados. They kill lots of people every year. I'm looking at this as a mythic adventure of Western and Midwestern America. So I can call the tornado a dragon.

"The entirety of the work is based on naturalistic, documentary recordings of the Midwest. You start real, and then you ask, 'What do I remember and what am I afraid of about a tornado?' So we talked to people who had seen tornados, and we watched lots and lots of tornado documentaries and listened to every time they discussed the sound. I'm not looking to them to listen analytically; I was looking for people who are not sound or audiophiles to tell me stories about how they *felt*.

Creative Cafe

Stephen Hunter Flick left Weddington Productions and his longtime partners in the late-summer of 1995 to open Creative Cafe with his wife, Judee. After brief stops in the Varitel building, then Director's Sound, they purchased 6,000 square feet on Glendale Boulevard South in Los Angeles. On October 6, 1995, the day they moved in, they began cutting.

The space is light, open and airy, with a '50s diner decor. The first thing you notice on entering is a working 1946 jukebox that plays 78s. The reception area is dominated by the front end of the cherry-red killer car from *Christine*, which has been made into a desk. Diner-style chairs and cafe flooring add to the charm. There is a gym downstairs for editors to keep fit. An onsite chef cooks breakfast and lunch for the staff. A healthy crew is a happy crew.

The main room consists of compartmentalized cubicles for the assistants. Each station has been designed and optimized for specific tasks, with the apprpriate computer horsepower—one station for Exabyte backup, another for printing log sheets, etc. Editing/design rooms surround the central floor, with an additional four design rooms and a transfer room downstairs. All in all, there are 30 edit bays.

Creative Cafe is a Pro Tools/Avid house. On the day I visited, they were evaluatining Pro Tools 3.21 from Digidesign, and the Avid Media Dock system had arrived in crates. Tour guide and sound supervisor Dean Beville, who serves as de facto system supervisor at Creative Cafe, says the plan is to convert the entire in-house DAT library to sound files that will reside in Media Dock, providing instant access to any station.

But many are in a position to buy equipment and, with the proper financing, open a shop. It's the people that make Creative Cafe, and it's the crew that the Flicks most like to talk about. So, for *Twister*, here is that crew:

Supervising Sound Editor: Stephen Hunter Flick

Sound FX Editors: Warren Hamilton Jr., Gregory Hedgepath, Richard King, Charles Ewing Smith, Marvin Walowitz, Teresa Eckton

ADR Supervisor: Judee Flick

ADR Editors: Beth Bergeron, Nicholas "Von Loopen" Korda

ADR Mixer: Bob Deschaine

ADR Recordist: Tami Treadwell

Dialog Editors: Rick Freeman, Staphanie Flack, Ben Wilkins

Foley Editors: Solange S. Schwalbe, Charles Maynes, David Spence

Foley Artists: John Roesch, Hilda Hodges

Foley Mixer: Mary Jo Lang

Foley Recordist: Carolyn Tapp

1st Assistant Sound Editor: Linda Yeaney

Sound Assistants: Catherine Calleson, Baylis Glascock, Jeff Etcher, Don Likowitz, Chris Smith

Special Sound Design and Field Recording: John Pospisil, Ken J. Johnson, Eric Potter, Charles Maynes, Martin Lopez

Recording Assistant: Mollie Gordon

Sound Transfer: Matthew Beville, Eddie Bydalek

Temp FX Editor: Bruce Stubblefield

Temp FX Assistant: Dana Gustafson

Trailer Editor: Paul Berolzheimer

Interns: Bill Wagner, Stephen Rafferty

And Outside of Creative Cafe:

Re-Recording Mixers: Steve Maslow, Gregg Landaker, Kevin O'Connell

Music By: Mark Mancina

Score Engineered By: Shawn Murphy

Score Mixed By: Steve Kempster

Music Editor: Zig Gron

Assistant Music Editor: Rupert Nadeau

Executive Music Producer: Bud Carr

"One person said, 'A thousand pigs squealing.' Other people said repeatedly, 'freight trains,' 'sounded like a jet,' 'I heard pops and booms.' Then I had looked at how my naturalistic sounds worked and how traditional methods of musique concrete preparation worked with animal voices. Then I looked at the essential sonic literature of radio and film, mainly *The Wizard of Oz*. I looked at all this to figure out what people reacted to when they thought about tornados and what made them afraid."

In many senses, *Twister* provided Flick and his team with a chance to re-examine what sound effects are. It was a time to re-assess, he says, a return to his roots. After the long, hard year of *Speed* and *Apollo 13*, Flick stepped back to study the nature of wind and how physical acoustic devices could make and control the sound. Before he could talk about dragons and monsters and the audience's collective id, however, he needed original material.

In the summer of 1995, Flick sent sound recordists Eric Potter and Wayne Bell to Texas to gather authentic prairie ambiences. At the same time, he met with Foley artist John Roesch and sound recordist/designer Ken Johnson about collecting wind sounds. They decided to build two wind machines—one brand new in the traditional spindle style, and one that fit in the back of a pickup truck to capture and manipulate real wind. One generates wind, the other sort of captures and manipulates real wind. There is a difference.

"Wind machines don't make wind," Flick explains. "They make the sounds that people conventionally understand as wind. We built one of those. Then Ken built this wooden box—he called it Dr. Marvel—and he strung piano wire and fishing line, bungee cords, wood strapping, metal strapping, loose and hard, tuned and out of tune, Coke bottles full of fluid, all sorts of things. We put it in the back of a pickup and drove it down hills in the desert at 70 miles an hour with a pair of mics well-wind-screened in the back. Every time we added something to modulate the wind, it sounded different. And we could control the pitch by the acceleration of the vehicle, and by having some fast stops. A mobile Aeolian harp.

"We had already done about six months of documentary-style recording, and we had all these great growls and grumbles and naturalistic winds. What we needed was that core pitch shift. And the only way you can get that is to build a controllable device, or by varispeeding it. We found we were able to change the pitch and create the sound of acceleration, because drama, as we know, comes with a pitch shift and a change in volume. Volume is a piece of cake. But to create winds that would physically shift pitch on cue, you have to manipulate them in some way. And it has to have a realistic place to start acoustically."

The amount of material, nearly all of it organic, that went into any one tornado is staggering. Animal voices, real winds, train-bys, whistle-whines, buffeting thumps—all of it layered and assembled in Pro Tools, most of it by sound designer John Pospisil. He was the tornado guy who delivered finished voices to the editors for placement and further manipulation. There were angry winds, soft winds, gentle winds, percussive winds, monster winds, growling winds, high winds, low winds and midrange winds. Much of the processing took place in Pro Tools or with a Lexicon PCM-80. The only dictate was that the wind had to keep moving. Static winds are death.

"You can't have constant wind," Flick explains. "Some of the people we interviewed said the tornado pulsed, so John took some low-end tones of animal voices and created a low-frequency undulating tone that wasn't in the pitch area of rumble, one that would pulse and undulate—kind of like a more aggressive soft ocean wave. And it had to be arrhythmic, because rhythm becomes music. That doesn't mean our sounds don't have rhythm and meter and structure. It just means that we deal with rhythm and meter and structure only as it relates synchronously to visuals. This is a 5/4 tornado in a 4/4 movie."

THE EDIT

Despite the large number of units, this was not a large audio post crew by blockbuster movie standards. At most, there were 25 editors, including assistants, working on the film at Creative Cafe, Flick's new editorial house that he co-owns with his wife, Judee. To ensure consistency, editors were not just assigned reels, they were assigned responsibilities. And in addition to hard effects, they delivered multichannel premixes to the dub stage. Gregory Hedgepath and Charles Maynes took on the moniker of "Twister Twins."

"I would say Charles was a little more synthetic in his treatment, where I was going with animal sounds," Hedgepath says. "But any effect we put in had to have movement, because if you put in a steady and play it loud, it may sound great, but then 10 seconds later, you say, 'Okay, what next?' Consequently, we both tended to do more premixing on this film than I would suggest an editor do when I supervise films. I would duck effects and swell them up, but never the same movement on every track.

"For example, I put together a 4-channel mix where a tornado comes right up on the characters and begins to stroll around," he continues. "I recorded my fader moves on my CS-10 MIDI mixer at half-speed and swirled them around the room—picking up speed as it got close to them and slowing down as it moved away. Then I would take those four tracks and maybe do two other groupings of different wind sounds—like maybe a nice constant wind, where the faders give you the movement, and maybe a buffeting wind. One is high, one is low, so you pick up three colors. Start with the high, add the medium as they get closer to it, then when it's really upon them, the low wind swells up. Then they go away and you reverse it."

Automated or volume-mapped edits are not recommended, especially without consultation with the re-recording team. Because of the time constraints on the final and the massive number of elements, it worked on *this* film. "One of the pivotal expeiences for both Greg and me was the sweeteners on reel 1 tornados for the final, because it was the first time we had done heavy automation to the point of predubbing in our systems.

"Charles and I are both mixers as well as editors," intercuts Hedgepath, "which gave us the confidence to premix without tying the mixers' hands in the final."

"We needed more movement," continues Maynes, "but we found it difficult to convey our intentions by just laying the units up and doing fades. There was plenty of discussion at the shop about whether we should do this. Old-style editors said we were trying to do the mixers' job for them. But we just felt there was too much information, and we didn't think we could make up units that would play to the degree of activity we were looking for. Steve Flick is big on having an editor go to the dub stage to dub their reel. He is one of the finest supervisors because he has his ego in check."

The 4-channel treatments worked well on the wind, and there was plenty of swirling at the final. But this story is also about layers. When cutting the first tornado effect for the film, Maynes was working on *Mulholland Falls* and came across a fast-but-smooth merry go-round sound in the DAT library, recorded from the Scream Machine in Santa Monica. Run through a PCM-80 (with some modifications on the Finish Line patch, a sort of multivoice Doppler), it became a subliminal building block for the tornados.

Meanwhile, Martin Lopez of Digital Sound Design in San Diego came up with some stunning 4-channel recordings of train-bys, which were "massively limited" in L1, a Waves plug-in for Pro Tools, then dropped in. Hedgepath came across a vey slow diesel freight train that added a crunchy sound, which he described as "wind made of razor blades." Maynes also made regular use of the Focusrite TDM plug-in, which allowed him to notch out and boost certain frequencies to place individual colors or sparkles inside a much larger and more violent wind sound. The L1 became key, and distortion ruled the day, replacing reverb as the treatment of choice. Warren Hamilton, who the Twister Twins referred to as their Godfather of sound effects, would walk by and tell the two: "We need more grit. Grit it up."

A view from the machine room.
At left, reels of Foley; at right,
boxes containing the 600 DA-88
cassettes for effects alone.

"When the twister is upon you, like in reel 4, it's always great to add the old constant-acceleration effect," Hedgepath says. "You take some sort of whine that increases in pitch and you lay it over itself so it appears to keep going up. It's a tension-building device that was used in the trench war in *Star Wars*—the X-wing fighter was always accelerating. Ben Burtt taught me that. So I got an inertia starter out of the library—similar to the effect used on the cartoon Tasmanian Devil when his feet start moving. I pitched it down two octaves, then four octaves, then overlaid them on top of each other, then ran it through two L1s, and you get this tremendous, increasing, distorted whine that goes up in pitch. Something really bad is coming at you."

"I'm a big fan of L1," adds Maynes. "We figured out that when we put two of them in a line with maximum limiting, it made the most ungodly distortion. You could run an interesting moving wind through it and end up with something that sounded like the world ending. Then we put that into our spinning automation and it ended up fascinating."

"That's something I got from Randy Thom up at Lucasfilm," Hedgepath interjects. "His famous saying when I used to work up there was 'Distortion equals art.'"

So much energy and so much of the drama is focused on the tornado that some excellent Foley work, ADR and music may appear to get short shrift in these and other pages. Flick, who has edited some big films, including cutting on *Raiders of the Lost Ark*, says this was by far the biggest Foley show he's ever done. Wind, by itself, is not that intersting, Flick maintains. It's the dust and debris it whips up that adds the color. Not to mention flying objects—from truck crashes to knives and shards of glass being flung by the main character's ears and into a barn wall. Kudos to Foley artists John Roesch and Hilda Hodges.

Judee Flick cut more than 1,200 lines of ADR for the film, which isn't at all surprising considering they had two jet engines on the back of a flatbed during production to generate wind, along with ice machines to shoot hail, regular wind machines and lots of dialog in cars. ADR was recorded to DA-88, then loaded into Pro Tools for editing.

Music was composed by Mark Mancina, who also scored *Speed*. There is actually a surprisingly small amount of music for such a big "quest" film—roughly 44 minutes of score and 32 minutes of source. But according to all sources, De Bont shoots in a way that provides effects moments and music moments, where by and large music will carry a scene until you see the tornado, then effects take over. Mancina was invited to a few advance screenings of the trailer last December so that he would have an idea of how the sound effects were going to be played. The score was recorded to 48-track analog, then loaded into Pro Tools through Apogee converters.

"Jan is one of the top directors I've worked with in terms of being aware of the potential conflict between music and effects," explains Zig Gron, music editor on *Batman Forever*, *Assassins* and *Don Juan DeMarco*, to name just a few recent credits. "I'm a music editor who happens to believe that if the music needs to be lowered or dumped because of the emotion of the scene— which is unusual because music normally plays emotionally— then I'm all for lowering it if it will make the film better. I believe music can work with effects.

"Mark delivered the music separated onto 16 tracks of Pro Tools—left-center-right orchestra, left-center-right percussion, left-right brass, left-right synthesizer, left-right guitar, left-right choir, left-right woodwinds," he continues. "That gave us control, because we didn't really know what we were up against sound effects-wise. So if sound effects were going crazy, percussion is one of those things that can get drowned out. So we ended up boosting the percussion about 2 dB all the way through the movie, just to give it some drive. In another scene, we ended up going with choir to cut through the big effects."

"On *Speed*, there were a lot of very literal visuals working with sound," Flick adds. "See something, hear something. But in this picture, there is a lot of sound driving the drama—we hear a tornado offscreen, and it moves the drama forward, or in the house sequence, we hear noises and the characters react. It's in the writing and in the way it's photographed, and by having sound more entwined with the drama, as opposed to being sound *with* the drama, he's become a much more complex film-maker, which is a delight for me."

"When I started to think about soundtracks in a whole sense in the early '80s, as opposed to earlier, when I was just cutting sound effects, I realized that with any modern picture where you have lots and lots of sound, and the score is dynamic, you have to trade licks. You have to be able to produce a unified, whole process."

TRADING LICKS AT THE MIX

The music metaphor of the tornado is not a stretch, and in many ways, the sound of the individual tornados can be thought of as jazz pieces, fluid and arrhythmic, with complex tonal layers. While the editors are essentially concerned with making "musical" effects—in fact, Flick says, he only hires editors with a music background—the re-recording team strives for that delicate balance between dialog, effects and music, the unified whole referrred to by Flick.

You won't find a better re-recording threesome than Maslow, Landaker and Kevin O'Connell, who was brought over to help on *Twister* from his regular gig as a lead mixer at Sony. It's not just the technical chops, or the awards or nominations—though they each have plenty of both, with Landaker and Maslow each holding three Oscars and O'Connell with nine nominations. It's more in the way they can put an entire dub stage at ease and inspire complete confidence. Universal's Stage 3 is their house, and despite the pressure of a big film and the fatigue of three months of 12- to 16-hour days, they are relaxed and jovial just two days before the print master. The three can create an entire comedy routine out of the curly fries at lunch, trading licks in the same manner they do behind the Otari Premiere (with Concept 1 sidecar) on the stage.

"We knew going in that this had the potential to be a loud movie," says Maslow. "So we went in with the premise of letting me set the dialog to what I felt was a comfortable level, and that gave me a frame of reference. Everything was based around that level—all the tornados and winds and music—everything was bobbed and weaved to facilitate hearing every word. Kevin came in next with the music, and then Gregg supported it with effects."

"At no point is Gregg trying to override until it's time to let him go," explains O'Connell, who in addition to mixing music served as an extra pair of hands on the effects premixes. "If we tried to do this film the old-fashioned way, with effects trying to overdo it, we'd still be mixing the movie. It took us 150 films to get to this point," he says, and they all laugh.

Bobs and weaves, peaks and valleys—this particular film mix was all about movement. "We picture Jan's films as roller-coasters," Landaker says. "You take an audience, have them grip ahold of their seats and say, 'Omigod! Here we go!' They go through the falls, through the terror, and then relax. *Speed* was a quick-hitting roller-coaster; this is more about long undulations into terror. And at the mix, that's mainly done by not playing all 800 units at once, even though you have them. It's built from maybe five units here, then another 30 to 40 feet in, you introduce something else, then something else. It's constantly moving on the sliding scale of intensity.

"I approach sound effects mixing thinking that I want to have the audience walk out and say, 'What a ride! That was worth seven-and-a-half bucks.' I want to create a 3-D theater environment illusion for them, something they can't get at home. I want the sound of that twister 15 feet in the middle of the room. I want them to feel what they see. If we just play it flat-screen, then it becomes simply watching a movie. I want the audience involved; I don't want to be invisible."

Certainly, the 5.1-channel digital film sound formats (*Twister* was released in DTS, Dolby Digital and Sony's SDDS) play a large part in creating the 3-D environment. But all three mixers are adamant that the 5.1 channels are not about making a film loud; they're for enveloping the audience. The surround work is not overdone, though it does provide the swirls. And surprisingly, Landaker, perhaps influenced by O'Connell, is a recent convert to the use of the subwoofer—he did not employ it on *Speed*.

"After *Crimson Tide*, I really got to know subs," O'Connell says, pun intended. "From the second the tornado arrives until the second it leaves, you could literally drive the subwoofer at 100 dB and it would be fine—most mixers would have done that. We never did that. We modulated that subwoofer in and out, and what we put in the sub is not a steady rumble track, no pink noise down at 20 Hz. It was a modulated, very dynamic track that would make the sub key on and off, on and off. Same with the surrounds. We never played things straight."

"This picture deals with a lot of mid- and low-frequency information," Landaker cuts in, "so we can create a sound pressure level in the room that is not assaulting, where the audience shies away from the screen. This crew is trying to be very preservative and very conscious of levels, of not reaching the point where OSHA is saying, 'Guys, you are too loud.' This crew, and the crew that Kevin works with—and there are very few teams out there who think this way—are very conscious of not hurting the audience. There's no need for it. We can make apparent loudness without shredding someone's ears with digital sound."

"The way you do that is by lowering what's in front of the shock event rather than making the shock event so loud," explains O'Connell.

"We're trying to preserve the audience's ears," adds Landaker. "We want to involve them, but we don't want to hurt them."

"I'm going to go out on a limb here and say the responsibility of the level on the dubbing stage begins with the mixer," Maslow says. "Everybody tells you it's the director who's forcing you to make it louder, or an editor who's making it loud. But in the end, it's you who has a finger on the console."

To be sure, there seems to be a backlash in Hollywood and across the country about films being too loud, both in the sense that dialog can be buried (the ultimate sin, according to most editors and mixers) and ears can ring. There are loud moments in *Twister*, but as Landaker says, its *apparent* loudness, grip-your-seat loudness, not an assault. Critics may pan the script, but audiences are guaranteed a ride—a true audio-visual roller-coaster.

CHAPTER 12

Sound Design for The English Patient

Clockwise from top left: director Anthony Minghella, ADR supervisor Marc Levinsohn, re-recording mixer Mark Berger, supervising sound editor Pat Jackson, and film editor/re-recording mixer Walter Murch

PHOTO: STEVE JENNINGS

The English Patient is not an easy book. The Booker Prize-winning novel by Michael Ondaatje opens in southern Italy near the end of World War II, in a bombed out villa-turned-hospital. Hana, a young nurse, is caring for a severe burn patient with no identification, whom officials believe to be English. Gradually, and often in morphine-inspired prose, his past is revealed through poetic, sometimes unsettling flashbacks to the deserts of North Africa, the chaos of Cairo in the 1930s and travels through war-torn Italy. It's a love story about time and displacement, about people who have nowhere to call home—from the Bedouins who rescue the patient as he leaps burning from a plane, to the patient himself, who ultimately reveals his Hungarian roots.

And as anyone who has read the book will attest, it would not appear to be an easy movie to make. The weaving in and out of time, which works so well on the printed page, is challenging in film, where the pace is not controlled by the viewer. As film editor/lead re-recording mixer Walter Murch says, the mental

This article appeared originally in the December 1996 issue of Mix.

Music editor Robert Randles

inertia of reading is much less than the investment required when viewing sound and image combined, and what would appear easy on the page does not necessarily translate to film. It is the difference, he says, between trying to stop a pickup truck and trying to stop an 18-wheeler.

"Our biggest challenge," Murch says, "was figuring out how to put the film together so that the flow back and forward in time felt organically part of the story. So that the audience would be able to engage with the story at any one time period, but then be willing also to move from that period to another without feeling cheated or frustrated. Any film with these kinds of time transitions rides that line, but *The English Patient* does so more than any other film I have worked on. If there are too many transitions, or the transitions occur at the wrong places, we would wind up inhibiting the audience's identification with characters and situations, jerking them around to the extent that they either never commit to the story emotionally, or they do commit and then become annoyed when we take them away from it. It's a bit like taking a sports car through corners along a twisty road, without losing traction, so that your passenger feels exhilarated and safe at the same time."

The challenge of the film was also its biggest attraction. Writer-director Anthony Minghella's background was in stage, radio and television before he broke through with the art-house favorite *Truly, Madly, Deeply*, followed by the "Hollywood" film *Mr. Wonderful. The English Patient* was shot over the course of five months in Tunisia and Italy, with a bit of set work, most notably the patient's room. As in most films of this scope, the story evolved in the editing room. Murch says the number of transitions in the final print is roughly half of what was in the script, which was probably a fourth of what was in the book. And three-quarters of the transitions were created in the edit.

As has become increasingly common, picture changes were made right up until the final mix. But because the Miramax release was finally locked at 2 hours, 42 minutes (18 reels), changes typically involved far more work than would be required on a shorter, more linear film. The relatively tight temp/premix/final mix schedule was made easier by two factors: The Saul Zaentz Film Center, where the film was edited and mixed, has the most extensive Sonic Solutions network in the world (see sidebar), with original units, temps and alternates available on hard drives; and Murch wore the two hats of film editor and lead re-recording mixer, an unusual but effective arrangement. When he and Minghella made picture changes, the Avid output was dumped directly to 3/4-inch video for going into the temps or premixes.

Even with all the high-end technology employed at the Zaentz Film Center, the glue that held the project together was a core crew that has worked together on and off for the past 20-plus years. Re-recording mixer Mark Berger and supervising sound editor Pat Jackson were hired by Murch for *The Conversation* and *Godfather II* back in the early '70s, and the relationship with Zaentz goes back to before *One Flew Over the Cuckoo's Nest.* As Jackson says, "This is the Saul Zaentz company doing a Saul Zaentz movie, so there's a lot of excitement about it."

THREE WORLDS OF SOUND

Transitions in and out of time are traditionally the domain of the composer and the music editor—a prelap or postlap cue, perhaps a single piano note to trigger an event or a memory. And while those types of transitions certainly lent a great deal of emotion and coherence to *The English Patient*, as will be discussed later, the groundwork for the audio transitions was laid in early discussions about the three main settings covered in the film.

"There's the desert, there's Italy at the conclusion of World War II and there's the monastery," explains Jackson. "We conceived of those as three separate universes, and they each have their own audio world. Anthony was very clear that he wanted the monastery to be a refuge from the other two worlds, so early discussions with Walter were about how to create the feeling that the monastery would be a sanctuary. That meant it had to be a sanctuary *from* something. The world of the army in Italy is noisy, and it has artillery and clattery elements going on—it's chaos, it's war. The desert is another kind of assault, which you certainly see in the sandstorm. And Cairo [which, technically, could be considered a fourth world] is a babble of people, an exotic chaos. Then, when you get to the monastery, the present, it's very serene."

"The sections of war are such that almost all of the sounds you hear are manmade sounds—motors for the most part, explosions, guns. Nature plays a very minimal role," Murch adds. "When he goes to the monastery, that's when nature takes over, and the war, the mechanism, disappears, and we suddenly start hearing birds for the first time in the film."

"The monastery has a lot more birds," Berger agrees. "There's a lot more movement of the rustling of winds and branches and trees. It's a warmer sound, a friendlier sound. There aren't a lot of sharp edges, and there's more echo surrounding you, enveloping you in rooms, so you tend to feel enclosed and safe."

This is not a loud movie, but as many editors and mixers intuitively know, apparent loudness is key to a dynamic mix, which explains Jackson's statement about the monastery, the hospital, being a refuge *from* something else. Sometimes you know how quiet an area is by what you can hear, Jackson says. Small sounds, slightly exaggerated, can convey: "This is really quiet."

"There's a wonderful moment where Hana has come up to the patient's room for the first time, and she brings a plum," Murch says. "She chops the plum up and feeds the patient. It's probably the first time he's had fresh fruit in months, if not years. And at the same time, all of the ambiences that were playing had been reduced so you hear very clearly the sound of someone eating a plum. But also at the same time, two miles away, you hear the sound of a distant church bell. There's kind of a synesthesia of the sound of the bell and the taste of the plum. We're asking the audience to remember what a plum tastes like, and in a way, that distant bell is the sound equivalent of: 'Oh yeah, I haven't heard this in a while.' That's the first time in the film you've heard anything like that. I said earlier that you begin to hear nature at the monastery, but at the same time, you also start to hear what remains of civilized humanity, which in this case is symbolized by the church bell. Everything up to that has been bombardment."

Many of the flashbacks have a sound effects or music trigger, sometimes both. They are subtle in most cases, as there is always the danger of sounding too perfect or contrived. Some examples: As a medical tent is bombarded by artillery, the lamps in the tent clang together, and the clanging dissolves into the tinkle of a medicine man's bottles as he arrives at a desert oasis to treat the patient's burns. In another, Hana is alone playing hopscotch, and the English patient hears her footsteps in

Sound effects editor Kyrsten Mate Comoglio

rhythm to the beat of Arab drumming in the desert as he falls into a flashback. Or, the patient Kip (an Indian bomb expert, temporarily housed at the monastery) and Hana are joking about the patient drinking all of Kip's condensed milk. As Kip taps on a new can before opening it, the tapping helps the patient drift back to Cairo, arriving after a sandstorm, to the sound of metalwork in an open-air marketplace.

Those examples were planned, either in the script or in the picture edit. Sometimes, however, those "happy accidents" take place at the mix, where all the elements are in place and, as Jackson says, "movie magic happens."

In a scene where Hana watches and the English patient hears Kip and a partner drive away on motorcycles, the sputtering triggers the sound of trucks coming across the desert. "We had designed this to overlap, for the motorcycle to trigger the truck effect," Jackson explains. "At the mix, though, there was music right on top of it. We had been struggling anyway to get the motorcycles and the trucks to connect, but it became apparent that it was overly complicated, and that we needed to let the motorcycle go away, let the patient have a moment to breathe while the music sort of wafts over you, and then go into the trucks. I wound up feeling that it was the sound effects making it complex. So let's let the music carry it through."

In another fortuitous moment at the mix, during the final on reel 11, a quiet reel, the English patient asks Caravaggio (a former spy who's come to the monastery) why he's wearing bandages on his hands. A Benny Goodman tune, "Wang Wang Blues," is playing on the Victrola. As Caravaggio rises to unfurl his bandages, there is a cut to the Fall of Tobruk, during the war, where the story of his bandages is explained. "As part of the premixes on the Tobruk scene, we had put in an air-raid siren, synched with picture," explains Murch. "But there was suddenly something about Benny Goodman's clarinet that reminded me of the siren, and as this clarinet rolls up in pitch, I thought it would be a good idea to start the siren a little earlier and have the sound come out of the clarinet. So we laid up that track, slipped it and put it in. It doesn't happen on the frame, but you go from relative quiet to as loud as the film gets within a couple of feet."

"All we had to do was move the air-raid siren 12 feet, and it makes a beautiful music transition," adds Berger.

The war in Italy is loud, with distant artillery ringing in the backgrounds, and the scenes in Cairo are packed with urban ambiences. This is the age before air conditioning and before, as Murch says, the internal combustion engine has taken over. The shouts and babble outside the open windows depict an active, dense human environment. There are not a lot of car honks or trucks—just street life and open markets. The only place like it today would be Venice, Murch says.

The desert, where the English patient—actually a Hungarian desert map maker known as Almasy—both finds and loses love before crashing in a burning bi-plane, presented its own set of challenges. At times it was deathly quiet, described by Berger as "a constant search for that perfect air, the air that isn't there. What is the sound of the desert when nothing is happening?" Murch called it "varieties of air, with a few particular kinds of insects. On the production tracks from Tunisia, we heard this dry cricket sound, almost a pure sine wave-type chirp, very unlike crickets in temperate zones. There are insects where the sound itself speaks of dryness."

"It's dry, it's hot, it's windy," adds Jackson. "There are insects, desert birds of prey. The relentlessness of the desert is what we were trying to create. Even the contrast can sometimes make it work. When the English patient crashes early in the first reel and is discovered as a smoking ruin by the Bedouin, there's sand and wind and a camel caravan. Then he's taken to an oasis, and it's pretty subtle, but you can hear the sound of water in the oasis, in a way that makes you realize by its soothing quality what it's like everywhere else in the desert."

Many effects transitions were discarded as picture changed, others were created in the temps or at the final. Filmmaking is a constantly evolving process, a moving target, but by the end, right up to the final mix, the only wild card left was the music.

MUSIC BY DESIGN

Actually, because of the way composer Gabriel Yared worked, music was not such a wild card, which could have been problematic in a film of this length that was so heavily dependent on timing and transitions.

"One of the things that helped is the composer had actually done scratch mixes that were used in the temp mixes very early on," explains Berger. "The cues were done on synths, so the timbre and the frequency ranges that the music was going to be in—and where there was gong to be music and how big—was all available for working against early on. So all the sound effects editors and the music editors knew from the temp mixes and the screenings what their various areas were going to be. They were able to mark out their territories—'I've got the low frequencies here, and you can have the high frequencies. This is going to be a music scene, so let's not get too detailed. Or, we're going to be working back and forth here.' Because music was conceived of very early, there has been a lot of collaboration and a lot of synergy."

Music editor Bob Randles echoes the glory of collaboration, which he says is made much easier through the use of the network. Basically, from his Sonic Solutions setup in Room 309 at the Zaentz Film Center, he can call up individual scenes and listen to the dialog edit, effects edit, or any combination of the previous temp mixes. "For example," he says, "in the main titles we have an airplane, and we have basses in the orchestra in about the same pitch range. So we pitched the sound of these airplane propellers to follow the music. It's a very subtle pitch change and would sound natural as an airplane engine, but it also fits with the orchestra because of the pitch. This is the sort of collaboration that is easier to do when you are on the network."

There are numerous other examples of effects and music working together, especially in the transitions. Part of that may have to do with the fact that Randles does more "music design," piecing together bits and adding textures, than regular music editing. And on this film, that was necessary because of the short time Yared had with the orchestra.

The score was recorded over two days, four sessions, at AIR Studios in London. Not a lot of time for a long movie. The 60-plus piece Academy of St. Martin in the Fields orchestra was recorded to 24-track by Keith Grant. Rather than trying to cover every scene, there were times Yared asked for cues in a certain key, or a coda, with instructions for Randles to use them where they would fit best. Sometimes they got only a single take; other times they were able to only record the rehearsal. Tapes were

Chief engineer Jim Austin, left, and systems engineer Vince Casper in Transfer B; the Sonic network loading station is pictured through the window at right

PHOTO: STEVE JENNINGS

then flown back to the Zaentz Film Center and mixed by Michael Semanick to eight tracks (L-C-R-LC-RC-LS-RS-sub) directly into the Sonic Solutions system, using the 18-bit Sonic converters. Some synth passages were also added at this point, to spotlight certain Middle Eastern instruments.

One of the more interesting textures Randles added after the fact was low, low tone clusters. He recruited six voices from the San Francisco Gay Men's Chorus and San Francisco Opera. Rather than tracking specific cues, he recorded them 3-track into the Sonic, singing in various pitches down to A below the staff. Those tracks were then doubled or quadrupled and added where it helped fill out the tracks. In one case, director Minghella wanted to repeat a quiet, plaintive clarinet and harp passage against the backdrop of the desert, when Almasy is going to rescue Katharine. To avoid repetition, Randles dropped in the tone clusters. He also put them into a sorrowful Hungarian lullaby that is heard inside a cave, added them to an airplane scene and put them in the 70-plus tracks of "Silent Night" at a Cairo Christmas party.

The Christmas party scene had to be premixed in the Sonic down to a more manageable 24 tracks for the dub stage. The actors had sung it in production, and Randles added untrained voices of whoever was roaming the halls at AIR Studios. Low tone clusters were added, and antiphonal parts—not too perfect—were recorded. And holes were allowed for the orchestra to creep through, although Randles had to piece together a part from synth tracks, as the orchestra hadn't the time to record it. Finally, because a player is visible roaming around the shot, bagpipes were recorded at Fantasy Studios. But, bagpipes can't play the melody to "Silent Night" because it doesn't fit into the scale. To improvise, Randles wrote out the harmony on the spot and popped it in.

The music is very European, epic in scope, and at the same time it's intimate—a simple piano note from a Bach aria, a spotlighted oud or doumbek that leaves an emotional trail. In many cases, it was a solo clarinet. "The clarinet solo was kind of a surprise," Randles explains, "in that Anthony said if Gabriel had told him he was going to write a clarinet solo or clarinet accompanied by harp, Anthony said he probably would have told him that's not what he was hoping for. But when he heard it, he said, 'Bob, make sure you sprinkle that liberally throughout the picture, because this is the voice of the movie.'

"There's a story point about Arab vs. Hungarian and English," Randles adds. "The English patient who isn't English, but Hungarian. A folk song that sounds Arabic but is really Hungarian. There's all this play. So I think it's entirely appropriate that we start out with an optical of sand that isn't sand, but parchment that becomes sand. And we start out leading the orchestra solo with the English horn, which is neither English nor a horn."

THE MIX

The mix schedule was not particularly short by today's standards, but it did get congested because of the length of the film. Temps were being put together by Murch for screenings in New Jersey and California (often just the 4-channel Avid output) as dialog and effects premixes were put together by Berger and David Parker, often on the night shift, sometimes on a second stage. Murch had premixed the first seven reels of dialog, but as he became busy with picture changes in preparation for screening number 2, Berger took over while Parker did effects. Then Berger may have spent a day on loop groups or ADR, while Parker continued with effects. "Every possible combination of time and function was involved in getting ready for the final," Berger says.

The film was mixed against video (the Avid output) on Stage 3 at the Saul Zaentz Film Center, on a 96-input Otari Premiere console. Music was played back directly from the Sonic Solutions system on the stage, which was fiber optically linked to Randles' editing room. Dialog, which was recorded 4-track on the Nagra-D, was edited in the Sonic and played back from 6-track mag film. Foley, which was traditional in that there was 100% coverage ("There was a lot of attention paid to the gritty sound of walking instead of the click-click-click of a sterile floor," Berger says. "There was a lot of dirt thrown down."), was recorded to 2-inch, 24-track and played back from the same. Effects came off of 6-track mag film. At any time, however, the mix team could access any bank of effects, ADR lines or dialog lines from the online Sonic systems residing in any of the 18 rooms at the Film Center. And it was not uncommon to hear Murch or Berger say, "Give me Room 209, tracks 3 and 4," meaning the Sonic in room 209 was functioning as a playback dubber.

But for all the ease of access, both Murch and Berger are adamant that it is irrelevant where the sound is coming from, and it in no way changes their approach to a mix. Sure, some operations are faster, and when you need to search for "scrabbly air" to fill out a ballroom scene, it can be flown in and essentially edited at the mix. But the approach is the same. And they don't distinguish between premixes and final mixes.

"Premixes are in fact the final mix," Murch says. "I don't distinguish between the two—you are mixing. It's just that in the premixes, you're focused on a certain area of the orchestra. If you were talking about orchestral rehearsals, you would be rehearsing the strings section, and so you're just focused on the strings and how they're working to each other, although in the back of your mind, you have to know that they're going to have to work with the woodwinds. So you don't want one to do something that steps on or eliminates something another section is doing. The premixes are a good example of that paradoxical state you find yourself in in films a lot, which is extreme attention to detail, but at the same time trying to maintain an idea of the big picture. You can get into trouble if you wander to either side of the road."

The Sonic Solutions Network

About four years ago, under the direction of facility executive vice president Roy Segal, the Saul Zaentz Film Center began assembling a Sonic Solutions editing network. Chief engineer Jim Austin and systems engineer Vince Casper started with four rooms and a couple of Sound Designer II sidecars. Today, the company boasts 18 Sonic-equipped rooms, with more than 60 4-gigabyte drives accessible from any room, at any time. But, the facility has not thrown out its Sondor mag recorders, and DA-88s and Pro Tools systems are used throughout.

"The whole time this technology is developing, we're making feature films," says Casper. "So our original intent was to make the network work side by side with mag, with the understanding that this is an evolutionary process. Each show, we have added more digital rooms.

"The main thing Sonic contributed here, and I guess Andy Moorer is the genius behind this, is the MOFS [Media Optimized File System] file structure," he continues. "This is what allows the multiple mounting of drives. This is what allows several people to use the same file. This is what allows transfer to be recording on a drive while someone is playing back off it. About two or three software upgrades ago, we were given the ability to mount any of these Sonic drives on the Mac desktop, which is a wonderful feature because it allows you to do Finder tasks to the drives—drag-and-drop copying, searches, lists.

"We've learned a lot here coming from four rooms to 18. It's very, very advantageous having file servers as opposed to having individual rooms with hard drives. Traditionally, if you have a stand-alone system and want to move material or troubleshoot a crash, you have to shut down the system and stop editing. You then sneakernet the hard drive to another room or repair the system. That takes time. Using the network and the drive servers, a local computer can go down, and the rest of the editors continue to work without interruption. Here, any Sonic station with a MediaNet card can be a server in an emergency."

On a typical show, the transfer department will first load and deploy the server room, which consists of four Mac IIci computers, each with eight 4-gig drives. (As the Sonic network card handles the file and all SCSI activity for the net, state-of-the-art computers are not required for this function. Editing rooms are equipped with Quadra 950-class machines.) Then, when more drive server space is needed, individual rooms—the ones not in heavy use—handle the overflow. In the case of *The English Patient*, there were servers for ADR, Foley, dialog and effects, with additional stations for temp mixes (so editors could edit multitrack mixes, and still go back to original elements) and a guide track. "Originally we were putting guide tracks in with the dialog system," Casper explains, "but we realized that it's such a dominant player on the net that we had to give it its own server. Anyone who's cutting wants a guide track to play against." Daily backups are done to Exabyte, from 5 to 9 in the morning, and at

Steve Shurtz, Saul Zaentz Film Center director of operations, and Roy Segal, right, executive vice president

2 a.m., via automatic macro-dash scrips, running Retrospec backup software. Casper performs low-level formatting of the drives about every three months as a preventive maintenance measure.

There are a number of sub-networks involved, including the music net, which allows a direct fiber optic link to the dub stage and allows music editor Bob Randles (who has a mirrrored set of six 4-gig drives) to switch to the larger editing network as well. Because music is played back directly from the Sonic, in case of drive failure, he's up and ready to go in minutes from his music editing drives. Also, there is an AppleTalk network, known as Walter World Wide Web, for picture editor/re-recording mixer Walter Murch, which is linked with supervising sound editor Pat Jackson and two of her assistants. This net is for exchanging FileMaker III database updates containing picture change information, and, of course, the ever-present e-mail. The print station AppleTalk network consists of two Quadra 610s running Trackit cue sheet software, with an HP LaserJet 4 as their target. Also, there is the company office network which extends onto the dub stages and the client lobbies for administrative tasks.

Perhaps one of the big bonuses for sound designers is that the Film Center has made Pro Tools sidecars available in the effects rooms, what Casper refers to as the hybrid rooms. "We've set up a digital switching situation where we can route digital signals from Pro Tools to Sonic/Sonic to Pro Tools/DAT to Sonic, using Z Systems sample rate converters and Zsys switchers," he says. "We bridge the two platforms by moving things digitally—maybe not the most efficient way, but until all the file structures are compatible through something like OMF, it's probably the only way. It allows these hybrid rooms to do an assortment of tasks, and it lets the designers who want to do something in Pro Tools then just move it into the Sonic. It's been an interesting evolution for the Pro Tools people, when the first time they open up the Sonic Manager and see they have access to that many hard drives, their eyes pop out. I think the next step you'll see around here is putting Sonic MediaNet cards in Pro Tools computers and literally allowing the ability to mount a Sonic drive on the Pro Tools desktop."

Cruising With David Lynch Down the 'Lost Highway'

The Lost Highway re-recording team, at the three-position Euphonix board, L to R: David Lynch, John Ross, Derek Maicil and Frank Gaeta

This article appeared originally in the January 1997 issue of Mix.

Nothing about a David Lynch film is "normal." Not the script, not the visual stamp, not the editing and certainly not the sound. His films tend to occupy the Hollywood fringe, as well as the subconscious fringe, in a manner that defies genre-coding or "typical" definitions. Now, after a six-year absence during which he made directorial forays into television, music videos and commercial spots, he's back in features with the October Films production of *Lost Highway*. And he says he's back in features to stay.

You will not find a director today, inside or outside of Hollywood, who is more involved with the creation of the soundtrack than David Lynch. From his very first short film, *The Alphabet*, through *The Grandmother, Eraserhead, The Elephant Man, Dune, Blue Velvet* and *Wild at Heart*, he worked in tandem with Academy Award-winning sound designer and close friend Alan Splet, one of the true gentle giants in the history of film sound. (The duo even shared sound design credit on *The Elephant Man.*) The mechanical-industrial dissonance that marked his early films established a sonic perspective that blurred the lines between music and effects, opening up sound montages that could be labeled backgrounds, but more appropriately called atmospheres.

"For me, a director designs everything, because [the film] has to pass through this one person for it to be cohesive and whole," Lynch says during a break from the final mix on reel 2AB at Digital Sound & Picture, Los Angeles. "That's not to say you don't rely on people, and that other people don't have a great deal of say and talent and do a lot to help shape the film, but it all passes through one person. I love working on sound. If I could have more time, I would like to be working with the people making the sounds, and who knows where it would lead.

"When I worked with Alan Splet, we were always making sound effects—before, during and after the shooting," he continues. "A lot of times, a piece of music or a sound effect up front gives you ideas that will help you in the shooting. And then I listen to the music while I'm shooting, so the more I have up front, the better. It helps the picture. I'm an action and reaction person. I have to hear something, and then we go from there."

Lynch lost a dear friend and the industry lost a gifted talent when Splet passed away in December 1994. For the past few years, Lynch has turned to John Ross, owner of Digital Sound & Picture, for his post-production needs. Frank Gaeta, on staff at DS&P, supervised *Lost Highway* and admits to a bit of anxiety upon getting the assignment. "For me, or for any sound person, David is an icon. So of course it's a thrill to work with him. But at first I thought, 'What can I say to David that he doesn't already know about his film—a director who seems to have done everything and explored everything?'" The picture was in-house for a month prior to the five-week final in July, but Lynch and Gaeta began talking about and previewing sounds as much as six months before that, soon after shooting wrapped.

It would be impossible to describe *Lost Highway* in the *Player*-esque 25 words or less. Bill Pullman plays Fred Madison, an L.A. jazz saxophonist who, through a surreal chain of events, witnesses a murder (of his wife, played by Patricia Arquette) that he may or may not have committed. While on Death Row,

David Lynch, front, and John Ross at the custom Euphonix

Madison morphs into Pete Dayton, played by Balthazar Getty. A highway is involved, we know that, and Dayton morphs again. Beyond that, it's hard to predict from a three-reel preview where the film ends up. But we know where it starts, and with this film, it seemed to start with music.

MUSIC AND FIREWOOD

The first thing that needs to be stated is that Lynch mixes his own music at the final, and has since *Twin Peaks*. He's right there on the left side of the custom three-position Euphonix console (Ross chained three together years before Euphonix offered a film version of the CS2000), with Ross in the middle and Gaeta and Foley/background editor Derek Maicil to the right. Lynch is a composer as well (he's released a CD of original compositions with his longtime musical collaborator

Angelo Badalamenti), and in a sense, he creates a music track right there at the final. No score at the last minute, competing with effects. This is music by design, and the bits and pieces he's assembled, literally from all over the world, he refers to as "firewood."

The primary arrangements and bits of firewood were written by Badalamenti and recorded in Prague. But pieces came from avant-garde jazz string sessions, written by Barry Adamson and recorded at Capitol Studio A in Los Angeles; synth sessions recorded by Arthur Polhemus at Excalibur Studio in New York City; and a three-day stint at Trent Reznor's studio in New Orleans, where Lynch sought "drones"—guitar tones that contributed to many of the atmospheres and supplemeted some of the more ominous sections of the film's sound design.

"Since Fred Madison is a jazz saxophone player, I was thinking kind of crazy jazz at the beginning," Lynch explains. "Barry [Adamson] and I wrote in kind of a '90s bebop sound, which Angelo nailed pretty well. Then I like this composer Górecki and I like Shostakovich—they've been a big influence, and Angelo can tune into that and still do Angelo, as well. But there's something about the sound from Prague that I really like."

Because the studio in Prague was not familiar with the 5.1-channel digital format for film, Ross accompanied Lynch to Prague to track and mix the orchestra, which at times numbered 80 players. "I know how David works," Ross says, "so I wanted to make sure we had the material recorded in such a fashion that we could pull it apart. I didn't want to come back with an LCRS recording, where either you have the cue or you don't. I wanted to set up the mics to get the split surrounds acoustically, in that space. We mixed in Prague, but nobody was familiar with the 5.1 environments, so we pretty much had to rewire the control room to make it work."

Schoeps mics were used on individual instruments and, with MD capsules, for the room, including a delta configuration over the conductor. Ross mixed a 5.1-channel live version, as well as down to the 24-track analog machine, then mixed the 24-track down to a 5.1-channel version. In most cases, that multitrack mix was brought to the final.

It was not, however, as if Ross was mixing songs. These are motifs, passages, moods. "The pieces that were done in Prague were very open-architecture," Ross explains. "There were long, dark string moves that we could take and use as components— we could cut the front section, merge it into the middle section, and so on and so forth. Some of the relationships between the keys from various cues were designed in such a way that they can be overlaid on top of each other or stripped back. A lot of the percussive elements were singled out. He would also divide the orchestra into various components and let them create sounds, like effects, on the instruments. Each player was basically given the responsibility to do their own little piece of time—it wasn't an organized event—and as a result, it was an interesting cacophony created within the orchestra, which we can then use as a color in overlaying another piece of orchestral music.

"In some sections, we recorded the orchestra the conventional way, as well as directly into containers—two long tubes and a large wine bottle. [Neumann mics were placed inside a large carafe and at the end of long piping tubes, then hung above and behind the conductor.] These sounds were then used to mix in with the orchestra, and we pretty much had no idea how it was going to play. I took sections of the bottle, copied it, looped it, and David used it as an overtone to some of the orchestral pieces. Very difficult to guess how that is going to sound. It has this reedy overtone, which David used as a high-frequency element to sting things with.

"We might take some of those elements into the workstations and process them and it comes out as a sound effect at the end of the day, or what would traditionally be a sound effect," Ross adds. "But it started out as an orchestral piece. So there's a real gray area between what is a sound effect and what is music.

"We've done things where he's pretty much taken a piece of music, reversed it, dropped it down an octave and played just the reverb return of that. Think of it more as music design. That's why he's physically sitting here. He wants a mood against the picture, and where he feels it, he puts those faders up. Sometimes he has no idea what's underneath those faders—it's pure surprise to him—but he brings it out, and if it works, great. If it doesn't work, we might take it, do something backwards and

132 Sound for Picture

forwards, drop another element. Sometimes you get some really interesting results. No composer in the world is gonna sit there and say, 'Let me write this backwards at half-speed'—it doesn't work. David has a totally nontraditional approach, and he's comfortable with taking these chances."

"Score is a weird thing," Lynch says. "On a lot of pictures, directors don't really get to work with the composer until the eleventh hour, and then they're saddled with a score. I've done that. But I prefer that Angelo builds me modular music that can go here or go there, and get fiddled with. Beds and all kinds of little builds. Small pieces, long pieces that are meant to be fiddled with.

"There are sound effects, there are abstract sound effects; there's music, and there's abstract music," he adds. "And somewhere music turns into sounds, and sounds turn into music. It's kind of a strange area."

EFFECTS AND BACKGROUNDS

Because he is essentially creating the music track during the mix, Lynch avoids any semblance of the age-old conflict between music and effects fighting to be heard. In fact, he finds the notion of competition on the stage absurd. Music becomes effects; effects become music. It's the way he's always worked, and it's led to some incredibly inventive sound montages, from the eerie early squeaks of *Eraserhead* through some of the sawmill/industrial backgrounds of *Twin Peaks*. But as Ross and others point out, it's not really fair to label them backgrounds. They are atmospheres, designed to create a mood. More than once on the stage, Lynch pulled back on an effect—whether in a prison background, footsteps or a hard door-close—because "it sounds too real."

"When you think about backgrounds on a normal film, you think about birds, winds, traffic, etc.," says supervising sound editor Frank Gaeta. "On this film, we're talking in abstract terms, a feel rather than a sound. David would say, 'I want it to sound oppressive, or I want it to sound ominous.' So we take tones and pitch them down, process them and make them run backwards, and that becomes a background for a scene, like the prison sequence we're in right now. Our first talks were all in

Chapter Thirteen **133**

terms of musical quality. And it's all atonal. When I sat down with the videotape to begin thinking about the elements, I had the music that David had been putting together. It was a big priority to have the music with the work copy, but it's very unusual."

"In some of the house sequences," adds Ross, "we've taken such elements as church reverbs, church room tones, air conditioners, refrigerators, and slowed them way, way down, then mixed them up to create this industrial background, this industrial tone, which we use in a house that is essentially quiet—which a conventional director would play quiet. There are no birds in these sections. The backgrounds are made of unusual elements, and in certain places they feel like music, in that they tend to suck you in, and they're played fairly loud. Music tends to do this function on certain shows, but we're using sound effects to do it."

Backgrounds and Foley were edited on DAWN workstations— Ross was an early supporter, as he tends to be with new technology, and now owns 22 systems, some of which serve as recorder/players on the stage. Effects were edited in Pro Tools and created in a combination of Pro Tools and Sample Cell cards, triggered from Studio Vision. One of the more interesting design elements in the film involves a series of videotapes, delivered mysteriously to Fred Madison (the Bill Pullman character). The series of tapes, with the images and static-like crackles, convey some of the horror and tension as the film builds. Madison plays them back on a standard television, with very unstandard crackle and sparks.

"John had built this tube preamp," Maicil says of the root video static sound. "So we took this sound Frank had of the cord being pulled out of an amplifier and basically overloaded the input stage of the tube, creating tube distortion out of tube distortion in the process. That makes it a little more earthy and takes the edge out, but still makes it cut through. It's not like pink noise, and it could very easily get that way. At some point, when you run out of volume, you start going for EQ to make things come up, but that sound is right in the range where it can be painful, so the tube really helps to lighten that up a bit."

That distorted tube sound was then miked in an open room to add grit and drone, then processed through an H3000 for a wider and thicker feel. Then, as the camera moves in on the television and the electro-static becomes more pressing, Gaeta added some reversed metal doors. "That was a David thing," Gaeta says. "One of the first things he told me was, 'Frank, I like things pitched down, I like them reversed, I like reverb.' His whole concept was that he wanted [this static] to be harsh, very steel-like and metallic, grinding. And he's always looking for sounds that cut through."

There are two huge effects moments—the transformation scenes—where Lynch wanted it pedal-to-the-metal, Gaeta says. "We have already started introducing the sounds that are going into Fred's transformation, in which we sort of follow the character along in the film," he adds. "The basic notion was that there is going to be a lot of motion, a lot of static and a lot of turbulence. It's not your typical Hollywood morph special effects. It's done very cool through the way they shot it, on good old film.

"I got a lot of inspiration for the sounds from some of the drones and tracks that David played me of what Trent Reznor was doing," he continues. "Basically, I came back to process things, and they were sounding too sweet. So I took some screams, put 'em through reverb and let 'em repeat—loop and loop, over and over—so that it would build as constant acceleration. Then I put a microphone in the middle of my room, in front of the speakers, to get the feel. I recorded that sound, and it will play somewhere in the scene. It's rough and full and gritty and as ugly as anything we've heard."

LIVE AT THE MIX

The film sound industry has a reputation for accepting new technologies slowly. Workstations have made their way onto mixing stages, and DA-88s have become de rigueur, but each facility seems to be working out its own transitional hybrid methods of working, often with an integration of the best of mag and the best of disk. At DS&P, though they can work on film, the transition to completely sprocketless, tapeless post was made about four years ago with the purchase of the DAWN systems, which also act as player/re-recorders.

"There is no sound effects prelay or anything along those lines to send to a multitrack format, whether it be DA-88, 24-track or mag," Ross explains. "It all runs directly from the DAWN workstations. We can work in the conventional manner, as in hanging everything on the screens and just mix. But often our clients, and David in particular, want to make changes—they want to interact with the audio evironment. David sees things and makes calls based on his gut reactions at the time. It's difficult to predub in that sort of situation, so we keep everything pretty much hanging live here, except for Foley. That's the only thing we predubbed, just because it requires a fair amount of finessing, and I prefer to put that time in up front.

"Everything we have here, for a particular show and in our libraries, is published on a LAN [local area network]," he continues. "So all our editors can make sure that whenever we come into the main character's front door, it's always this group of sounds that is used, and if we make changes on the stage, where we want to add or subtract elements, we have access to those same databases. So we hang all the units directly from the computers, mix through the Euphonix under automation, and go down to six stems on DA-88.

"The flip side of mixing a show in this maner is that the dialog tracks have to come to me pretty smooth, so as a result, the editors are making some decisions that may have been made by a mixer in the past. But I can always undo those decisions. It's not as if they've mixed something and given it to me on tape. Same thing with sound effects. Our editors are set up with surrounds, so they can actually do a fair amount of panning, movement and the like under controllers—not actually as part of the sound but as automation controllers."

There was no standard premix, though there was a temp mix, sort of a "fleshing out" period, a few weeks before they went into the 25-day final. And the nice thing was that the moments they liked in the temp were used from then on, perhaps augmented and updated, but pretty much intact. This is not by any means a new standard for the way audio post works in film, nor is it recommended for those who don't enjoy the challenge of pulling a soundtrack together all at once. It works for David Lynch, and it works at Digital Sound & Picture.

A New Way of Working

The whole industry has been waiting patiently for digital dubbers as a means to make changes and conforms much easier on the mixing stage in this age of shortened post-production schedules and constant picture changes. For Ross, they arrived years ago.

"Think of our workstations as intelligent digital dubbers, if you like," Ross says. "They are digital dubbers in that they are running to the picture in sync and playing back the sounds. The difference is that I can *see* the sound. I can interact with the sound. What's the difference? It's a hard disk device that plays back sound digitally.

"I understand that some mixers like to mix in reverse—set automation and make EQ decisions as the film is in rewind," he continues. "But you don't need the rewind. I can hear a piece of dialog far better running forward. If I want to get rid of clicks and pops, work around a piece of dialog or interact with my props, it's easier to do that in a maner that they were designed to work, which is forward. If I want to match a piece of ADR with production, I highlight a start point, highlight an end point, and just put the workstation on a loop in front of me and EQ it as much as I want. I don't have to see the picture—sometimes I can actually get a clearer sense of what it sounds like without picture. Obviously, I then play it against picture to make sure it's a wonderful thing, but I think the conventional philosophy was that if the picture rolls, you have sound; if the picture is not rolling, you don't have sound. There's no reason for it to be that way. Ultimately, it all rolls as a single entity, but I think you can do far more productive work without having the burden of dragging this 35mm piece wherever you go.

"The trick to this whole operation is that the projector is actually slaved to a 3/4-inch videotape, which is the master for everything. So there's a Lynx device that locks up the projector. I have local [video] monitors at my mixing positions and also in various places within the room, so that we can see time-code, we can see feet and frames, we can see those relationships. So if we need to have a particular hit of music occur at a certain cut, I can scrub it backward and forward using the DAWN driving the 3/4-inch machine via Sony 9-pin control. When I park to a partiuclar area and snap the sound at that location and go back and hit 'play,' the projector comes online and locks up very quickly.

And on the big screen, we see 35mm film, we hear the full mix, but the projector is not driving it. The projector is a back-base device that is fairly dumb: It can count pulses one way or count pulses another way; it doesn't have any more smarts than that. Dealing with timecode, it's a lot more flexible [to work in video], and that's why we made the projector the slave. But, you have to have a good projector. We have a Sondor machine, which is an excellent device. We go from the beginning of a 2,000-foot reel, play it back then go back to the head to do fixes. By the time we sit and discuss the few changes in the reel, we're ready to go."

"David wants to hear every element, and you can't do that when you premix traditionally, with a BG mix, a Foley mix, a dialog mix," Maicil says. "We have to keep everything separate. You can see that David has these tracks in his head all the time. He can say to you articulately what he wants, and when he hears it, that's it. Don't touch it. Accidents happen, and as you see, they stay because they work. He has an amazing attention to detail and knows evey little click and pop. He'll say, 'The third pop should come down a little bit, with the fifth one as we move in on her face.' Very few directors seem to have the focus in that amount of detail."

"The one thing I've learned from working with David is that there are lots of ways to solve a problem," Ross concludes. "There are ways to look at a problem area and find various solutions. He's definitely not a 'See a dog, hear a dog' kind of guy. He's more, 'See a dog and possibly imagine what the dog is thinking.' "

Titanic

Sound Design for James Cameron's Epic Ocean Saga

L to R: Mix Technician Tony Sereno; Re-recording Mixers Lora Hirschberg and Gary Rydstrom; Sound Designer/ Re-recording Mixer Christopher Boyes; Supervising Sound Editor Tom Bellfort; Re-recording Mixers Tom Johnson and Gary Summers; Mix Technician Gary Rizzo.

PHOTO: STEVE JENNINGS

First, *Titanic* was going to come out on July 2, 1997, capturing the big holiday crowds. Then late July. Then rumors of Labor Day, before Paramount and director James Cameron settled on a December 19 domestic release. "Something must be wrong," went the typical Hollywood buzz, seemingly eager to trash a big-budget, epic-style film before the first test screenings. Not once was it conceded that maybe, just maybe, the extra time could mean a better film and, consequently, a better return on the $200 million-plus investment.

No doubt the extra time gave Cameron a chance to tighten up the edit, which originally came in at 25 reels and was trimmed to 20 (3 hours, 16 minutes, including credits). And it must have given Digital Domain, the visual effects company Cameron co-owns, time to polish and perfect tremendously complicated

This article appeared originally in the January 1998 issue of Mix.

sequences. But it also gave the edit and mix crew at TEC Award-winning Skywalker Sound the opportunity to complete a much fuller, richer soundtrack and rely on first-call editors, many of whom were booked on other films based on a July 2 release.

"What the extra time gave us," says supervising sound editor Tom Bellfort, "was the ability to come to terms with all the material and try to articulate all the possible sounds that would create the sheer size and elegance of the ship before it hits the iceberg. It also gave us the time to approach the job [in the post-iceberg section] in less of a mechanical way. It's easy to do a mechanical job as compared to a more of an emotional and psychological rendering of what's going on aboard the ship while it's sinking."

Of course the later release also gave more time for the mix. Premixing began in early August and was finished in late October, in time for the world premiere at the Tokyo Film Festival on November 1. The schedule might seem luxurious in today's film sound climate, but the length made it essentially two movies, and the complexity of the material (127 speaking parts, 4,000 principal loops, intricate water Foley, at least three big, protracted action scenes) was daunting. By all accounts, it couldn't have been done without the stage setup on the new Mix A at Skywalker, which includes the 156-input AMS Neve Capricorn digital console pictured on last month's *Mix* cover, along with two Pro Tools systems for effects fixes, two Studioframes for dialog and a Sonic Solutions system for music. Premixes and finals were recorded to Skywalker's Sondor mag machines with Dolby SR.

"With a digital, fully automated console, we were able to audition alternate effects that we premixed, and we could cut elements on the stage," says effects re-recording mixer Gary Rydstrom. "I could take those inputs to the board, and since it's fully automated, I could pan it, EQ it, make it echo, and it sits right in. It's almost like being able to edit, premix and final mix at the same stage. So it gave us a lot of flexibility."

Working with Cameron demanded flexibility. He makes full use of the four outputs on his Avid system during the picture edit and creates a detailed temp mix (which was used at the first test screenings). The re-recording team would then solo those tracks before going into a reel to isolate Cameron's ideas. Sometimes he wanted the single effect from his temp, sometimes he wanted a different sound or more fullness. And because he was so involved with other aspects of the film at the time, there was really no way of knowing before he sat in for the final, at which point he would inevitably ask for changes.

"Jim [Cameron] is very good about pacing when he does his temps," says music re-recording mixer Gary Summers. "He is very conscious of where there's going to be effects only, where there's going to be music, the interplay of them, and how dense it is. When you say he likes effects big, well, he also likes music big, but he's very, very selective. I remember that from *Terminator 2*—at any given moment, there's only certain things you're going to hear."

IN THE BEGINNING

When Bellfort, Rydstrom and sound designer Christopher Boyes flew down to Los Angeles in early March to meet with Cameron, the film was really "a rough assembly of scenes," according to Rydstrom, and clocked in at 5-1/2 hours. The job seemed a bit overwhelming; the obvious place to start was field recording aboard ships.

Many of the water and ship recordings come from four sessions aboard the Liberty ship Jeremiah O'Brien, an old working vessel with roughly the same engine-type as the Titanic, docked in San Francisco Bay. The Jeremiah O'Brien actually had been used in filming for some interiors of the engine room, so Boyes thought it would be ideal to get the sound of the engine, which he knew would be crucial in selling the size of the ship and the drama of switching to full-reverse when the iceberg is hit. But as is usually the case, he says, "The real sound never really works." (For the curious, the basic building blocks of sound of the Titanic's engine, which was the biggest steam-driven device ever built, are a piston from a racing-engine block, a massive air compressor and a stamper machine, combined and played on a Synclavier.)

The O'Brien sessions weren't a complete wash, however, as the recordists came back with plenty of metallic door closes, hatch openings, distant engine rumbles (which run throughout the film, to give the sense of movement), bells, clangs and the like. The O'Brien also was taken out into San Francisco Bay, so the sound team was also able to capture a tremendous variety of bow wash, mid-side wash, propeller wake, hull laps and other water

Sound Designer/Re-recording Mixer Christopher Boyes in his Chris Pelonis-designed sound design room, complete with 40-input Oram BEQ console, Pro Tools and Synclavier (monitoring through Tannoy AMS 10As).

movement sounds, which occupy much of the first 11 reels, before the collision with the iceberg. The O'Brien crew even threw the engines into full-reverse about 20 times, simulating the climactic moment, which provided a wealth of creaks, groans, distant rumbles, perspective shifts, and countless backgrounds used to re-create the factory-like ambience of the steerage compartment.

Water and metallic groans became the signature effects of the film, established in the first half and lending what Rydstrom calls a "sort of haunted house" tension to the second half. Each portion of the film posed challenges: Pre-iceberg, the job was to sell the audience on the size and elegance of the world's largest movable object.

PRE-ICEBERG

"It was Cameron's idea that every time we could, we make use of differences in sound perspectives on different points of the ship to remind us of just how vast this ship is," Rydstrom says. "Steerage obviously had a certain sound that was very mechanical and rumbling, and the pipes are gurgling. Then in first-class, it's low but still rumbling to give you a sense that the ship is still moving, but it's very quiet and elegant. You hear clock ticks and the period cloth on the women's dresses—all these audio clues that this is a high-class place, but always pointing out where we are on the ship, both in location and class.

Chris "Bear" Barrick in the central machine room

PHOTO: STEVE JENNINGS

"Another great scene is when the ship is first launched and the engines kick in," Rydstrom continues. "Again, Cameron cuts from a close-up of a propeller starting to turn, with all the churning water and rumbling of the ship, up to someone in first-class where you just hear a slight rumble and the clink of a teacup. Playing up those contrasts was really important."

Out on deck the relationships of wind and water sounds provided the audio clues. The sound of bow wash had to be very different from mid-wash and stern wash. And the wind had to vary, from sea winds to the fateful windless night, when what you hear comes only from the motion of the ship (the source, Boyes says, was wind cutting through telephone wires near the Point Reyes lighthouse). As the Titanic nears the iceberg, the music from a quartet playing in a ballroom adds yet another audio reference: "Jim was always very conscious of where the characters are on the ship and where the band was in relation to them," music re-recording mixer Gary Summers says. "He always wanted it to feel that the quartet was still playing. Then you have the total destruction of the ship and lives are going to be lost and the despair, and you hear this waltz playing—this really nice counterpoint he's creating."

THE CRASH

The crash sequence was one of the first things Boyes and Rydstrom worked on, in order to get a sense of the size of the engine and the size of their biggest effects reel. Although Rydstrom helped design some of the big scenes and collaborated throughout, he passed on taking a sound design credit, saying, "It really is Chris' movie." After working as Rydstrom's assistant on films such as *Terminator 2* and *Jurassic Park,* Boyes has gone on to do sound design and re-recording on such films as *Mission: Impossible, Eraser* and *Volcano.* Nothing, he says, has matched the scope of *Titanic* And few scenes have matched the complexity of the crash sequence.

"One of the things that Gary once said to me a long time ago, which I've come to learn is absolutely right, is that sometimes when you make sound effects, you can't go for the biggest sound," Boyes says. "You can't go to a really large device that makes huge sound to get that huge sound. Often, it's the smaller things that make the more interesting sounds, that sound bigger than the big things, if that makes sense."

The night of the crash was moonless and windless, and the Titanic was clipping along at 23 knots. A huge engine is roaring away and water is thundering past the hull. The sense is that you are moving fast and can't be stopped. Then deck officer Murdock spots the iceberg, issues the order to full-reverse with a turn, and sets up an intense audio drama, culminating in the lethal rip along the hull.

"Jim really wanted to tell the audience with audio how difficult it is to take this massive engine from full-speed forward to full-speed reverse," Boyes explains. "I found a recording from one of the cargo holds of the [Jeremiah O'Brien] during the ramp-down/ramp-up of the engine—not a straining, but sort of this steel moaning, crying sound. I started applying ramp-down square waves to it and came up with these sounds that feel like a tremendous amount of power winding down, then later winding up."

Boyes took that sound, along with the piston, compressor and stamper effects, but still wasn't getting the rhythm he wanted. "So Gary and I sat down and basically created a loop on the Synclavier keyboard that I was able to apply speed to," he says. "I could slow these four main sounds down so that they came apart and you could hear each of the sounds distinctly from one another, and then as we sped it up, they would sort of blend into each other and reach full syncopation. It felt like you had the throttle to the engine of the Titanic in your hand right here on the Synclavier."

The Titanic Crew

Titanic required a massive and incredibly detailed film sound job, involving editors in Los Angeles and Northern California, with the bulk of the work done at Skywalker Sound in Marin County. Supervising sound editor Tom Bellfort says, "This is one of the few films where I feel that *every* member of the sound crew and *every* member of this facility did just an astounding job. And I think I've been on some fairly difficult jobs, but really nothing like this one." Here is that crew:

Re-recording Mixers: Gary Rydstrom, Tom Johnson, Gary Summers, Christopher Boyes, Lora Hirschberg

Supervising Sound Editor: Tom Bellfort

Sound Designer: Christopher Boyes

Assistant Sound Designer: Shannon Mills

Sound Effects Editors: Ethan Van Der Ryn, Scott Guitteau, Christopher Scarabosio

Supervising ADR Editor: Hugh Waddell

ADR Editors: Suzanne Fox, Harriet Fidlow Winn, Richard G. Corwin, Cindy Marty, Lee Lamont

Dialog Editors: Gwendolyn Yates Whittle, Claire Sanfilippo, J.H. Arrufat, Richard Quinn

Supervising Foley Editor: Thomas Small

Foley Editors: Scott Curtis, Tammy Pearing, Dave Horton Jr.

Supervising Assistant Sound Editor: Scott Koué

Supervising Assistant ADR Editor: Jonathan Null

Assistant Sound Editors: Beau Borders, Jessica Bellfort, Mary Works, Michael Axinn

Paramount Foley Mixer: Randy K. Singer

Foley Artists: Sarah Monat, Robin Harlin

ADR Mixers: Dean Drabin, Brian Ruberg, Tony Anscombe

Composer: James Horner

Scoring Engineer: Shawn Murphy

Supervising Music Editor: Jim Henrikson

Music Editor: Joe E. Rand

Recordists: Cary Stratton, Ann Hadsell, Joan Chamberlain, Scott Jones, Darren McQuade

Re-recordists: Ronald C. Roumas, Scott Levy, Al Nelson, Mark Pendergraf

Machine Room Operators: David Turner, Steve Romako, Christopher Barron

Mix Technicians: Gary A. Rizzo, Tony Sereno, Sean England, Kent Sparling, Jurgen Scharpf

Director James Cameron talks with Leonardo DiCaprio on the set.

Then the engine came to a two-beat "equipause," as Cameron called it, before the reversing lever is thrown and the ramp-up begins, setting up a thunderous, warbling, torquing sound in the hull of the ship. In between are cuts back to the bridge, where things remain calm, shots of the quartet playing, underwater shots of the propeller churning, dampers being closed to cut down the fire and, always, the bow cruising toward the iceberg.

"I can't honestly say what raw elements went into the ship hitting the iceberg," Boyes admits. "Basically, I got out every powerful steel impact sound I had and came up with probably a combination of ten different sounds, explosive-type deep, echo-y impacts. Obviously, I wanted a deep cracking sound, too. I had recorded a bunch of footsteps on ice up in Yellowstone, and from that I made a very sharp, articulate ice-crack sound, which I combined with the metal impact to become the iceberg hit.

"But that's only the beginning of the iceberg hit, because it continues to bounce along the hull from all different perspectives," he continues. "Jim said, 'You know, it's been described by passengers as the sound of somebody running down the side of the hull with a sledgehammer and hitting it.' So we had this string of very articulate, metallic, echo-y impacts." Meanwhile, up in the bridge, the hit barely registers, the only real clue being the slight rattling of the ship's wooden wheel.

Then a 1,500-ton chunk of ice shears off the iceberg and lands on the deck; the camera cuts to the huge rip in the hull and a tremendous amount of water rushing in; watertight doors begin to seal, trapping boiler-room crew members inside; and there's a huge rush of steam, subtly played—the last gasp of the engines. Then Cameron cuts to an interior, first-class.

"We've just been through an amazing amount of noise—articulate, but nonetheless powerful," Boyes says. "We go to first-class and a woman comes out of her door and says to the steward, ' Excuse me, why have the engines stopped?' I felt a shudder. In that hallway, we have literally nothing but her dialog and the cloth movement of her dress and her footsteps. And those three elements alone make you realize why it's so incredibly unsettling. Suddenly, with the absence of the rumble and in the absence of any air at all, you realize something's deathly wrong."

The iceberg hit occurs in reel 11, and the ship splits in two and sinks in reel 17. That meant a slow build back to chaos and climax, with appropriate room to breathe. Pacing became very important. "From the moment you hit the iceberg to the time it sinks is a long period of film time, at least an hour and a half," Rydstrom says. "So you have every different type of effect in the water category—everything from drips to the sound of water building up behind a wall, water seeping under a door crack, then building up to three inches in the room, then several feet, then climbing to the ceiling, then the big explosions and crash through the glass dome. It was very important for that long hour-and-a-half stretch that everything—creaks, water—have a real sense of progression.

"My first law in terms of sound is to have variation," he continues. "A steady blast of sound tends to lose interest. So my instinct is to mix so that the water has splashes and explosions—the water I'm talking about here is the type of water that floods through a hallway and comes rushing at the two main characters and just sweeps them off their feet. But every once in a while—and this is Cameron's idea, really—you just go for the firehose effect. We just hit every speaker with a roar of water with no modulation, and the lack of modulation in those few scenes gives you the sense that this is more water than you can believe coming at these people."

Many of the more intricate water effects, and all of the ones that involved people moving, were done by Foley walkers Robin Harlin and Sarah Monat on the Paramount stage in Hollywood. That particular team had just come off *The Flood*, had use of a heated, 30-foot-diameter Doughboy tank, and had developed specific water miking techniques. Effects sources came from everywhere, including geysers at Yellowstone, a "geothermal mud and water bubbling cavern" that Boyes recorded in a blizzard-wracked Yosemite, a sea cave, water treatment plants and an aquarium that dumped 1,000 gallons in one fell swoop.

But it was the creaks and groans that most dramatically inspire terror, the sense of impending doom, from the first distant creak when Kate Winslet goes below deck to find Leonardo DiCaprio, to the final rip in two.

PHOTO: STEVE JENNINGS

*Mark Pendergraf at the Sondor
dubbers*

"The groans have to constantly change in character, and they have to be moaning, squeaking, straining, twisting, breaking— the whole gamut," Boyes says. "I tried to stay away from the classic sound design technique of mixing a metal impact with a lion roar or some animal vocal. That sort of gives you that classic high-tech dramatic sound that we've come to hear from action films of the '90s. I had this notion that it's 1912, and I wanted it to sound like you're living in a giant steel chamber that's coming apart. This is the height of the Mechanical Age.

"Actually, the most powerful elements for the groans came from my assistant sound designer, Shannon Mills, who went down to a pier at the San Francisco Maritime Museum, where this ship was tied to the dock with large steel chains and ropes," he adds. "The dock has this sort of steel pinion and ramps, and he came up with these recordings of the most powerful straining, moaning, twisting steel sounds. He thought they were okay, but not great, because of background crowd noise. But once I started to play with them—applying all sorts of pitch bends and certain amounts of reverb and EQ—I found that by going way down in the sections where there were voices, the voices themselves added this ghostly quality. That combined with straining steel became the basis for the metallic groans and the ship sinking."

The scene of the ship sinking, Rydstrom says, is as big as anything he's ever done, and this from a guy who won Oscars for *T2* and *Jurassic Park*. But for Cameron, and for the sound crew, this is a dramatic film, not a disaster movie. So the rush of the people, and the chaos of the last few hours onboard, form the heart and soul within the horror and cacophony.

"The loop group was a very important component in this film," says supervising sound editor Bellfort," because from the time the ship hits the iceberg, the people occupy the main dramatic element of the film. And you can't have people screaming for nine reels, so you create these ebbs and flows, these spikes, and decide when to use them. Compounding the problem were the problems of languages. The Titanic was a very international ship, insofar that first-class was primarily made up of British and American passengers. The crew itself had to be made up of various British classes—the waiters, for instance, were not as 'lower class' as the stokers. And you had the international makeup of steerage, so you had Russian voices, Lithuanian,

Jonathan Greber in dialog transfer

Arab, Polish, Swedish, Irish—the range was phenomenal. The loop group was truly one of the threads that linked the last nine reels, from the time of the impact to the scenes in which there are fewer and fewer survivors screaming in the ocean at the end, until you reach silence."

The silence was actually pegged in notes as "the presence of water." Cameron wanted the feeling of being surrounded, without really having an effect, which proved challenging. It was a sound Boyes didn't come up with until the final mix, and he has his 8-year-old son to thank.

While mixing the trailer for the film, Boyes received a call from his son saying he was going to Hog Island for one of the last nights they would allow camping in Tomales Bay, an hour and a half north of San Francisco. Having worked a grueling six months, he decided to skip out and spend time with his boy, so he got a ride in a motorboat and arrived at the island around 9:30 p.m. "I woke up about 2:30 in the morning," Boyes recalls, "and I just crept out of my tent and set up my rig. It had become calm and we were encapsulated by water. It was tough because it was one of those recordings that was just on the edge of technically what a preamp can deliver without applying noise to your recording. I got this sense of feeling surrounded by a mass of water without really feeling surf. No lapping. More of a presence.

"The other sound came from the Foley crew down at Paramount," he continues. "I had requested that they record the sound of frozen hair, because toward the end of the film, Rose is left on a raft in the middle of the Atlantic and you can see the icicles in her hair. So I asked them to try freezing celery or green onions or something of that nature and give me a crunchy effect every time she moves. Between the frozen hair and the presence of water, I think we leave the audience with an absolutely chilling emotional moment. And it worked out magically."

So much more could be written about the tracks for this epic, which is not so much a disaster movie as it is a love story, on a scale with *Doctor Zhivago* and *Gone With the Wind*. The dialog edit alone could fill an article, with its 127 speaking roles, more than 4,000 principal ADR lines and the fact that it sits in a frequency spectrum that competes with water and wind. Or the Foley, perhaps the largest assignment of its kind on film, with its frantic action and its quieter moments, such as the scene in which DiCaprio sketches the nude Kate Winslet, and she removes a barrette as he sharpens his charcoal then sketches on paper—a favorite of Boyes.' Or the dramatic score (composed by James Horner, recorded by Shawn Murphy, with synthesizer sweetening delivered LCR), which at times moves from sweeping, panoramic love themes to driving, action-packed, pulsing rhythms.

As surprising as it may sound, both Rydstrom and Boyes spoke of the sound design for *Titanic* as an exercise in restraint, in pulling back and building to the proper big moments. It's not always about big sounds or a massive number of tracks, they say. ("I don't know what I would do with 120 inputs for effects," Rydstrom says.) It's about choosing the right sounds and articulating them. They are aware that films are getting bashed for being too loud. In a film as long and heavily dramatic as *Titanic*, they say, there has to be time to breathe. And in a sense, the most memorable sounds of all may be two key moments of silence: when the engines shut down, and when a final survivor slips into the icy ocean.

CHAPTER 15

Bringing Down the House

Sound for Brian De Palma's "Snake Eyes"

Do not arrive late to *Snake Eyes*, Paramount Pictures' late-summer thriller directed by Brian De Palma. Reel 1AB, set around a championship boxing match at the fictional Millennium Casino in Atlantic City—with an oncoming hurricane as a backdrop—is about as energetic and frenzied as movie openers get. There are no car chases, no comets hurtling from the heavens, no monsters from the deep. Just solid, well-paced editing, an amped-up Nicholas Cage and the excitement brought on by 14,000 fight fans anticipating the main event.

The film actually opens outdoors, with a glimpse of the Millennium sphere (a 20-foot-diameter ball atop the casino) and a television reporter announcing the fight and warning of the approaching storm. It then quickly moves inside the casino, where the camera follows Rick (Cage), a local cop-on-the-take, through the labyrinthine passageways of the in-house arena. It's a complex scene, with Cage wandering through the arena, moving through hallways, popping up in the dressing room, descending an escalator and finally circling the ring en route to his front-row seat. All the while he's delivering rapid-fire dialog on pay-per-view camera, in negotiations with bookies and even setting up a post-fight celebration with his girlfriend on a cellular phone. And for the first 11 minutes, until the gunshots, there is no music, so dialog and effects carry the film. The environments change continually, the rush of the crowd adds a full, all-consuming background, yet you hear every word: It's a tribute to the entire audio crew, from production sound mixers James J. Sabat, Patrick Rousseau and Keith A. Wester, to dialog editors Laura Civiello (supervising dialog editor), Dan Korintus and Marlena Grzaslewicz and re-recording mixer Lee Dichter, whom many label the "dean of dialog mixing." All editorial and mixing was done at Sound One in New York City.

This article appeared originally in the September 1998 issue of Mix.

The opener is essentially an intentional exercise in "controlled confusion," say co-supervising sound editors Maurice Schell and Richard Cirincione. The plot revolves around an assassination attempt at the fight, which throws the arena into chaos. Throughout the next hour-and-a-half, Cage tracks the conspirators through the casino-hotel, and through a series of flashbacks/replays, complete with alternate visual and aural cues, the layers of the conspiracy are peeled back. It was, Schell and Cirincione say, an exciting approach for the sound team.

"We knew we had to start off very full," Cirincione says, "where the audience doesn't really know particularly when the fight begins—you hear the crowd and you hear the commentators through the handheld radio, but we had so much going on that you don't know what to listen to. In subsequent flashbacks, little by little is revealed and the tracks unfold. We had so much material from production that we never had to play the exact same tracks. For a particular crowd reaction, we would play a different take because everybody remembered the moment differently. That applied to both picture and sound, where, for example, Tyler, the fighter, might remember four shots, when in the opening sequence we had seven or eight."

Because De Palma wanted the energy of the arena at the same time he wanted to protect the dialog, the scenes were shot with a silent crowd and Cage, Gary Sinise and the other actors on lavaliers, with the occasional buried mic. Consequently, Dichter received very clean dialog, which had been recorded to DAT—everything stereo—then loaded into Sonic Solutions workstations for editing, then dropped onto the Akai digital dubbers for playback at the mix. (It should be noted that all dailies were loaded, not just the printed takes, and eight discrete guide tracks, rather than the usual four, came from editor Bill Pankow at the Lightworks. Loading and track management became a time-consuming issue.) Alternate readings were always available; sometimes, individual syllables were slipped in right on the stage, transferred from the Sonic to the left of the Neve onto the Akai DD8s.

Some of the crowd roars were also delivered on DAT, later augmented by individual spikes from group ADR. (Schell and Cirincione went so far as to employ a lip reader to get exact readings.) Crowds, like rain, can be troubling at a mix for a number of reasons, chief among them the frequencies they eat up and the danger of monotony. Because production provided a number of crowd recordings, Schell and Cirincione were able to provide Dichter with enough variety and perspective shifts to keep the roars interesting, assembling different crowds for the challenger's rooting section vs. the champ's and the front-row vs. the cheap seats, often pulling from 20 years' worth of their own libraries, as well. Then Dichter premixed down to as many as six crowd groups. His challenge at the final was getting dialog to poke through.

"When you're putting dialog over a loud background, such as a crowd, it needs a different type of equalization and compression," Dichter explains, "because it would feel oversqueezed and overequalized without the background. A lot of that I learned in mixing TV commercials, which I did for the first ten years of my career. Many times after we would mix a commercial, we would play it back and one word wouldn't be heard, so the producer would say, 'Lower the music.' And I'd say, 'Why lower the music for one word when I can raise the one word, or the one syllable? Or equalize the one syllable?' I brought that technique into film mixing. For me, if you can't hear every syllable in a film, then we've done something wrong. Go back and get a replacement, or equalize different syllables in different words differently. I don't go with one setting for a dialog shot and ride the level or compression. I'm constantly riding equalization as we're rolling.

"And I'm talking about a tremendous amount of rolling equalization—bringing lines and words and syllables into focus with tremendous EQ shifts," he continues. "You notice in music that people will contemplate, 'Oh, should we add 3 dB at 2,300 cycles, or should we add 1 dB at 5,000 cycles?' I'm taking those equalizers and ripping 'em. I'm going 15 dB at one little word, then back off again—really swinging it, drastic moves to dig out that one word. I'll punch into a line of dialog with a tremendous EQ boost, then get back to normal two or three frames later. I use the technology to get that dialog to really sing and sit on top.

Co-supervising sound editors Maurice Schell (top) and Richard Cirincione joined Lee Dichter (front) at the Neve during the final mix.

"Also, you have to remember that sometimes the longer reverbs will get soaked up. If you took away the backgrounds, two or two-and-a-half seconds would be too long, but with the BGs, you're losing half a second to three-quarters. [In the opening scene] I'm constantly riding reverb as he walks along. And it's definitely in stereo, to give you the space and feeling."

Then the crowd is seated and the fight begins. Punches, roars, paranoid activity in the front row—Kevin Dunne (Gary Sinise), who is guarding the Secretary of Defense, leaves his post to investigate—screaming, whispers, then bullet impacts. More gunshots are fired, then people duck, chairs scrape, people scream, flashes are seen in the crowd—effects have taken over.

"The intention with the gunshots was that it was supposed to be somewhat confused, so we stretched some of them in the first reel," Cirincione says. "The audience isn't quite sure what it's hearing—is it thunder? And the first shots were with silencers, so we're just hearing impacts. There's so much going on in Reel 1AB that we don't notice the assassin getting shot in the back of the room, but we hear it."

Then the arena empties as the crowd streams for the doors. Cage seals off the casino, as all 14,000 fans are potential suspects or witnesses, and the search for the killer begins.

"After the fight, we tried to keep a quiet, reverberant atmosphere in the arena, where they're taking away the bodies and picking up the chairs," Schell explains. It's quiet, with light movement, and that's where we begin to introduce the outside world, with thunder, police sirens and ambulances. That's the first chance the audience gets to catch its breath."

EFFECTS: HEAR THAT STORM A' COMIN'

Schell and Cirincione got a first look at *Snake Eyes* in late December 1997 and had to be ready for the first temp mix by mid-January. Their first impression was that the film was deceptively big, with a large amount of crucial effects, including gunshots (where the number of shots become a plot point), boxing punches (ditto) and the impending Hurricane Jezebel (essentially a character).

Sound for Picture

"From the very beginning, we're told there is a storm, and it is set up as a driving force," Schell says. "The next thing we're introduced to is the ring, and those two components become the driving force for the whole film. But we had to use them carefully to accommodate the energy. For instance, Brian [De Palma] told us at the beginning that he didn't want any storm in the pay-per-view booth or the casino, but everywhere else he said 'be my guest.'

"We were worried about the storm in that we didn't want it to be repetitious," Schell continues. "We were constantly trying to make it change as we went along so it never stays steady—adding a new element, playing with rain on different surfaces. We had layers and layers of maybe 20 different types of rain—from rain on umbrella, rain on a raincoat, rain on boardwalk, rain on cement, blizzard sounds, blizzard rains."

Sometimes rains had to be removed, sometimes lowered. In a key scene, where Cage is beaten mercilessly by the conspirators in the boiler-room bowels of the casino, a loading door is open, and the storm is raging outside, but it's played for emotion. "Rain on metal would have interfered with the dialog at the mix," Cirincione explains. "And the drama is of the guy getting beat up. Gradually, after he's thrown on the boxes and it quiets down, we introduce the rain-on-metal more. Before that, it's mostly basement and thunder, so we try to be careful. It's a big, dramatic moment."

The storm also figures prominently in the climax. As the action builds toward a showdown, as the chief conspirator is tracking Cage and Carla Gugino, both the storm and the Millennium sphere begin their assault, with the latter rolling along the boardwalk and the former manifesting itself in a huge tidal wave, headed for the shore. Both have been properly introduced as threats, and by the end, they are running completely in parallel.

"The biggest challenge in getting the ball to work was the many, many, many tracks," Cirincione says. "Because of the intensity of the ocean laid on top of it, it took a bit of doing to get the proper balance so you can hear both menaces at the same time."

Machine room operator Harry Higgins helps keep the Akai DD8s and DR16s running at Sound One.

"They're both in the same sound area—too much bottom end," interjects Schell, "so we tried to make one distinct from the other. One thing was to try to make the ocean feel wet, with a wash and waves, some peaks to poke through. And the ball of course was many things put together, trying to make it organic. One of the elements was a bowling ball in a gutter. Another was a tank. Then we used wheels going over wood for that echo-y feel. And earthquakes and avalanches. But usually, to be honest, we don't in most cases reveal what we use because people tend to focus on the element and they hear it differently."

The climax is huge on effects, to be sure, and without judicious mixing, it could easily have fallen into a dull, albeit loud, wash of sound. "I tried to protect certain frequencies so that the ball had room to cut through," Dichter says. "The wind and water combination can just fill up the soundtrack, the total spectrum of the sound envelope. So for the ball, I found a frequency somewhere between 150 and 200 cycles that I overemphasized to give it a voice, to get it to cut through the water. I also compressed it tremendously to give it power. Then, the closer we come to it, we used the subwoofer for the ball only, so the low, low rumble—that 30 or 40 cycles down below—was another element used to give the ball voice and presence. I kept the rain and water completely out of the subwoofer."

MARRYING THE MUSIC

Because of previous commitments, Dichter was not onboard for the various temp mixes. De Palma apparently wanted a full-blown stereo mix by the fourth go-around in order to give Ryuichi Sakamoto (*The Last Emperor*) something to write the score against. Sakamoto, who has a studio in New York, has been actively producing for interactive media, even producing a live Internet concert where people could send MIDI information in real time and play along with his symphonic work. For *Snake Eyes*, there are roughly 56 minutes of music and 34 cues, four of which are source cues. Of the remaining 30, three or four are completely electronic, according to music editor Nick Meyers, though viewers will be hard-pressed to distinguish which ones they are.

Sound for Picture

"This is not your normal film score," Meyers says. "It's very dramatic, and Sakamoto has a style that's very much his own. He's loyal to his own inner ear. It has a very contemporary feel, and it's modern music, but I hesitate to say that, because when people think of modern music, they think of atonal composers who are more for a concert audience. This music is not that. It's accessible, yet it uses tonalities that are not immediately recognizable as film music tonalities.

"Tension in any film is set up by the visuals," Meyers continues. "One of the wonderful scenes in this movie is the sequence where the two characters are chasing the female lead through elevators and hallways, and it's about a six-minute cue, the longest in the film. Most movies don't have chase sequences lasting quite that long, and it's hard to sustain a 'hunt' cue for that long. The tension that you feel is all about this inevitable meeting that never takes place, which, of course, is reserved for the end of the film. It's a constant tease that keeps you on the edge of your seat."

The orchestral cues were all recorded to 48-track digital by engineer Goh Hotoda at The Hit Factory in New York. Fernando Aponte mixed the tracks on the Capricorn at Right Track to 3-track left-center-right, with splits for certain instruments and overdubs on a separate channel. The mix was digitally transferred to DA-88, then loaded into Meyers' 16-channel Sonic system for editing, with electronic instruments kept separate, basically untreated.

The music, with its film noir sensibility and thoroughly modern approach, works beautifully in the film. And it never seems to compete with effects. Apparently, De Palma was so enamored of the temp mix on the final reels that he was willing to go with just effects if it worked out that way. But then Sakamoto's score was created to interleave and was woven in masterfully ("weave" was a word that cropped up a lot at the final, Meyers says), particularly in the tracking scene leading up to the final confrontation, where screeching metal effects punctuate the rhythmic, pulsating score. It's a scene that could be used in film schools to illustrate the blending of music and effects.

Snake Eyes opened nationally on August 7. If you can, see it in a properly aligned theater, because it's a big film, with big moments, and it never gets too loud. And most importantly, you hear every word.

CHAPTER 16

The Delicacy of War

Creating the Soundtrack For Terrence Malick's "The Thin Red Line"

Robb Wilson, J. Paul Huntsman and Hugh Waddell

Something special occurred in Hollywood during the last half of 1998, something only a handful of people will truly appreciate because most of it was orchestrated largely behind closed doors at Warner Bros. and Fox. Terrence Malick, the reclusive director of *Badlands* and *Days of Heaven*, had returned to filmmaking after a 20-year absence. It was as if the Prodigal Son had come home in the '90s, and the town was buzzing about his new project: *The Thin Red Line*, a WWII drama based on the raw and gripping James Jones novel about C-for-Charlie Company and the siege of Guadalcanal.

This article appeared originally in the May 1991 issue of Mix.

Once word began trickling out, it became clear that Malick had made a different kind of war movie, one that is highly impressionistic and personal. As composer Hans Zimmer said, "I said to Terry at the beginning that the one thing I'm not interested in doing is yet another war movie where you go, 'War is horrible, war is terrible.' That's been said millions of times, and I have a feeling Steven [Speilberg] just said it better than anybody else [in *Saving Private Ryan*], so let's not go there. Terry wanted poetry, not prose."

The challenge from the start, it seems, was to make a "delicate" war movie—what Malick would often describe, whether in picture or sound, as "oceanic," "flowing," constantly moving. That proved quite a challenge for the sound crew, considering reels 5 to 13 (it's a 17-reel film, nearly three hours) are essentially one long battle, complete with light weapon fire, ricos, mortars and howitzers. The key, according to supervising sound editor Paul Huntsman, was to look at the film itself, the way it was shot and edited, "which asked nothing more than to simply be expressed in some beautiful, soft way that forced you to think in simplistic scenarios. And that funnels right into Terry's sense of a minimalistic approach to sound—only the things that you really need to hear, and just make damn sure they're the appropriate sound."

ON LOCATION: PRODUCTION MEETS POST

"Minimalist" sound does not mean few sounds, or the absence of sound. It's more about the "appropriate" effect, or the single, long, dynamic note, or the right breathing on the battlefield. In fact, the crew at Warner Bros. Post-Production Services, the core of which has worked on Huntsman's most recent five pictures, had mountains of material. Ships, landing craft, additional weapons and winds were recorded in and around L.A. by John Fasal and Jayme S. Parker. But the bulk of the material, about 250 hours worth of elements on DAT, was sent from location in Australia in what Huntsman calls an "absolutely novel" collaboration between production and post.

Production sound mixer Paul "Salty" Brincat, an animated 25-year veteran from New South Wales, and second unit mixer Greg Bergmann proved to be the unsung heroes of the film. At every spare moment, they recorded backgrounds, vehicles, birds, soldiers walking through grass, you name it, even going so far as to spend two additional weeks on the Solomon Islands recording birds (Malick is an ornithologist and was particular about getting the birds right), ambiences and specific effects. Indigenous music was recorded in coordination with Claude Letessier, a colleague of Zimmer's at Media Ventures. When production wrapped, Salty spent additional days recording light weapons and howitzers. All this was in addition to turning over "excellent, excellent dialog work, the best I've heard in a long time," says ADR supervisor Hugh Waddell.

And it couldn't have been easy. More than a million feet of film were shot, according to reports, and principal photography took place over about six months in Australia, including 12 weeks on a hill for the battle sequences—actors on the run, diving down, leaping up, screaming, whispering, in rain, in wind. "I went in thinking this would be a pretty standard feature," Salty recalls. "But as we started to get into the shoot a couple of weeks, I thought, 'Boy, I gotta change my ways here.' I started thinking that I had to get back to where I was when I was put into the field to do docos [documentaries] and put in situations to capture sound as simply as I could and be sure to get what I could get. Obviously, I needed to get feature sound for them but approach it in a documentary way. [Terry] kept the pace moving. He kept it zooming and he kept rolling. My best choice, I gotta say, was when I decided to have two boom operators."

Rod Conder and Gary Dixon ran the hill with the actors day in and day out, carrying Sennheiser 816s and 416s on the end of 18-foot fishpoles. It was tiring work, and Salty sang their praises. "These guys really did work it," he says. "They were using Steadicams and running through battles. That's why we had to use booms. You can't put body mics with full webbing gear and thick terrain. You might get slightly tighter, but at the same time I would have lost more by getting rustle, getting thumping, possibly getting a mic ripped if one of the actors dives down because of an explosion effect, then gets up and charges, then dives down to do their dialog. It made sense for us to radio-mike the booms themselves and just run free. And I mean run free— they could run up to 200, 400 yards away in a sequence. And they'd be running up hills. It was pretty demanding on the guys, and they did fantastic.

"It's funny," he continues. "I hadn't used the 816 for quite awhile, but I tell you what, she's back in the truck and she's staying with me because she worked it out. I guess it's getting back to docos, 'cause in the old days you used an 816 when you didn't know your distances. And you were always ready."

Paul "Salty" Brincat, on location in Queensland, was constantly asked about "coldies" in his "esky," but inside his cooler were an Audio Development mixer, Fostex PD-2 DAT machine, preamps and a built-in fan.

Because of the terrain, Salty didn't have the luxury of a cart, and he scaled back his rig considerably. About three years ago, because he works extensively in the tropics and around sand, he converted an esky (what we in the States would call a cooler) into a portable sound-protection unit. The preamps are housed in a custom-fitted lid, a fan was built into the side, and inside he keeps an Audio Development 206 4-channel mixer, a Fostex PD-2 DAT machine (primary recorder), a backup Sony TCD-8 DAT Walkman, a Comtek to feed the timecode slates, and a feed for the director and whoever else wanted to hear program. That esky, plus a mic bag, plenty of HHB DAT stock and batteries, and a "brelly" to shield the sun and rain.

When Salty and Bergmann went out to record effects, atmospheres and weapons, they usually took more equipment, including a 6-channel Pico mixer, AKG C552 stereo mics (atmospheres, in an X-Y pattern), AKG 568 and 300SBs Blue Line condensers (interior tents), and Nagra 4.2 and stereo recorders (gunshots and explosions). Bergmann even borrowed a Sony PCM-800 8-track from the picture-editing department for recording vehicles and aircraft. Two weeks were spent in the Solomon Islands, recording the landing scene on Guadalcanal, followed by a four-hour trek into the jungle to record atmospheres and choirs, the most stunning of which was a 60-voice Melanesian ensemble, recorded in a church that the art department built. Various themes, as well as original material, were brought back by Letessier and have wended their way into portions of Zimmer's score.

The need to record authentic, period weapons, both small arms and heavy artillery, was obvious. Producer Grant Hill called Salty and arranged for him to spend a day (which, because of wind, turned into two days) with the Australian army on a firing range outside of Sydney. After faxing mic plots back and forth to Huntsman, mics were set up all over the 400-yard-long field, especially near the impact point, where they were firing into sand and grass walls.

A couple of weeks later, Salty took Rod Conder with him to record the howitzers, the 105mm cannons, in Victoria. He was expecting one gun and got 12. The regiment set him up in a camouflaged truck in the middle of the range and fired over him. Then they offered him the unique opportunity to record the troops rolling the cannon up a hill (part of their training) to fire into a dirt mound a kilometer away. "You see the round leave the gun," Salty explains. "You see it hit, you see the white flash, you see the dirt rise up, and about 15 seconds later—an unbelievable amount of delay—you hear this huge crack that comes back at you. Absolutely fantastic.

"We chased and got live rounds," he continues. "The crack in the air was just fantastic. I've never been able to get that involved in post. I gotta say, that excited me to run around and be able record all the gear. And the director gave me the time and direction to do it. It's one thing for a director to say, 'This is what I want.' It's another thing for a director to say, 'Hey, there's the time, go get it.'"

"I have never seen this kind of work done on a film," Huntsman says of Salty and Bergmann. "And I've never seen such dedication and concern about it. Good record keeping, great recording work and an enthusiasm that absolutely shows in their work. A lot of what this movie is about in terms of how it sounds has to do with the care and deliberate nature of the way these guys went about their job."

J. Paul Huntsman fed the final mix from his Fairlight station on the Zanuck stage.

BACK IN HOLLYWOOD

Huntsman and his crew were finishing up *Deep Impact* in late spring, but every couple of weeks they received anywhere from six to 20 DATs from Australia. First to come were backgrounds, then vehicles and aircraft, then weapons. At the same time, Huntsman, an avid reader, was poring over WWII literature and diaries. One of the most valuable, *Touched With Fire*, was recommended by Malick and included first-hand reminiscences of the siege on Guadalcanal.

Then in the last week of June, in the midst of assembling libraries, the film was turned over and the sound team was treated to a rare opportunity to view the rough 4.5-hour cut, an experience Huntsman termed "mesmerizing, a treat beyond any, and a wonderful place to start out as a crew." Right before they began editing, the crew lobbied to divide the work according to effect—one for guns, one for vehicles, one for BGs, etc. Huntsman, who typically turns over whole reels to editors, agreed.

"Two things swayed me," he says. "I knew Jayme Parker would be the perfect individual to cut backgrounds on this movie. He is a quiet, hardworking, well-read, extremely focused guy. The other thing was that we had recorded this gigantic gun library—the entire, legitimate arsenal of what the American and Japanese armies carried into Guadalcanal—from three different shoots, and I needed somebody to construct that library of material. And Chris Aud became that guy." John Bonds took on heavy weaponry, meaning anything that exploded, and Andy Sommers handled vehicles, aircraft and miscellaneous elements.

While Huntsman spent the last three-and-a-half months of the process on the dub stage, his co-sound supervisor Robb Wilson managed the crew back at Warner Bros. "with aplomb and a genuine sense of inspiration." Dialog and effects were edited entirely on Fairlight MFX3 Plus systems; Foley and ADR were recorded directly to Fairlight drives. Foley was supervised by Jeff Rosen and edited by David Horton Jr. Dialog was cut by John Reynolds, Patrick Foley and Virginia Cook McGowan.

"My first thoughts were, 'How do you make a battle movie soundtrack work that is long and has sustained portions of gunfire?'" says Huntsman. "How can you keep an audience sitting in their seats and still play guns, mortars and ricos and not drive them out of the theater? How do I control the dynamic so that it doesn't become an offensive wall of material after a while? Easy-on-the-ear gunshots was the concept I came up with originally. I knew I wanted something that had power in the weaponry but not the kind of edge that would wear on your ear. There's a couple of moments in the movie where you're close to a soldier firing an M1 rifle and you can practically feel the kick of the gun, but it's not hard to listen to. It doesn't hurt your ears. It just feels solid.

"Then Terry's first conversations with me were about dynamic range and perspective," Huntsman continues. "We never really talked about the sound of the movie as much as the structure of the sound of the movie. There was always the necessity of having something in the foreground so that whatever played in the background had even more weight and perspective. It's the equivalent, I guess, of the deep-focus shot. There are always these layers of imagery, and I think that's what Terry wants to hear. He wants to hear the whole scene. He believes, and I agree with him, that having the appropriate material in the fore- ground acts as a lens that allows you to see more deeply into the background. Group ADR and the vocal nature of the battlefield would be a good example."

ADR Supervisor Hugh Waddell also worked on *Titanic*, so he was not intimidated by the amount of material needed, most of which was alternate readings and offscreen changes. But he did find the edit a bit tricky in that Malick demanded such a natu- ralistic feel to the dialog. "You can't just present him with wall-to-wall loops and hope to get away with it," Waddell says.

"You have to literally use two or three words from production, then maybe three words from loops, then back to production. You really have to piece it together. It's very difficult to tell what's looped in this film because we have mixed it up so much."

Most of the ADR was recorded at Warner Hollywood with mixer Tom O'Connell, and a military adviser and Japanese interpreter were present at all times to ensure period authenticity. The bulk of the work involved generalized, wild recordings of group ADR by an all-male cast from L.A. Mad Dogs. Specifics were avoided until the "dying gasps" of the premix, according to Waddell, so that they didn't overshoot.

"We were going for a documentary feel," Waddell says, echoing the production process. "We came up with a way for the loop group actors to say lines in a way we called 'nondescript dialog.' They said lines, but they didn't say the actual words. If you put it behind people speaking, you just think it's people talking offscreen, but your ear isn't drawn to it. It would just lie there as a bed, and you can play it relatively loudly and it just fits in with the scenes.

"So we put those nondescript lines in the background," he continues, but in the foreground, especially during heavy battle sequences, Terry's had us record a lot of very close-up, very personal, intimate kinds of sobbing and moaning and sighing. When you're looking at a field full of men dying, suddenly you'll hear a moan or just a sigh—very up close and very personal, and it sort of pulls the whole scene toward you."

Breathing, another element used to personalize scenes, was recorded for every character. And 80 to 100 hours of voice-over/narration were recorded; some of it was in place for the final but most of it was expected to be added during the last week of the mix.

Foreground/background was also dealt with in effects, perhaps most notably in scenes of soldiers crawling, diving or running through grasslands. Using the library of material from Australia, the crew might spread rather broad M-S recordings of 50 soldiers moving through grass, coupled with an X-Y version of the same track, somewhat offset, along with Foley and production. In the background, then, rests a deep, rich, hypnotic wind. The result, Huntsman says, is the "*crème brulée* of sound effects."

"[Once we started listening] we could all see a way to make this movie delicate," Huntsman says. "[In] one of my favorite shots in the movie, you see maybe 100 or more Americans hunched over and moving through very tall grass. You're looking up this hillside, and the lieutenant in the foreground stops and does a hand signal, and all these men drop down behind him. These guys literally disappear in the environment where they're probably going to die. And it's so allegorical to the thoughts of these men and what might lie in store for them. At the same time it's absolutely descriptive of the environment that these men find themselves in. If you don't get it when you see that shot, it's because you're thinking about popcorn or something. It's just a wonderful moment. There's not a lot of sound there, but what sound is there is really appropriate and you just get caught up in it. Then it's gone."

Still, for all the delicacy, for all the times the term "oceanic" was used to describe the tracks, it is a war movie with an all-male cast, and Malick often spoke to Huntsman in terms of "the fighter." A fighter moves quickly and jabs, often so that you don't know where the punch came from. But the jab, Huntsman cautions, is not effective if you do it all the time.

"There's a spot where a mortar shell comes in all by itself, over a long period of time, and it lands close to one guy," Huntsman explains. "We put a little treat in there toward the end of it so that it's almost as if you hear ringing in your ears. And it goes away before you can quite figure out whether it was ringing in your ears or a ringing on screen. It crosses a line and internalizes the experience on the screen if it's done effectively. If it's a little overdone, then it becomes just a very obvious sound effects ploy."

MUSIC AND TRUTH

The final weeks of the mix were not for the faint of heart. Picture changes occurred almost daily. Recordings done in the morning would be shuttled to the stage that afternoon to play against picture. Alternate lines were flown in. And despite spending roughly seven months on the film, composer Hans Zimmer was under, perhaps, the most pressure, which he handled with grace. Up until the end, he was writing new orchestral cues, recording taiko drums and sitting beside Malick in the editing room with picture editors Billy Weber, Leslie Jones and Sar Klein.

The Sound Crew

Huntsman prefers to work with a small, tightknit crew, regardless of the size of the film. At Warner Bros. Post-Production Services, that crew, most of which will be working on Renny Harlin's *Deep Blue Sea* as you read this, included:

Sound Design and Sound Supervision: J. Paul Huntsman
Co-Sound Supervisor: Robb Wilson
Sound Effects Editors: Christopher S. Aud, John V. Bonds Jr., Jayme S. Parker, Andrew M. Sommers, Mark Mangino, M.P.S.E.
Foley Supervisor: Jeffrey Rosen
Foley Editor: David Horton Jr.
Special Sound Effects Design: John Fasal
Dialog Editors: Patrick J. Foley, John F. Reynolds, Virginia Cook McGowan
ADR Supervisor: Hugh Waddell
ADR Editors: Lee Lemont, Karyn Foster
Conforming Editor: Hugo Weng
Assistant Editors: Jeff Cranford, David Werntz, Todd M. Harris

From Media Ventures:
Music By: Hans Zimmer
Scoring Engineer: Alan Meyerson
Music Editors: Adam Smalley,
Special Sound Design: Claude Letessier

From Fox:
Re-Recording Mixers: Anna Behlmer, Andy Nelson, Jim Bolt
Assistant Chief Engineer: Denis St. Amand
Recordists: Bob Renga, Craig "Pup" Heath

From Australia:
Production Sound Mixer: Paul "Salty" Brincat
Assistant Production Sound Mixer: Greg Bergmann
Boom Operators: Rod Conder, Gary Dixon

Adam Smalley, sitting, and Alan Meyerson surround Hans Zimmer.

"We never really had a spotting session," Zimmer explains. "The way it started, which seemed like a good idea at the time, was that I would write the music first and Terry would cut the picture to the music. We are doing that sometimes, and sometimes we are not. It's been intensely collaborative, and it's been wrought with frustration because you're striving for that level of excellence and simplicity and truth.

"The question of truth always hangs over my head," he continues. "After about the first month, I realized that I have never been a composer, and now I'm slowly learning to become a composer. I think I had about 25 very good themes that will never make it into this movie because they're just not appropriate. It's been a lot of that—writing things, putting them up against picture, and having the picture just reject the most beautiful piece of music. You try to find what's appropriate, and things have gotten pared down to become more and more simple. There's one piece now that has for the last few months been my cornerstone. It's just an 11-bar phrase that's stretched over eight minutes. If I played you the music, you would never know this is a war movie. All I'm doing is playing subtext and trying to find humanity, trying to find brotherhood, trying to find comradeship. That's what I'm writing about."

For the first time, Zimmer, a known gear hound, recorded strictly orchestra—no samplers or synths. The score was recorded on the SSL 9000 J at Fox and mixed on the Euphonix CS3000 back at Media Ventures by Zimmer's longtime engineer Alan Meyerson. The music is not fast, Zimmer says, yet it is very concentrated and poses challenges for the orchestra. "I don't know if people realize how difficult it is to play one long note beautifully, as opposed to lots of fast runs," he says. "The detail of going from different dynamics to different dynamics within one note is very difficult."

The film's music moves from the intimacy of the orchestra, to the rolling thunder of taiko drumming, to the explosion of the "cosmic beam," essentially a large wooden horizontal beam strung with piano wire and played with a metal bar. Francesco Lupica, a Long Beach performance artist, has been playing the instrument for more than 25 years.

"The first recordings we did of it were terrible," Zimmer admits. "Nobody knew how to tackle this thing. You can't just walk up to it and put your ear next to it because you wouldn't have any ears left. The first recordings wouldn't translate [to the mixing stage], especially the bottom end, because it's not just a matter of shoving it in the subwoofer and hoping it will live there. It has enormous range. Basically, you need a lot of Bruel & Kjaers because they're the only mics that can handle the volume. We were in a 26,000 square-foot space so that the bass could really develop. And Alan [Meyerson] was hanging mics from the rafters of a 40-foot ceiling. I think he had 14 mics on it, and we would just walk around and find where the sweet spots on the stage were. There's a certain corner of the building where the bottom end will stay pure."

THE FINAL, FINAL MIX

Nobody on the film was surprised by the fact that they never really had locked picture. They knew going in that Malick preferred working that way and developed schemes around it. For the sound crew it meant limiting the number of times they conformed the audio tracks to fit the picture changes. The fact that the sound editors were working on Fairlights, editing across 24 tracks and making use of the macros, sped up the process and freed them to think creatively.

"Andy Sommers is a really creative guy who understands the workstation like he built it," Huntsman says. "He and Jayme Parker figured out that if one of them sat down and conformed the stems from one version to another, or in any one project, and recorded all their moves, they could then export that macro to other machines and use it to do an autoconform, in essence.

Now what works for backgrounds doesn't necessarily work for gunshots, but you can quickly change the reel from that and then go back and fix any bad edit. You'd have to fix it anyway. But the machine 'resunk' the material. The most mundane, mechanical thing we do is resync material we've already made work once. It's nice to have that kind of flexibility with your tools; it frees up the creative side.

"I've always maintained that movies only have to be in sync a few times," Huntsman continues, "namely, whenever they are being screened for temp mixes, premixes and finals. And if you chase changes between those points, it's not about making the film sound good. We conformed once to get ready for the premix, then again for the rehearsal mix, and we're going through another huge conform from that rehearsal mix to the final mix. Three times on a film that's changing every day. As a result, I think my crew has been able to think more about what the movie should sound like as opposed to where any particular audio event occurs."

The film was mixed by Anna Behlmer (effects) and Andy Nelson (dialog and music) at the Daryl Zanuck Theatre on the Fox lot. The stage is centered around an SSL 5000M console with a Harrison SeriesTwelve sidecar, for a total of 224 inputs. Playback was from a variety of sources, including Fairlight DaDs, multitrack, DA-88 and Pro Tools. At any one time, up to 11 workstations were available on two stages, including Huntsman's MFX3 Plus system (plus five more Fairlights) and Pro Tools for music editor Adam Smalley and Lee Scott. The film was recorded to 6-track mag with Dolby SR.

Crucial to the process was re-recording mixer Jim Bolt, who labored largely alone upstairs on another Harrison console, incorporating fixes and updating the premixes in order to feed the main stage and keep the movie current. And, according to Huntsman, the film would never have gone so smoothly without the first-rate work of assistant chief engineer Denis St. Amand (along with recordists Bob Renga and Craig "Pup" Heath in the machine room), who kept all the systems running.

"Anna is dubbing this movie—with enormous amounts of changes going on—with no, what we affectionately refer to as 'binkies,' which are cheat sheets that say, 'This predub contains these things at these footages,'" Huntsman explains. "The movie is so straightforward in its execution that she can set up almost every reel exactly the same on her console. When somebody says, 'I want to lose that offscreen explosion,' it doesn't matter what reel you're in, it's the *same* fader you take it down with."

The making of the soundtrack on *The Thin Red Line* was at times enlightening, stimulating, frustrating, demanding, invigorating and enriching to those involved. Certainly, it was challenging, both to their skills and their concepts of what film sound can be.

"In terms of my involvement on this movie," Huntsman concludes, "somewhat even beyond my wonderful experience of working with a guy as interesting as Terry, I'm really pleased with the way my crew has just socked themselves into this film and responded with absolutely splendid work. I feel blessed and fortunate to work with these people, and they have done both the craft that they work in and this movie a tremendous credit in their professionalism and their dedication to executing the concept that we've come up with. We've stuck with it and stayed true. When I say I've been enriched, I suppose to a degree a good part of that is the sense of working with a group of people who are all dedicated to something that is a little outside themselves."

CHAPTER 17

Oh, Behave!

Shagadelic Sound for the Austin Powers Sequel

Standing L to R: Bill Smith, Matthew Waters and Joe Barnett; seated L to R: John Ross and Frederick Howard.

Comedy, to paraphrase Woody Allen, is timing and delivery—a pregnant pause that lends anticipation, an infectious giggle to lighten the double entendre or a change in inflection that is loaded with satire. These are the types of moments that make us laugh out loud in a darkened room full of strangers. And few actors working today excel at comic timing and delivery as much as Mike Myers. Think back to his goofy, delayed head flips as Wayne, or listen to Austin Powers' signature "Yeeaaahhh…" Vintage timing.

Granted, most of these moments derive from the performance, but the issues of timing are critical in the audio post-production process, as well, and working on a comedy can be every bit as challenging as working on a special effects blockbuster. *Austin Powers: The Spy Who Shagged Me*, released in June by New Line, has its big effects moments (most notably the final battle sequence), but it's the intricacies and feel of the track, along with the subtle timing issues, that add yet another comedic flavor to the film.

This article appeared originally in the August 1999 issue of Mix.

Supervising sound editor Fred Howard praised the Foley team, especially for the tent scene where Heather Graham is rummaging through Austin's survival bag. He then found himself using some Foley elements in design. "The line between Foley and effects merged on this film," he says. "When the Fat Bastard character enters, I needed elements for his footsteps. I wanted the sense of everything coming loose every time he takes a step. I will take some traditional Foley elements and cut in a more traditional sound effects style."

Much of the fine detail work—some of it more traditional editorial—took place during the final mix. The post schedule was relatively tight, with only six weeks between the wrap of principal photography in late December and the first temp mix, then less than three months till the print master. So it helped that the sound crew at Digital Sound & Picture in Los Angeles was largely intact from the first Austin Powers film, and that the working method at that facility allows for the ultimate in flexibility.

"The dub is where all our layers come together," says director Jay Roach. "The systematized approach at DS&P—the way editorial feeds the stage, the way the whole process works—is so fast and efficient. We were under a tight schedule, and John [Ross, co-owner and lead mixer] has it all in place."

All versions, including the Avid tracks, are hung in Pro Tools for playback through the final and can be unraveled, modified or completely replaced at any time. Twenty-one Pro Tools-based edit bays can upload to a central server or feed the three-position Euphonix on Stage 1 directly, and stems are updated as the mix progresses. In essence, sound is conformed as changes are made.

DS&P tries to construct full-blown 5.1 temp mixes of all the films it works on, and, with Austin II, it seemed especially important because of the pressure to deliver a sequel that topped the original and the desire to put the best foot forward for test audiences.

As the film editing team began roughing out a first edit, supervising sound editor/sound designer Frederick Howard was shipping them signature effects, backgrounds and such from the first film, along with newly designed material in as complete a form as was possible early on. At the same time, film editor Greg Hayden was cutting in bits and pieces of George S. Clinton's score from the original so everyone would have an idea of music placement.

"As we were completing scenes and assembling chunks of scenes, we would send them to Fred Howard, and he would send us back sound effects on DAT or Jaz drives," explains Jon Poll, who shares an "Edited By" credit with Debbie Neil-Fisher, editor of the original film. "He was constantly giving us effects, and then, of course, we would turn over reels. It gave us something of a template so that even by the time we got to the temp dub, we had worked some areas out in rough form. The back-and-forth worked very well, and the temps went smoothly. In fact, a lot of the stuff we're hearing in the final has been in from the beginning."

"We had given them several gigabytes of sounds on DA-88, all categorized and organized," recalls Howard. "We also gave them quite elaborate sound design material, where we literally built whole scenes. Some scenes were a bit complex, so we cut them and somehow managed to squeeze them onto eight tracks so they could pull them up on their Avids or pull out certain elements."

After each temp screening, the picture department received the music, effects and dialog stems, input them and cut a new version, with updated scenes and/or visual effects. When the picture was turned over again, the sound crew had the original Avid tracks plus the updated stems delivered again on DA-88 and loaded onto the DS&P server. (Note: On this film, the OMF utilities for Avid/Pro Tools were not used.) For the next temp mix, then, the Avid tracks are carried to the stage because that is the director's reference.

"It's good to be able to slide in the [Avid effects] if new material we're presenting doesn't quite hit it on the nose," explains Ross. "I like to put the Avid tracks into Pro Tools so I can see them. Often, the picture editors don't know where they put a particular sound effect, which may have been mixed with something else. I can see the waveform of the discrete eight tracks, and I can go in and grab a particular sound effect. I can see it without having to hunt through Track 1 or Track 2 or somebody forgetting to write it down."

SIMULTANEOUS SOUND DESIGN

Howard came onboard in late December and immediately began feeding the picture department. At the same time, he viewed a rough cut and began thinking about sound design—particularly the time-portal transitions, comedic nuances and various ambiences.

"I really had the same kind of thoughts and ideas in mind that I had on the first film, as far as having it be low-tech and fairly organic, sound-wise," Howard says. "We wanted to shy away from anything that didn't really fit in, and that's a fine aesthetic line, because obviously we have modern scenes, like with the NORAD control room. And there's modern beepage in there, but there's also a layer of classic short-wave tuning and that type of sound—something you might imagine in a '60s spy film at spy headquarters.

"I wanted to pay homage to the world that spawned Austin Powers, the '60s intrigue-espionage movies," he continues. "There's a look and feel and sound to those films. For example, when they're traveling through time, I felt that wouldn't be served by being real high-tech. So we gathered wind sounds and other elements to suggest the movement of air, a movement into the seventh dimension. Sort of like a vacuum. The laser was conceived correspondingly. A lot of real high-tech sounds could have worked there, but we pulled together a lot of elements and went for quintessential laser beams of the Hanna-Barbera-type. Then we add a lot of movement from the surrounds forward, and it gives a good sense of motion."

Supervising ADR editor Susan Shin in her editing bay, where she managed some 1,000 replacement and alternate lines. "I specifically wanted Mini-Me to come in and do more 'eeeee's,' which is his only line from production," she says. "I wanted him to sound a little more menacing. He's a totally sweet person, with a kid-like voice. For the laughter at the very end of the movie, we wanted him to sound a little more evil, more disturbing."

The visuals and sight gags are funny enough, so the sound crew made a conscious decision not to go cartoon-y, unless the film demanded it. One example is the fight scene between Austin and Mini-Me in Dr. Evil's lunar station, where the "ding" of Mini-Me hitting the pole was intentionally modeled after the classic "anvil on the head" we all recognize from childhood. And the punches lacked variety intentionally, paying equal homage to the Three Stooges and World Championship Wrestling. "There are some sounds you just hear and say, 'That's funny,'" Howard says.

"A good example for me of funny, but not cartoon-y, was the scene where they unveil the time machine," Howard says. "Dr. Evil goes running up to it, says, 'I'm going through time!' and bounces off it. It's not turned on. The visual is very funny when he hits it. I combined a few elements to get a metal flux kind of a '*bonk!*' It plays very funny. Then the body falls, and I made it kind of hard and pratfallish—'*calump, calump, calump.*' That's also about timing. I've learned, working on these shows and comedies in general, how important timing is, both to the sound effect and the joke. Quite often, the payoff to a joke is in the sound of it, a sound cue that is the other foot dropping. If it drops too soon or too late, it isn't as funny."

Often that would mean slipping a reaction or an effect by a frame or two at the mix, once Roach and Myers had seen it. "A lot of Austin's delivery has little nuances, little giggles, that are spaced out in his performance to make him goofy," Ross adds. "He'll say a statement that is quite clumsy, then he'll giggle about it a few frames later, and that timing is critical. Those things all need to be heard and acknowledged by the audience. Otherwise, that punctuation, that orchestration of his line, doesn't work."

Some of the signature backgrounds were pulled from the first *Austin Powers*, and again were cut by Benjamin Cook. But Austin moves around a lot, and, in this second installment, he enters Dr. Evil's new lairs inside a volcano and in a moon station. "The lava lair wanted something with low end," Howard explains, "something that spoke of a real viscous, thick environment—a little bit of hissing, some gaseous elements in the midrange, and a little bit of steam for the upper reaches. Then you could pick out some gloops and glops occasionally.

"Then in space," he continues, "we were trying to add a little bit of tension, a little bit of mid-low nebulous hum, if you will. But we didn't want to get too scary. In fact we toned it down after one of our temps because we had some tones that were just a little too dark and ominous for this film. For the most part, it's a pretty light film."

The Spy Who Shagged Me was the second film (after *Star Wars: Episode I*) to come out in the Dolby Digital EX format, with a matrixed center-rear channel. (Kind of Loud Technologies developed a software-based panning system specifically for DS&P.) Nearly all BGs were cut with "6.1" in mind, but the scene in the NORAD control room, intercut through a TV monitor with footage from *The Jerry Springer Show*, perhaps illustrates the new format's use best.

"We had a lot of mini-vignettes that we built to go on these various monitors," Howard says. "Then we had the general 'spy' type of interior for the room. At the same time, we have to push into *The Jerry Springer Show*. The discrete surround allowed us to push in and move the NORAD room around us, and you can still get into *The Jerry Springer Show* without forgetting you're in the room."

"We used [EX] in cases where the picture dictated it, where you can create a nice panorama of sound," Ross adds. "In the *Jerry Springer* sequence, we were able to create an atmosphere back there with beeps and police radios and scanners and other things that didn't intrude upon the screen, but had its own left-center-right behind you. You could split the theater in half."

Ross also made use of the EX format in firing the laser, which would typically rip forward (or to the rear) in the classic 4 o'clock-8 o'clock position, during the climactic battle scene: "You can stretch this illusion of traveling sound by delaying what goes in the surrounds, and now you have a second arrival point, which can make the theater feel longer."

Recording the Score

Because of the desire to have full temp mixes, film editor Greg Hayden cut in music from the original *Austin Powers* early on. Because music editor Mike Flicker was busy with the score at the time, Hayden also cut in the source music, hand in hand with music supervisor John Houlihan (who wrangled new songs, supervised the scoring and is really a story unto himself). That gave the advantage of fleshed-out temps, but it also carried the danger of being restrictive, the inevitable "temp love."

"It can be restrictive, but it can also be instructive," admits composer George S. Clinton, who also scored the original and whose credits include *Mortal Kombat I* and *II* and the summer release *The Astronaut's Wife.* "The challenge is to retain the sense of comic timing that they've worked so hard to get, and yet not have it be the temp score, but have it be something new."

New themes, new textures. Clinton begins by writing pieces of music with a beginning, middle and end; he doesn't think in terms of cues. At his home studio, he writes at the piano or at his Kurzweil K2000 controller. He also uses two K2000 modules, two Roland JV1080 modules, an Akai S5000 sampler and an Apple G3 running Digital Timepiece. Monitoring is through Tannoy Series 10s.

Director Jay Roach (L) checks the charts with composer George S. Clinton.

Clinton says he tries to write from inside the character's head. "There are light moments," he says, "where I use sort of a *Pink Panther*, Henry Mancini-esque approach to the rhythm section and sort of an *In Like Flint* approach with the organ and twangy guitar. And I've also enjoyed the flavor of the '60s style James Bond—the big 'wall of steel' sound that John Barry patented."

One of the first tasks was updating Quincy Jones' classic "Soul Bossa Nova" for the synchronized-swimming opener. The piece was recorded on the "retro-sounding" API console at O'Henry's Studio B, with Fairchild 670 limiters across the left-right channels. "We didn't ignore the vintage technical aspects of it," says scoring/mix engineer John Whynot, who has worked with Clinton on a number of films. "But it's all in the attitude of the playing, and the sound of the brass and rhythm sections. The musicians were into it; it's one of their favorite records."

Bagpipes and percussion/rhythm beds for the 70-piece orchestra were also recorded to Studer 24-track analog machines at O'Henry, and all the music was mixed there, directly to 24-bit Pro Tools from the SSL J9000 (which has a "tricked-out" film monitor module, allowing for the creation of up to five or six independent 3-, 4- and 5-track mixes). The orchestra was recorded over two days to analog 24-track on the SSL J9000 at the newly refurbished Fox Newman Scoring Stage.

"It's not a terribly radical setup," Whynot says of both the seating arrangements and the miking. "I have a typical three-TLM150s setup on the tree, and I

Clinton with orchestra on the Fox Newman stage

spot-mike every section pretty extensively. On violins and celli we used MKH-40s. For basses I used 414s and EV RE20s. Ribbon mics on the brass, with a couple of TLM170s for the big brass. For woodwinds, the M149. Then I basically have MKH-40s for all the percussion, with a single TLM150 omni over the tympani and a 414 on the bass drum. Then I make two separate mixes— one with the room mics to get them sounding right; then I turn them off and get all the direct mics to work as a single mix. The way we have it set up, it sounds really good with just the close mics. The room mics become a giant enhancement."

Clinton has said that his score is an homage to '60s spy thrillers and spoofs, and perhaps nowhere is that more evident than in the brass section. "John Barry called it his 'wall of steel,'" Clinton says. "It's just brass and percussion, big gongs and cymbals, anything steel that you can either blow on or hit—it makes you pay attention. The five trombones, with a bass trombone and tuba, four trumpets, four French horns. It's not any bigger than a lot of other brass sections, but used in the right way, it makes an impression."

"I think George underplays what he really does, because he has good comedic sense," says music editor Mike Flicker, who works with Clinton at every step of the process, from feeding him bars and beats to cataloging the takes. "We [on the music team] take Austin seriously. He takes himself seriously. And the music plays that. The two hardest movies to score are heavy walking-talking drama and comedies. You have to play the music in a way that nails the emotion but doesn't get in the way of the dialog. As soon as the music tries to be comedic, you're cartoons."

Flicker and his assistants literally finished editing at 2 a.m. the night before the final began. Each night during the process, he returned to his Burbank office, where he had duplicate sets of the entire score, and backed up all the updates on Zip cartridges. If he made changes, they were updated and flown into his rig at console-left in the morning. Most timing changes, however, took place on the stage.

"In the first movie, it would be: action cue, drama cue, romantic cue, 'Austin on the move' cue," Flicker says. "But in this one, within one cue it might start up action, then all of a sudden it would be romantic, then pull back and be dramatic. It's down to all these complex stages."

"The thing I wanted to do, and I feel like everybody associated with the movie wanted to do, was to build on the first movie," Clinton concludes. "I wanted to be able to reuse thematic material but add new themes as necessary. A guy asked me yesterday what my dream project would be. I thought a few minutes, then said, 'Well, doing a sequel to a hit, where I've been identified with a genre or music that I love.' I'm living the dream!"

The predubs and final mix took place in Stage 1 at DS&P, at a three-position Euphonix 2000 with eight Pro Tools screens at the meter bridge, monitored in a THX-approved JBL environment. (Three more full Pro Tools rigs were on the stage for flying in music changes.) Playback was from Pro Tools; premixes and stems were recorded to DA-88, then loaded back into Pro Tools for playback.

Ross and Joe Bennett handled the premixes in two long shifts each day. First they did a dialog and Foley pass through the whole film. Those were played back while the next pass was made on backgrounds and sound effects. "By monitoring the predubs from Pro Tools sessions, you can make changes to the previous discipline as well," Ross says. "If one particular sound effect was too loud because you didn't know there was going to be a piece of dialog, you can go in and modify that one item—raise it or lower it—by updating the automation. Then when you get to the final, you've already done some work on your old predub stems. You don't get into a situation where you'll fix it in the final. We can get in and mess with all the units all the time."

Consequently, the final mix was relatively relaxed—regular hours, two days ahead of schedule. Ross mixed dialog, Bill Smith mixed music, and Mathew Waters handled effects. All of the original source material was hung and metered in Pro Tools, below the stems. If a modification was needed (such as when the inflection of the word "now" by actress Heather Graham was inverted in PurePitch to make it more serious), the tracks could be unraveled in seconds on the stage. The lines were blurred between the edit and the mix.

"Often when editors are making decisions, they are working in small little stops and starts, like on the ADR stage, for example," Ross explains. "They make decisions based upon what's good for the moment and not necessarily what's good for the sense of the whole movie. When it comes together as a film and we've run the reel down, and something doesn't feel in the same spirit as the rest of the film, then we need to make changes. Yes, these are things that were classically editorial—grabbing alternate production takes and laying them up—but at the end of the day, Jay [Roach, director] is sitting three feet away from me, and it's like he's sitting in an editing room. But now he can evaluate the whole painting and go back in and re-choose the type of red used on the cheeks."

Except for the final battle sequence on the moon, this is not a "loud," special effects movie, and the tracks are wonderfully spare and detailed at times. Likewise, the use of the subwoofer channel is judicious and constantly varied. A lot of time was spent on creating rich low-end information, then holding back on it in the mix. "We tend to be picky about what we put in the subs," Ross says. "When it does happen, it's an event that wasn't there for the last 20 minutes. When it comes up, it re-surprises the audience."

With his writer's ear and comic vision, Jay Roach had no trouble elucidating what he wanted during the final. By the time Mike Myers returned from Cannes in late May, the tracks were in order and changes were minimal. "He basically took a grand master approach to why a scene is funny," Ross says. "There's a scene in the volcano lair where Mini-Me is driving Dr. Evil around on a bicycle and honking the horn. Mike wanted the horn so loud that it nearly obliterated the dialog, which was against my instincts. But on a grander scale, the comedy is not what he's saying but the fact that he looked like an idiot, talking about how he's upholding the dignity of the organization while he's being driven around by a midget going ballistic on this horn. Coming from someone as well-versed in comedy as Mike is, these are the types of things we focus on."

CHAPTER 18

It Was 31 Years Ago Today

The Beatles Remixed in 5.1 for Yellow Submarine

by Tom Kenny and Chris Michie

It had to happen. Some day, some way, somebody was going to remix The Beatles for 5.1. As it turns out, all it took was a lot of perseverance and a little push from Hollywood, for a film called *Yellow Submarine.*

No doubt, there will be purists who scream, "Sacrilege!" And debates will rage about the simple-yet-detailed beauty of the original mono mixes. But The Beatles were experimental, and had 5.1 been around in 1968, it is likely that the lads would have been driving the surround bandwagon.

Now, with the blessing of the three remaining Beatles, moviegoers will have a chance to hear "When I'm Sixty-Four," "Sgt. Pepper," "Eleanor Rigby" and "Nowhere Man" in stunning wraparound sound. The film will be shown in art houses in nine U.S. cities during the week of September 6, followed by the DVD and home video debut on September 14.

The project began, innocently enough, in the fall of 1995 in a Los Angeles video store, where Bruce Markoe, VP of feature post-production at MGM/UA, went looking for the film to show his 5-year-old daughter. Markoe took home a 1987 laserdisc but found that not only was the picture quality poor but the sound—originally mixed in mono but now billed as "video-phonic stereo" (with the songs direct from the album mixes)—needed major improvement. Markoe's daughter, however, "loved it," so he began exploring the idea of restoring this neglected modern animation masterpiece.

This article appeared originally in the September 1999 issue of Mix.

Markoe went back to the office and started his research in anticipation of a full theatrical re-release. Finding that the rights had
been tied up in a legal dispute since 1988, he called John Calley,
then president of United Artists. Calley, in turn, prodded the
legal department to settle the suit, which took a year. Meanwhile, Markoe looked into the status of the original elements,
knowing that he wanted to remix digitally for the 5.1 format. His
first call to Abbey Road was met with some skepticism, along the
lines of, "That's never been done; they're not going to allow it."
So he pulled back, figured out the process he wanted to follow
and called Neil Aspinall, the head of Apple.

"I explained how I wanted to take the songs and remix them
from scratch to 5.1," Markoe recalls. "I said that I didn't want to
just take the 2-track album mixes and spread them, because I
thought that would be a compromise of the sound. In movie
theaters, people are used to 5.1 digital sound, and 2-track mixes
would just sound wrong. [Neil] got back to me and he agreed to
let us do this, with the understanding that these 5.1 mixes were
specifically for the [theater] format. I think that was key. Obviously, The Beatles would have to approve, and if they didn't like
what they heard, the whole project would be killed. It was the
first step, and it was baby steps."

Yellow Submarine was shot in a 1.66:1 aspect ratio, the UK and European standard, and will be letterboxed that way for DVD (theaters will project it at 1.85:1). Two versions were made back in 1969, with the UK version including the song "Hey Bulldog" and a few extra minutes of animation that U.S. audiences never saw. For the renovation, the UK version was used, and Markoe went on a search for the best available print. (Note for hard-core fans: The final reel is from the U.S. version, as the last reel of the UK print was a mono composite, meaning that effects and dialog could not be separated.)

The original negative, he found, was in "horrendous condition. It was all beat up, and the color was bad. Lots of dirt and scratches." So Pacific Ocean Post (at the time owned by Alan Kozlowski, a friend of Paul and George) did a full digital restoration of the first 40 minutes of the movie. For the last three reels, Markoe located an interpositive element that was in "excellent, excellent condition. It even had the 'Hey Bulldog' sequence on it," he adds. "My big concern was color, because the movie is very vivid. We did the color timing at Deluxe, and it took awhile, but we were able to bring the colors back."

A transfer of the original film was sent in late 1997 to Ted Hall at POP Sound, Santa Monica. Provided with the original mono DME (dialog, music, effects), Hall started working on the dialog and effects. Markoe, in the meantime, flew to London for the first week of song remixing.

"I foolishly thought we could remix all the songs in a week," he recalls. "I had no idea about the complexity of how these songs were produced originally. The engineers at Abbey Road, and Peter Cobbin in particular, were very aware that we were treading on sacred ground and that we had to be very true to the integrity of the original songs. Beatles fans would be completely upset if these songs wound up sounding different. At the same time, we needed to enhance them and take advantage of the 5.1 format. Abbey Road set up this incredible marriage of the old technology that The Beatles used when they recorded and mixed these songs, combined with our state-of-the-art 24-bit digital machines."

The 5.1 mix project was started at Abbey Road in October 1997, with project coordinator and Beatles authority Alan Rouse acting as liaison between Apple Corp., EMI and Abbey Road. Rouse has an encyclopedic knowledge of the Beatles' archives and provided the necessary masters. As mixing engineer Peter Cobbin explains, most of The Beatles' recordings after the first two albums were made on 4-track, usually the Abbey Road 1-inch format Studer J37s, though some of the tapes he saw had been recorded on 1/2-inch 4-track at independent studios such as Olympic Sound Studios. [For session details, see Mark Lewisohn's *The Beatles: Recording Sessions*, Harmony Books, New York.]

"Between '64 and, I would say, halfway through '65, most of the things they did were on 4-track alone," Cobbin explains. "Then they became a bit more adventurous and wanted to go beyond 4-track. They would fill up one 4-track and then do a 'reduction' down to one track of another 4-track, then fill up the other three tracks [on the second 4-track]. If they still had other ideas, they would do another generation down to another 4-track. For the really adventurous songs, there could be up to three or four generations of 4-track tapes."

Though few would argue with the results, these progressive "reductions" inevitably reduced the options for subsequent stereo mixing. Cobbin cites "Eleanor Rigby" as an example: "The strings octet was the first thing recorded," he says, noting that the original 4-track tape features two instruments per track (two violins, two violins, two violas, two celli). This recording was then bounced down to one track of a second machine, to which Paul McCartney added two vocal tracks. "So even though they had the elements for a stereo mix, from that day on, the strings have only been heard in mono," says Cobbin. "Today, we can sync up the [component tracks], thus enabling us to use first-generation material. And it gives us options for placement and panning—for 5.1 that's a very significant advantage."

The signal chain at Abbey Road combined equipment and technologies spanning the past 30 years. From analog 4-track tapes, the archival recordings were converted to digital for manipulation and restoration in a Sonic Solutions workstation, then stored on a Sony 3348HR digital multitrack for playback at the mix.

The premix assembly process was laborious. First, the selected masters, predominantly 1-inch 4-track tapes, were transferred from the playback machine, a Studer A80 MkI, onto a Sonic Solutions workstation via Prism AD124 converters. Cobbin was agreeably surprised by the quality of the original tapes, all of which are now more than 30 years old. All of the Abbey Road sessions in the late '60s were recorded on EMI tape, a house brand that the company manufactured for its worldwide studio operations.

"When you look at the tape, it's still in immaculate condition," says Cobbin. "Not the slightest sign of shedding, and it's got an incredible full sound to it." Once on the workstation, the tracks were "NoNoised" and then transferred back onto a Sony 3348HR. "I'm not a firm believer in just denoising everything, because sometimes it does change the sound quality," notes Cobbin, who made sure that both the original and denoised tracks were copied back to the 3348 so as to have the option to use either when mixing.

Composite tracks were split into their components inside the Sonic Solutions system. "There could be five or six different elements on one track," recalls Cobbin. "There might be some sound effects, a backing vocal, a guitar solo, all on one track. I would actually split that off and create a separate track for each of those components. And suddenly, with some songs, I ended up with a fairly full 48-track. And, of course, that meant that when I came to mix, I could treat them differently, in terms of sound processing or EQ or surround placement. So that was one technique I used quite a bit, even for some of the simpler 4-track tapes."

Peter Cobbin at Abbey Road

MIXING FOR 5.1

Cobbin actually mixed the songs twice, once in 5.1 for theaters and DVD, and again in stereo for the "songtrack" CD (a soundtrack album containing all of the songs heard on the film soundtrack). Both mixes were done in Abbey Road's Studio 3 control room, which is equipped with a 72-input SSL 8000G console. Twenty-four-bit signals were monitored through Genesis converters and then-prototype B&W Nautilus monitors.

For the 5.1 mix, Cobbin routed outputs from the SSL to three 2-channel Prism AD124 A/D converters. "I knew that the mixes had to go to Los Angeles," recalls Cobbin. "I rang around and found that Tascam seemed to be the most acceptable format." Though the Tascam DA-88 is normally a 16-bit machine, Prism's MR2024 interface allows the extra bits to be stored on the last two tracks, which enabled true 20-bit recording. The final 5.1 mixes were to 20-bit DA-88 for delivery to Ted Hall at POP.

"It's a fairly radical thing to go back to the masters and actually remix them," says Cobbin. "Keeping to the spirit of the songs meant being fairly detailed and accurate in re-creating the original effects. We are lucky enough to have a lot of the old equipment still here [at Abbey Road]. And there's a wealth of knowledge of what happened—there are people still here today who were involved in the tail end of the Beatles' recording career."

For reverbs, Cobbin was able to make use of the famed Studio 2's echo chamber. "Abbey Road has three chambers, or they did in the '60s," says Cobbin. "One is now used to hold four vintage EMT plates, and the other is being used for storage, but we've still got Studio 2's chamber, which is basically the one that they used the most." Featuring a selection of clay sewer pipes scattered around the room, the chamber is miked with Neumann tube KM56s. "It's a unique sound, a very short reverb, but it's the sound on a lot of the recordings and mixes that they did," Cobbin notes.

Another vintage touch that Cobbin replicated was the mild distortion that can be heard on many of The Beatles' vocals. "Often they recorded through Fairchild limiters, and the preamps would just gently overload; that became the sound," explains Cobbin. "I don't think they were necessarily trying to hide or hold that back, it was just part of the sound of the day. It almost sounds desirable, particularly the tube-related distortion."

In addition to vintage Fairchild 660 limiters and Pultec equalizers, which were often used on Beatles sessions in the '60s, Cobbin also made use of Abbey Road's inventory of EMI equalizers and compressors. "They were part of the TG series that EMI made and they evolved through the '70s, but they offer a kind of characteristic that is different to modern EQs," he notes. "The other main thing, of course, was tape machines, which they used for tape delays and echoes and predelays to the plates, and ADT. Abbey Road could put all that stuff back together."

As Beatles aficionados are aware, several songs were pitch-shifted during recording or remix sessions, resulting in final mixes that run faster or slower than the multitrack masters. To ensure that his remixes were at the correct speed, whether for the songtrack or 5.1, Cobbin first created a reference by transferring the original 1/4-inch master to digital. "That ensured that we had the final definitive version at the correct speed," he says. "Once we got the right speed, we've got an old Q-Lock system which event-fires any machine, so with timecode we could trigger the machine to start at any point in time. We would then, if necessary, adjust the speed of the machine to match the master. The

Studer has a varispeed card with a very fine adjustment control, so we could match them up. I found that the best way to do that is to listen to what you're laying up and the final version as a sync reference. If you listen to one on one side, and one on the other side, the image should be perfectly in the center."

NEW PERSPECTIVES

At the time, Cobbin had never before mixed for 5.1. "I think it was still fairly new at that stage," he says. "Needless to say, some songs lent themselves to a more involving experience. The title song, 'Yellow Submarine,' has lots of weird and wonderful effects and waves and bells, so I could naturally be more adventurous. But given that we're talking about an important catalog item, I didn't want it to be gimmicky in any way.

"If something on the original stereo mix was coming out of the center, out of the phantom center or mono, and I wanted to replicate that, I found that the best way to go about it was to put it into the center speakers, and also put it in the left and right at a lower proportion," he says. "If I wanted something to the right, I might put 20 percent in the left, 40 percent in the center and 100 percent in the right speaker. That would give a strong feeling that something was panned right, without losing intelligibility if you happen to be sitting to the left of the screen."

In general, Cobbin created a surround mix that offered a strong reinforcement from the front and used the surround speakers to create a sense of space. Often, he directed effects returns to the rear speakers. "It's amazing the perspective that you can achieve," he comments.

RE-RECORDING AT POP SOUND

While the Abbey Road team was working out the songs, re-recording mixer Ted Hall worked up an effects library by pulling elements from the mono DME. Hall's experience with surround formats dates back to the early '90s and ranges from remastering *Ben Hur* to recent work on Tom Petty's live performance broadcast over satellite, and he has worked on music DVD projects including Madonna's *Girlie Show* and *Eric Clapton Unplugged*. He was given the mandate by Markoe to "be aggressive. We want to give everybody's home theater systems a big workout here. If it moves on the screen, move it."

Hall shies away from putting too much information in the subs or the surrounds, and he's adamant that renovation projects must maintain the integrity of the original mix. After attending a screening of the original mono print at MGM, his first thought was that he liked the character of the movie, "the whole feeling from this cruddy little soundtrack. But the idea," he says, "was to make this an E-ticket ride."

Hall first conformed the DME into his 24-bit AudioFile98 workstation, edited it, then passed the tracks to Norm McLeod, who cleaned up the dialog and effects in his Sonic Solutions NoNoise system. After getting the tracks back, Hall began pulling out individual effects and amassing his *Yellow Submarine* library, dividing it between hard effects and backgrounds.

"It was convenient for me that, back then, all their editing was pretty much linear," Hall explains. "There weren't many cross-fades between sounds, so there would be a hit, then a kick, then an explosion, and they'd be pretty much separated. I could extract each of those sounds and label them, say, 'Blue Meanie Bonk.' Pretty soon I had a library of 200 or 300 effects that we used throughout the movie."

Hall proceeded to build ambiences and stronger effects, "opening them up," as he calls it, for 5.1. He would double tracks, apply radical EQ from the AMS Logic 2, drop explosions down an octave and layer them, and spatialize sounds in the time domain. Often, he would pull effects from one part of the movie and apply them to another. "The original film is pretty thin," says Hall. "Whether because of time constraints, budget constraints or purely by design, many obvious effects are missing. Sometimes footsteps, for example, disappear when there's a perspective cut.

"And sometimes the Meanies would be shooting arrows and you would see maybe 50 shots from these cannons," Hall says. "but you would only hear two or three. So, of course, I put them all in there. Not only that, I would double them so they could fly over your head. The nice thing about doing it nonlinear is that on the AudioFile I have 24 tracks, so I can dedicate channels, say, to the flying glove sample and put it on its own joystick and do pans while all the other elements stay where they're supposed to."

Though the big Pepperland battle opener and some of the other busy shots might gather the most notice, the subtleties in the Sea of Silence backgrounds and other scenes also benefited from the 5.1 spread, where Hall's own stereo-izing techniques and phase manipulation created enhanced spatiality.

HANGARS AND HALLWAYS

The trickiest scene turned out to be the Hall of Doors scene, in which Ringo sets about gathering the lads for the trip back to Pepperland. A lot of left-right action goes on in the hallway, leading to a complicated effects mix. "At that point, they actually did have overlaps on the sound," Hall explains. "Of all points in the movie, that was one where they definitely spent time cutting the sound design together. I tried to take each of those moments and put them on a different track with their own panner. But sometimes the sound would include the sound of the next incoming object. When the pans are happening fast, you don't notice it as much, but if you were to isolate one sound, like a snail going right to left, you would notice that as it got to the left, you would hear, say, a bike effect in the right channel. So I would cut the beginning of that bike onto another track so I could accentuate the motion and hide the fact that I couldn't get in and cut them hard without the crossfades."

The dialog track on the 1987 home video is nearly unintelligible, and there are hard bumps when it cuts in. Hall fixed as many edits as possible and smoothed out the track, but in a few places it remains hissy, he says. He again applied EQ from the Logic 2 to take away some of the harshness, focusing on the 2k to 4k range, where it had been heavily boosted on the optical track.

MUSIC TRACKS

When the music tracks arrived in March 1998 from Abbey Road, Hall and his assistant, Shane T. Keller, put them up and "got goosebumps, totally mesmerized. You hear 'Eleanor Rigby' with a string quartet wrapped around you and just go, 'Oooohhh.'" But the music was not in sync with picture, and Hall began a bar-by-bar, song-by-song varispeed session, using a Hewlett-Packard function generator.

"I would varispeed the DA-88s against the original print and just phase it in by ear," Hall recalls. "As soon as you start hearing that Jimi Hendrix sound of phasing, you're really close to sync. Then I would digitally sample rate convert back to a stable 44.1 clock. People say you can't varispeed. Well, that's what they did on the original film."

The George Martin underscore came in from two sources: a mono track that Hall spread out (about 65% of the underscore) and a 5.1 spread of a stereo version that Martin re-recorded a few months after the film came out for the soundtrack album. "There were slightly different arrangements and sometimes radically different tempos. So it was lots of edits, lots of varispeeding, time compression and time expansion," Hall says. "Trying to get the themes to line up and the key changes to be correct. I think I got it pretty close."

In April 1998, Hall and Peter Cobbin brought the 5.1 stems on Sony 3348HR tapes to Disney Stage A to make the print master, so they could hear it in a 250-seat theater. Noted Hollywood re-recording mixer Mike Minkler sat with them and offered advice—a few minor tweaks, some more for the rears. Cobbin boosted some low end. The theatrical version was print-mastered in the DTS format, where, incidentally, the only other conversion outside the original A-to-D took place. The DVD was a straight 24-bit D-to-D into the Dolby Digital processor.

"The film is an amazing visual treat, in terms of being different and crazy and wild and a whole new world," Markoe concludes. "To me, a renovation is when you take something that's a classic piece of work—whether it's art or architecture or film or whatever—and you actually improve it while being very true to the integrity of the original piece. We set up playback of the songs for Neil Aspinall and Geoff Emerick because we figured if these guys didn't like what they were hearing, we needed to either change what we were doing or the whole thing would be killed. A week or two later, the three Beatles came in, and I'm told they were very happy with what they heard. Everybody who heard it was blown away."

CHAPTER 19

Walking The Green Mile

Designing the Soundtrack for Frank Darabont's
Death Row Drama

The re-recording team of,
l to r, Michael Herbick,
Bob Litt and Elliot Tyson on
Warner Hollywood Stage A

PHOTO: ENGLE MEREDITH

"The wide corridor up the center of E Block was floored with linoleum
the color of tired old limes, and so what was called the Last Mile at other
prisons was called the Green Mile at Cold Mountain. It ran, I guess,
sixty long paces from south to north, bottom to top. At the bottom was the
restraint room. At the top end was a T-junction. A left turn meant
life...A right turn, though, that was different...This is where you ended
up when you walked the Green Mile."

—Stephen King, *The Green Mile*

This article appeared originally in
the January 2000 issue of Mix.

Old Sparky, King calls it. The electric chair. The last stop on the Mile. Nothing can match it as a symbol of the power that men have over men. A body is strapped in and clamped down, from the ankles up, and a black hood is placed over the head. The switch is thrown, then a second switch, and the surge of electricity jolts the body violently and without mercy. It lasts about 30 seconds, then the body is carted away. Few people have actually seen it at work.

In the summer of 1935, Louisiana prison guard Paul Edgecomb (Tom Hanks) has to lead John Coffey, a large black man convicted in the murder of two 10-year-old white girls, down the Mile to the electric chair. The events and revelations leading up to the execution change his life forever and form the basis of *The Green Mile*, the holiday season's most talked-about film.

It's somewhat familiar territory for director Frank Darabont and much of the crew, many of whom worked with him on *The Shawshank Redemption* in 1994. Prison forms the backdrop; hope and redemption are the salvation. But where *Shawshank* occasionally turned dreamy and triumphant, *The Green Mile* is anchored in grit and stark reality. The horror is intentional, and Edgecomb's epiphany, revealed in layered flashbacks, is complex without being sentimental.

For the audio crew, the challenge was to capture that gritty realism—in the loneliness of death row, the violence of an execution and the magic of miracles.

BACKGROUNDS AND PRISON SOUNDS

"This film is three hours, and 2 hours and 20 minutes of it takes place on the Green Mile. So that's a background," says supervising sound editor Mark Mangini, co-owner of Weddington Productions in North Hollywood. "And yet the admonition was: 'The Death Row cellblock is isolated from the rest of the prison, and I don't want to hear anything else. I don't want to hear other prisoners. I don't want to hear offstage trains.' It's a brick building with a very high tin roof, and it's intentionally quiet there. As a sound editor, you're thinking, 'Well, how do we make a BG that's not boring for two hours.'"

Foley artist John Roesch was set up with a video playback system on the set, with the real concrete floors used in the film, while being recorded via fiber optic connections, back in Foley Stage F. The intent was to capture perspective and realism that you wouldn't normally get in Foley.

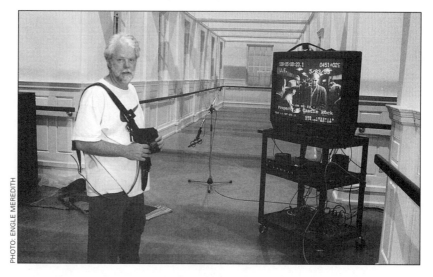

Mangini sent Eric Potter and Howell Gibbons to Fort MacArthur in Long Beach (later, effects elements would also come from Stateville Prison, Folsom Prison and the Lincoln City Jail) for a few nights of field recording in an underground bunker-like military brig. They shot 6-track "airs" for presence, which became the bed for the Green Mile—daytime, nighttime, early afternoon, etc. On top of that, they shot separate 6-tracks of what Mangini calls "ear candy."

"Eric and Howell amassed handfuls of little bits of debris," he explains. "Little bits of metal and wood and dust and dirt and grit. I had them walk around in their socks, in that 6-track sound field, and just drop things, because that's what you hear in real life if you sit and be quiet—you hear things settling and dropping. The whole idea of the prison was that it was supposed to be lonely and quiet. I remember an artist telling me once that the best way to make white whiter is to add blue to it. So I thought silence isn't good enough for loneliness. Reverberance is to me what sells loneliness. That's why I wanted to record that ear candy."

"Mark delivered the backgrounds on about 44 tracks," adds Elliot Tyson, effects re-recording mixer. "We broke them out into two background predubs—A and B. 'A' generally was the airy BG, and 'B' had what Mark termed 'pepper' [or ear candy], which was sprinkled with some vocals or metal twisting in the hot noonday sun, as if the room was warming up and cooling down. We would then weave those specific A's and B's so that you felt air kind of coming and going, with the pepper louder and softer. It always felt like something was moving in the room."

Emotional Score, Minimalist Bent

The last time composer Thomas Newman worked with director Frank Darabont he ended up with two Oscar nominations, for *The Shawshank Redemption* and *Little Women* in 1994. During a three-week hiatus from writing for *The Green Mile*, he wrote and recorded a gem for *American Beauty*. It's quite conceivable that he'll find himself competing against himself again this year.

"Tom has developed a whole type of music that is extremely emotional and extremely minimal," says his music editor, Bill Bernstein. "Normally, you think that if you need a lot of emotion, you have to saw away at the strings—they have to swell and sweep. What Tom does is go down to a very icy, cold, moving little melody and it's just heartbreaking. I don't know how he does it, but it's so effective. I think that's what makes him popular in temp music—he's able to get such emotion with such minimal touches. It's like Japanese painting."

For the brutal Delacroix execution, Newman wrote a full-on orchestral piece, loud and abrasive, Bernstein says. In deference to effects, however, and in a reversal of what usually happens on dub stages, it is there to poke through the lulls in the effects storm. But by the Coffey execution at the end, when emotion is at its peak, music plays the moment.

"By Coffey's execution, lyrical is the word," Bernstein says. "The music takes the forefront. You hear very little of the electric execution sound that you heard with Del. By the time the lights are exploding and everything is happening, it's slow motion. The sparks are floating down over Tom Hanks' stricken face, and the music is playing a beautiful haunting melody. It's piano backed by strings—still full strings but they're not playing a lot of notes. Then the strings take the melody. It's very sweet, what we called our 'Condemned Man Theme.'

"It becomes the theme for the movie," he continues. "It starts with Bitterbuck's execution. You hear it again as Del is marched to the chair. Then at the end of the movie, we realize we're all condemned men—'We all owe a death,' as the character says. That scene, the John Coffey execution, is where the theme finally pays off. I think he did a marvelous job with it."

Newman typically begins a project at home, prerecording some tracks from his sequencer or some improv sessions. On *The Green Mile*, he brought four to six musicians into Signet Soundelux for overdubs—for ambiences, sustains or woodwind noodles—recorded to 24-track. A slave was made for the orchestral sessions, which took place at the Todd-AO Scoring Stage. The orchestra was also recorded on 24-track and then mixed down on the Neve 8068 (LCR-LS-RS, with a boom channel) to Genex 8000 by Dennis Sands back at Signet. The non-orchestra pieces were often split into two LCR pairs on another Genex MO. By the time Bernstein loaded all the sessions into his Pro Tools system and prepared them for the stage, he had as many as 14 tracks per cue.

Bernstein had one 24-track, 24-bit Pro Tools online for the stage (monitor and keyboard only, with Cybex extender; the hard drive was in the machine room), which handled the quick fixes, and another in his cutting room just off the stage, for changes, alternates, emergencies or loading.

Perhaps the biggest challenge in the score was the same one Mangini faced with backgrounds: how to remain fresh, yet consistent, over such a long time. There are over 90 minutes of score in the film, the longest Newman has done.

"Early in the movie, there's a lot more fun, more humor," Bernstein says. "Then it gets very serious and dark, where the tone is more somber, moving and mystical. I think it was important in the music to view the movie in chapters. You'd introduce a new character, like Wild Bill, and use a lot of twangy, strummy, idiomatic Southern music. Then for the John Coffey miracles, it was more sustains and sort of icy piano drops. The movie had enough variation in tone to allow some different chapter music."

Other conventional prison sounds were approached with the same seemingly dual nature, where they needed to be consistent yet imply variety. There are four key doors on the Mile, so Mangini assembled elements from real jail cell doors, film racks and car jacks, among other things, and Howell Gibbons built "door kits." Those were then loaded in the scene-spotting program Weddington developed in conjunction with mSoft and used as the root throughout the 20 reels. It was the same for keys, which were handled in Foley.

"The keys were a big deal because that's a signature sound in that it's a sound of authority," Mangini says. "In normal movies, you play keys for cops and military and it can be too much. We have an ensemble movie with six guys in every scene. Do I do six individual passes of keys? 'My God, they're killing me!' We never actually did more than two tracks of keys, even for six guys, but they were a springboard for me to develop this new Foley process. We got the keys they actually used, these huge prison keys with a great, unique sound that a Foley prop wouldn't have had."

"My biggest concern on this film was the Foley sounding fake," Mangini continues. "To me, 99 percent of all Foley I hear, in my own movies and others, sounds crappy. It's an artifice. It's a function of the process that we've developed for ourselves, which is: You point a microphone right at somebody's shoes, which is unnatural, on a surface that isn't the real surface, in an acoustic space that has no natural environment. It's bothered me my entire career. On this movie, I knew we were going to constantly be going in and out of production to Foley and it was never going to match. So I thought this would be an opportunity to do something different. I wanted to reproduce production sound in the way that production sound really gets recorded. I wanted movement across the recording field. I wanted to feel real acoustics, not electronic reverberators. I wanted real props. I wanted the real shoes. I wanted the real surface. I wanted the whole thing."

First, Mangini and field recordist Eric Potter (who also recorded most of the sounds that went into the electrocutions) went to the Lincoln Heights Jail in downtown L.A. and shot some footsteps wild to DAT, from various perspectives, just as a test. Mangini brought the material back and hand-cut it against picture—the concept worked, but the location was right next to an Amtrak line.

So, he decided to scout for locations and found a school in Palmdale that had a long hallway with the right linoleum floor, and he knew that he could always shoot in the prison at Fort MacArthur. Mangini and Foley Supervisor Aaron Glascock built a lean rig, with big-screen TVs, a VCR and a portable Pro Tools system, planning to mike the footsteps M-S. Everything was set, then Warner Hollywood called, concerned that their Foley stage was no longer being used.

"Robert Winder said, 'You know, Mark, the sets are still constructed here on Stage 2, and they're on hiatus for four months waiting for Tom Hanks. Maybe you could Foley on the sets,'" Mangini recalls. "So I thought, 'Well, this sounds hare-brained, but I'll go check it out.'"

Foley mixer Mary Jo Lang, front, and recordist Carolynn Tapp provided remote playback and recording services for the 18-day session. Note the scene on the monitors, with a visual of Foley artist Roesch on the top monitors.

PHOTO: ENGLE MEREDITH

Mangini and Foley artist John Roesch brought a Hi-8 playback system and a non-sync DAT to the sets and did a test, synched to a scene where the guard Percy is walking down the Green Mile. He brought the tracks back and cut them in. Then, that afternoon, the same team, with the same scene, went into the Foley stage and constructed a 12-foot linoleum walkway so they could get at least some perspective. Mics were hung close and far to pick up room. That, too was cut against picture.

"The difference was night and day," Mangini says. "We brought Frank [Darabont] in and said, 'What do you think. We're going to try something new and actually do Foley on the set. It could blow up in our faces, but we wanted you to hear what it sounds like.' We played the tracks, and everybody, even John, said, 'That stuff on the set is the real thing."

At this point, Mangini still planned to bring in his portable Pro Tools rig and record to hard disk, right on the set. But again Winder came up with a plan to link the set with the Foley booth via fiber optics. Warner chief engineer Mike Novich handled the wiring and put in two 35-inch TV monitors on rollers, at either end of the Green Mile. They set up two microphones for recording and a two-way playback rig with a video tap. They even set up an infrared headphone system for when the artists needed to hear sounds in sync to what they were walking.

"While in the recording booth, we could watch John and Hilda [Hodges], and we could see the whole set," Mangini explains. "Aaron would be telling them, 'Move the microphone a little bit to the right, put the mic over there.' We had four different sets on the soundstage—we even did the Foley for the shack out in

Director Frank Darabont explains the execution rehearsal scene to Tom Hanks, while Harry Dean Stanton looks on and Barry Pepper peeks over the shoulder.

the woods, and the electrocution room. We had all the comforts of all the tools they have there, with a nice quiet monitoring environment. And yet we were getting production sound. It came out so well. If they had to do a 30-second walk-away down a 100-foot-long space, that's what they did. And it was like it was production."

All of the Foley (including exteriors, which ended up being done on Stage F) was recorded to 2-inch, 24-track by Mary Jo Lang and Carolynn Tapp. They also did keys, the guards' web belts, clothing, the mouse's footsteps and spool-rolling (yes, a real mouse is a main character), and everything else they could over an 18-day session. There was, Mangini admits, a lot of skepticism at the beginning, mainly to do with the noise floor and punching in to live Foley. "It's funny how hypersensitive we all get to extraneous sounds while in the artificial reality of a Foley session," Mangini says. "Like, it would be in the middle of a cue and you'd hear a little wood creak from somewhere off in the soundstage, and someone would go, 'We gotta go back and punch that out.' I would say, 'No! Leave it in! It sounds just like the Green Mile!'"

"It's no longer Foley, it's Mangini," jokes effects re-recording mixer Elliot Tyson. "We named it after him. If the legend is true that it was named after Jack Foley, why can't we name this after Mangini? On the stage, we would say, 'We gotta raise the Mangini here. Can we pull up the Mangini? Can we retard the Mangini?' When I first got the tracks, I turned around and said, 'Wow, this is amazing. Why can't all films be done like this?' It just laid in so well it was frightening. I predubbed it against [dialog re-recording mixer] Bob Litt's dialog predub, and you could take out the production and it would sound real."

Additional group ADR for the executions (in 1935, witnesses were in the same room—there was no glass to separate them) was also recorded on the set. And, Mangini figured that as long as he had access, he would make use of it, so he "worldized" the six source music cues (played them in a real-world environment) emanating from the radio on the guard's desk at one end of the Mile.

"One thing I hate almost as much as Foley is board futzing music recordings to make them sound crappy," Mangini says. "We got four old-time radios from a local prop rental company. Ezra Dweck put the cleaned up CD recordings on channel 1 of a DA-88 and fed that output to an AM transmitter that then broadcast the songs to the four radios, one at at time. Ezra miked the radios' speakers and sent that signal back to the DA-88 on channels 2-7. The recording was done on the Green Mile set with a 5-channel microphone setup—mono nearfield, stereo midfield and stereo farfield. We got natural acoustics, with a broadcast being picked up by an actual tube radio, and they sounded awesome. Some of them we'd tune off, just a little bit, to get a bit of that sideband modulation. It's a rig Howell developed for *October Sky*."

A similar setup was used to process the soundtrack of an old film for a scene near the end when John Coffey wanted to see a movie. It was his last request before walking the Mile. To approximate the sound of an old movie optical soundtrack playing in a large auditorium, the original film's magnetic sound track was played back using crackling 60-year-old movie horns in an old church.

THE EXECUTIONS

There are four executions in the film. None of them are easy to watch, even for the editors/mixers who have seen them hundreds of times. One of them is absolutely horrific, an execution gone bad because Percy, the guard, intentionally leaves water off the prisoner Delacroix's head before placing the

One Last Final Mix

Mangini and his Weddington crew began on the film at the end of March 1999. All editing was done in 16-bit Pro Tools, with roughly 250 gigabytes delivered for playback at the mix. Kudos, Mangini says, should go to Julia Evershade, who cut all 20 reels of dialog and ADR by herself.

The premix and final mix took place over 12 weeks from May to July at Warner Hollywood Stage A, with the team of Bob Litt (dialog), Elliot Tyson (effects) and Michael Herbick (music) sitting at a Harrison PP-1 analog console, serial number 002. Tyson brought in two 22-input PP-1 sidecars for effects. They returned on a weekend in mid-October to mix reels 1 and 20, the bookends. Dialog and effects were recorded to combo Fairlight MFX3plus from DaD systems, with music being recorded to mag.

Tyson, who now lead-mixes on a Neve DFC at Disney's Stage A (Disney graciously let him return for a final go-around on this film), says it was tough to revisit his old room. "It was like going back to 1935," he laughs. "No automated pan pots, no automated EQ, no automated joysticks, no automated routing. If I had been away from it for a few years, it would have been more difficult. But it comes back like riding a bike."

The Green Mile proved to be something of a swan song for the mix crew. Litt, considered one of the finest dialog mixers in the business, is rumored to be retiring. He and Tyson had worked together for 19 years before Tyson signed a contract with Disney last year, and Herbick's been with them for the last five. They mixed *The Shawshank Redemption* for Darabont in 1994.

helmet, just to watch him burn, literally. It lasts five to six minutes onscreen, and the director established early on that he wanted effects to carry the scene. For later executions, music would tie in, and drama and emotion would be played up. But for Delacroix, the idea was to capture the horror and reality.

"Essentially the body just burns up," says sound designer Eric Lindemann. "Parts of him explode. The flesh sizzles. It's probably the hardest scene I've ever worked on because of the horrific nature of it. But it's a very powerful scene. What will be conveyed to the audience is the sense of power—the power of electricity and the violence of an execution. That's, to me, the moral aspect of the scene."

Supervising sound editor Mark Mangini, who made the decision to go with location-based Foley, takes a break during the final mix.

Each execution is treated differently, but each contains two sound design moments: the surge of electricity, then the body sounds on the oaken chair. The clamping in and strapping down was handled in Foley on the set, and Mangini says the goal was to always make those sounds real, with the actual electrocution becoming hyper-real. When the guards throw the first switch, you get the sound of a generator winding up (a lathe motor base), followed by filament sounds of a series of light bulbs, followed by a second surge as they "Roll on two."

"There are about 12 incandescent bulbs that light up in sequence," Lindemann explains. "In my Pro Tools session I had about 14 sounds for each light turning on, and the sound would evolve so you get the idea that more and more power was being generated. I also added in electric arcs and things like that, which would modulate and give you a sense of power. After that, there's always a few moments before the final command where you can just feel the electrical energy in the room buzzing around. It's a subtle, delicate buzzing sound—very quiet and very scary. Then they throw the switch and all that power goes through the person being executed. You *feel* this jolt. We really tried to go for contrast, from very delicate to very large, nasty and scary.

"For the Delacroix execution, the thing that came to mind was that the electrocution device wasn't transferring the power to his body correctly, so it would be intermittent, like it was broken," he continues. "So I integrated sounds of metal ripping, dogs barking, pig squeals and other animals in pain. I took some human screams. Then I distorted them, pitched them and made them all work together. The idea was to make [the electricity] like scratching a chalkboard."

Eric Potter recorded most of the sounds that went into the surges and jolts, including transformers, the in-house degausser and microwave, an old Fender Bassman amp for some nice hums, and a plethora of "gnarly sparks," Mangini says. At one point they found Potter downstairs at Weddington touching wires connected to a transformer.

"That was a high-voltage transformer, designed for an old neon sign," Potter laughs. "One of the first things I do on a period picture like this is go on a scavenging spree at History for Hire, a prop house specializing in old stuff. I saw this beast of a transformer in the neon sign section. It looked old and scary—it was rated at 18,000 volts. So I dragged it back to the studio, and

The Green Mile Crew

Sound Editorial Services provided by Weddington Productions

Supervising Sound Editor: Mark Mangini

ADR and Dialog Supervisor: Julia Evershade

Sound Design: Eric Lindemann

Special Sound FX By: John P., Ken Johnson

Sound Editors: Howell Gibbons, Dave Stone, MPSE

Assistant Sound Editors: Sonny Pettijohn, Nancy Barker

Effects Recording: Eric Potter, Ezra Dweck

Foley Supervisor: Aaron Glascock

Foley Editor: Solange Schwalbe

Foley Artists: John Roesch, Hilda Hodges

Foley Recording: Mary Jo Lang, Carolynn Tapp

Re-Recording Services Provided by Warner Hollywood

Re-Recording Mixers: Bob Litt, Elliot Tyson, Michael Herbick

Recordists: Marsha Sorce, Kevin Webb

Production Sound Mixer: Willie Burton

Additional production sound mixer: Richard Goodman

Score Recorded at Todd-AO and Signet Soundelux, Mixed at Signet

Original Score: Thomas Newman

Score Recorded and Mixed By: Dennis Sands

Music Editor: Bill Bernstein

mindful of advice I'd gotten from Dane Davis, who worked with electricity during *The Matrix*, I coerced Weddington sound effects librarian Steve Lee into babysitting me during my experiments. He kept a vigilant hand on the power mains cable. I used my field recording setup, which is 100 percent battery-driven (Neumann KM-140 pair, Schoeps CMC-5 pair, Cooper mic pre's, Sony D-10 PRO II DAT).

"Soon I was playing that thing like a Theremin, changing and modulating the distance between the two bare-ended cables coming off the transformer to produce a ripping, white-blue spark of varying intensity and timbre," he continues. "Perhaps the most interesting moments were when the cable ends were

The tight-knit sound crew on the Warner Bros. stage.

about six inches apart, you could hear invisible static ripping across the field, when that first visible spark is trying to decide if it's going to make the leap yet. This makes for a subtle, creepy tension before they throw the last switch for the execution.

"Of course, one of the first things many of us think of when the subject of old-tech electricity comes up is the beloved Tesla Coil. I went to visit Park Meek, a marvelous propmaker who specializes in classic, mad scientist-style laboratory stuff. The Tesla Coil delivered as promised, a raspier, rapid-static texture. Then Park showed me his Jacob's Ladder—it looks like a big rabbit-ears TV antenna, eight feet tall and powered by *four* of those old transformers like the one I had just recorded, wired in series. The 60,000-volt arc would travel up the ladder, ripping and flanging all the way. I placed my Neumann capsules on a tiny X/Y mount, with active cables leading to the rest of the mic's electronics in my recorder bag. This allowed me to get a stereo shot from the narrow space between the ladder's twin poles, and track the arc as it traveled from bottom to. Some really strange effects would happen when I would stand on a chair and gently blow the arc back downward with my breath and try to keep it dancing in place.

"Originally I had intended to rent some of these devices and record them 'properly' in the studio," he adds. "But I soon realized the beauty of the shop's acoustics—high ceiling, tiled floor and a lack of soft surfaces. This lent a cold, harsh atmosphere to the wider room shots of the sparks—quite suitable for the execution room, and keeping with Mark's goal of a realistic recording environment."

If the executions symbolize the brutal reality, then the healing scenes speak to the magic. John Coffey is a healer, not a killer. He cures Tom Hanks of a bladder infection, he saves the warden's wife and he fixes up the mouse, in a real Southern, laying-of-the-hands style. During those moments, swarms of insects leave his body—a physical manifestation of the healing—accompanied by a more ethereal track.

"In the healing scenes you see the lights glow, so we have some filaments vibrating," Lindemann says. "But I thought it would be interesting to record some actual sounds that people make who do sonic healings using their voices. I wanted to have some sense that spiritual energy is moving through the room, an affecting presence. So I merged those vocals in with the filaments." Ken Johnson and John Pospisil then developed the insect sounds, the grand exhale when the poison leaves Coffey's body. To embody the evil that was manifest in the insects, Johnson processed Nazi war rally "Sieg heils" to add subtext and color.

The healings are crucial to the story and to the structure. The Tom Hanks character, through flashbacks and visions, comes to understand the gentle power of Coffey and the truth of how the two little girls were murdered. During the flashback scenes (introduced with knife rips), the sound is intentionally disjointed and oddly juxtaposed, sometimes offering signals, mostly mirroring the confusion.

"The whole movie is about the murder of the two girls," Mangini says. "So I wanted to plant clues all through the movie leading up to the discovery of who killed them. I recorded my 7-year-old stepdaughter, Jordynn, and her friends in the back yard on the swings—giggles, happy children-at-play sounds. Eric [Lindeman] then manipulated girls' laughter and used it in a variety of ways for some of the magic moments, especially as it associates with their killer. For example, there's a key sequence near the end of the movie where the killer's putting them in a barn, and he goes, 'Shhh. You talk, I'll kill her.' We took that 'Shhh' and used it as a sonic element in some of the magic moments. There's two other flashback sequences where we used girls' laughter for lights exploding and flashes of white light, massaged in different ways. I think it will be fun when you go back and watch the DVD after reading this article and hear all the clues we planted. I thought it was effective, without overdoing it.

Recordists Marsha Sorce and Kevin Webb

"There's another sequence where there's a flashback of Farmer Detterick [the girls' father] going into a barn with a hammer," he continues. "We took a screen door and made that a hammer sound, then we took the hammer sound and turned it into a heartbeat sound, which leads into a pulsing sound—tying all these moments together. The movie opens with a slow-motion shot of Detterick and a posse trying to find the killer. Very surreal music and sound effects. In the production track, he opens his mouth and screams, 'Katie! Cora!' Rather than hear him speak, we took the little-girls' laughter and modulated it to fit his mouth. It's really creepy. But you won't know what it is until you see the movie a second time." ·

The Green Mile will not be an easy movie to watch. A death row drama with a touch of magic, just in time for the holidays. Reportedly, some viewers had to walk out of early temp screenings because of the execution scenes. Yet it came in with the highest ratings from card screenings that Warner Bros. had seen in years. Executives were seen weeping at the early screenings, according to some reports, and it has generated significant buzz since the first-looks last summer. Don't be at all surprised if more than one member of the team walks up to the stage on Oscar night.

Glossary of Terms

By Larry Blake

This glossary appeared originally in the March, April and June 1999 issues of Mix.

Note that when you see a word in SMALL CAPS, this means that it will be defined elsewhere in the glossary.

A-2, A-4, A-7 *See* VOICE OF THE THEATER.

AB REEL Term for a 23-minute or less (max 2,050 feet, including head and tail leaders) reel of film that is shipped to theaters and that may originally comprise two "1,000-foot" edit reels. Projection reel 1AB would have been reels 1 and 2 during editing and mixing. In the event that reels 1, 2 and 3 together add up to less than 2,050 feet, the first projection reel might be called 1ABC, although this is rare. Sometimes films are edited in AB reels, a practice that is becoming commonplace due to the reduction in number of 35mm mag film units, which are very cumbersome to deal with as 2,000-foot loads on editing benches.

This is not to be confused with AB-roll printing, in which the camera negative is cut in two strands, allowing for simple optical effects such as fades and dissolves to be made when making original-negative prints (*see* EK NEG) or INTERPOSITIVE. This process is not limited to two (A, B) rolls, but can be as high as desired. Thus, a camera negative cut in four strands would go up to a "D" roll.

ACADEMY CURVE/ACADEMY MONO The name of the standard mono optical track that has been around since the beginning of sound. Standards were not codified until 1938, although it has "improved" slightly over the years. The response is flat 100 to 1.6k Hz, and is down 7 dB at 40 Hz, 10 dB at 5 kHz and 18 dB at 8 kHz.

ACADEMY THEATER   The Samuel Goldwyn Theater at the Academy of Motion Pictures Arts and Sciences on Wilshire Blvd. in Beverly Hills. Contrary to popular belief, voting for the Best Sound Oscar doesn't take place as a result of Academy members having seen the nominated films there. (All nominated films are screened at the Goldwyn Theater during the month-or-so voting period subsequent to the announcement of that year's nominations in mid-February.)

A-CHAIN   The part of the reproduction system in a theater that contains the sound pickup (such as OPTICAL analog track reader or digital sound format), preamp, noise reduction and MATRIX DECODING (if applicable), and the main fader. The B-Chain comprises the crossovers, equalizers, amplifiers, speakers and room acoustics.

AC-3   Dolby Laboratories' low-bit-rate coding scheme that is used in its 5.1-channel DOLBY DIGITAL film and television formats.

ADR   Automated Dialog Recording. The act of recording another reading of a PRODUCTION TRACK in post-production. Usually the actor will be looking at the cut picture on a screen and will be hearing a series of beeps in a headphone giving a countdown to the beginning of the line. *See* LOOPING.

AIRLINE VERSION   A remixed (and possibly re-edited) version of a film removing curse words, sex and violence. Airlines are an even tougher "room" than the broadcast networks, and so a version that passes the airline censors will almost always "fly" on TV.

"ALL-DIGITAL"   An advertising claim used frequently in the '80s. Now considered obsolete and rude.

AMPEX   Former manufacturer of videotape recorders, analog tape recorders and magnetic tape products. Name is an acronym based on the founder's name: Alexander M. Poniatoff EXcellence.

ANSWER PRINT   Classically means the first *composite* print of a film, i.e., with final mixed track and timed picture. In many contracts the delivery of the answer print is specified because it means that post-production has ended and release printing can begin, although the release printing is usually done from an INTERNEGATIVE. Should always be distinguished in conversation and film labeling from a BLACK TRACK answer print, which contains no soundtrack.

ASPECT RATIO The shape that an image is intended to be shown in, most commonly expressed in width relative to a height unit of 1. Standard television screens are 1.33:1, standard U.S. theatrical films are 1.85:1. Ratios are also sometimes expressed as a multiple of 3—TVs being 4x3 and widescreen TVs being 16x9 (or 1.85:1).

A-TRACK The primary dialog track cut by the picture editor. The B, etc. tracks will just be used for overlaps.

A-TYPE The original Dolby NOISE REDUCTION process, introduced in 1966 for professional recording. A-Type splits a signal into four bands for processing, while B-Type noise reduction, introduced in 1968 for home use, only affects high-frequency hiss above 5 kHz.

AVID Nonlinear picture editing system.

BABY BOOM a) The nickname of the Dolby 70mm process that dedicates two of the six tracks on a 70mm print to low-frequency information below 200 Hz. No longer used due to the existence of a dedicated subwoofer track in digital release formats. b) Post-World War II period of vigorous sexual activity followed by frequent child births. Generally considered to end in 1963.

BACKGROUNDS Sound effects that sonically define the time and place of a location. Called "atmospheres" or "atmos" in the UK. *See also* ROOM TONE.

BAKE OFF Hollywood colloquialism for the meeting of the Sound Branch of the Academy of Motion Picture Arts and Sciences in which the members hear 10-minute clips of the seven films that have made the semifinals of the Best Sound Effects Editing award.

B-CHAIN *See* A-CHAIN.

BENCH Film sound slang for the editing table, which consists of rewinds handling reels of 35mm picture and MAG FILM, a sprocketed synchronizer that keeps the reels in sync (in addition to providing a count) and a "squawk box," which is used to hear the tracks played back from heads mounted on the synchronizer.

BINKY Film sound slang for a mixing TOP SHEET.

BLACK-TRACK PRINT   Silent ANSWER PRINT of a film, made from the original camera negative. The first answer prints are usually "black track," in order to proceed with the color timing even while post-production sound is not finished.

BROOM   To not use a sound during a mix. "Site brooming" is when a director rejects a whole group of effects, often causing days of work to go down the drain.

BOOM   a) The pole that holds the microphone when recording production sound. b) Another outmoded name for the channel containing low-frequency enhancement. *See also* BABY BOOM.

BTSC   Broadcast Television Systems Committee. The FCC committee that decided upon the MTS standards for stereo television sound in the United States.

BUZZ TRACK   Alignment film used to set the lateral alignment of the "slit" in photographic (optical) sound reproduction systems. There are two different frequency tones

C.A.S.   Cinema Audio Society. Los Angeles-based organization of film and television recording personnel; founded in 1966.

CAT 43   The Dolby Laboratories "single-ended" NOISE REDUCTION device that turns a Cat 22 Dolby A-Type noise reduction module into a 4-band "noise fighter." The precise frequencies of the bands are optimized for production sound problems and differ from those used in standard noise reduction applications. In 1991 Dolby formally introduced the SR-based 2-band version called the Cat 430.

CHANNEL   A complete, self-sufficient recording setup. A "production channel" would include a recorder, mixer, microphones, headsets, etc. A "transfer channel" would include a 1/4-inch tape deck, a 35mm mag recorder, a RESOLVER and a monitoring system.

CHAIN   The group of equipment (frequently comprising DIP FILTER, GRAPHIC EQ, de-esser and compressor) that a re-recording mixer will have patched together in series, either inserted in a channel, on a console bus or in a REASSIGN buss. *See* IRON.

CINEMA DIGITAL SOUND The name of the theatrical reproduction format introduced by Optical Radiation Corporation, a division of Kodak, in 1990 (for the film *Dick Tracy*) for digital sound on 35mm or 70mm prints. The format lasted two years and is now obsolete.

CINEMASCOPE WIDESCREEN camera system developed by Twentieth Century Fox, which was responsible for popularizing the ANAMORPHIC format.

CINERAMA Widescreen system comprising three cameras/projectors running in interlock with 7-track MAG FILM.

COMOPT Laboratory term for "composite optical print."

COMMAG Laboratory term for "composite magnetic print."

COMTEK Salt Lake City-based company that makes portable wireless transmitters and receivers. "Comteks" have become generically used for wireless headphone feeds to directors and for wireless timecode feeds to slates.

CONFORM a) To re-edit sound elements to match a new version of the picture edit. b) To assemble sound elements (from their original sources) to match their location in a picture edit, often with the assistance of an Edit Decision List supplied in a computer-readable file.

CONTAINER Industry slang for a peak limiter designed specifically for controlling the dynamics of program material during SVA (*op cit.*) printmastering.

CPS Acronym for "cycles per second," cycles being the obsolete term for what is now referred to as Hertz (Hz).

CROSS-MOD Short for "cross-modulation test," which is a means of determining correct exposure on a TRACK NEGATIVE to result in minimum distortion on a positive print. Tests are conducted to determine the relationship of specific optical cameras to specific laboratories.

C-TYPE *See* SPECTRAL RECORDING.

CUE SHEET A track sheet for mixing that gives locations of sounds on a track-by-track basis, either in film footages or in timecode numbers. *See also* BINKY.

CUT EFFECTS   Sound effects that are PULLed from a sound library and edited; usually as opposed to FOLEY, which is recorded specifically for each film.

DAILIES   Uncut footage shot each day during production. If picture editing is on film, with picture and synchronized MAG FILM, those elements when edited together become the WORKPRINT and WORKTRACK.

DBX   NOISE REDUCTION system for analog recording. Type I is used for professional applications, while Type II was optimized for lower-speed consumer use. The name, properly spelled as dbx, referring to founder David Blackmer.

DECODING/ENCODING   In audio, encoding refers to the altering of a signal prior to its being recorded or transmitted, with decoding during playback/reception resulting in the original signal. In motion-picture sound this can have one of two meanings: *Matrix* encoding/decoding, used in 35mm DOLBY STEREO, encodes four channels into two in the studio, with the resulting optical print decoded from two tracks into four channels at the theater. For an explanation of encoding/decoding as they pertain to noise reduction, *see* NOISE REDUCTION.

DIGITAL DUBBERS   Film industry name for multitrack (usually eight channels per unit) digital recorders that use removable hard drives or magneto-optical drives as the recording medium. The term is partly a misnomer since previous film sound terminology had used "dubber" to distinguish from "recorder."

DIP FILTER   Parametric equalizer with an extremely narrow bandwidth ("Q") that is designed to remove noises, such as those from a camera or a light, whose offending frequency range is very narrow.

DIRECT POSITIVE   A PHOTOGRAPHIC SOUND recording that, when processed, results in a track that can be played and edited. A now-obsolete process.

DISCRETE   Refers to a 1:1 relationship of recorded tracks on a print and the resulting number of speaker channels. For example, a 4-track magnetic print will be reproduced through four channels—left-center-right-surround—in the theater. Obviously, the surround track/channel has more than one speaker. Discrete playback is often contrasted with matrix DECODING/ENCODING.

DISCRETE 6-TRACK   Traditionally means the five-speakers-behind-the-screen system made popular by the TODD-AO 70mm process (although it was first used for CINERAMA). In the current vernacular, though, discrete 6-track sometimes means six non-matrixed tracks, assigned left, center, right, left-rear, right-rear, and subwoofer.

DLT   Digital Linear Tape. Tape-based computer backup format developed by Quantum Laboratories.

DME   Dialog, Music, sound Effects. The three basic food groups of film soundtracks. Originally referred to the 35mm 3-track master mix of ACADEMY MONO films.

DOLBY DIGITAL   The 5.1-channel digital format created by Dolby Laboratories. In current usage applies both to the company's 35mm theatrical format (which contains the data printed optically between the sprocket holes) and its video formats (such as DVD, laserdisc, and DTV). First used in 1992 for *Batman Returns*.

DOLBY PRO-LOGIC   The Dolby Laboratories trademark used for home surround decoding devices that meet more stringent standards, and offer such features as band-limited pink noise for aligning channel balance, plus a separate, matrix-derived center-channel output.

DOLBY, RAY M.   The founder and sole owner of San Francisco-based Dolby Laboratories.

DOLBY STEREO   Many meanings! In the broadest and most common sense, the trademark that appears on movie prints, advertisements and posters means that a given film has been released in prints that employ Dolby A-Type NOISE REDUCTION encoding.

There are two tracks on 35mm *stereo* optical prints, referred to as LT and RT, which are matrix-encoded to contain four channels of information. The 4:2 ENCODING is done during the PRINT MASTERING, with the 2:4 DECODING occurring at the theater. *See also* ULTRA-STEREO.

In their standard form, Dolby Stereo 35mm prints are encoded with A-Type noise reduction. Beginning in 1987, Dolby Laboratories has made its SR (*see* SPECTRAL RECORDING) process available on 35mm stereo optical prints, with the advantage of greatly reduced optical noise and increased low- and high-frequency headroom.

All of the stereo optical prints—Dolby Stereo (A-TYPE), Dolby SR and Ultra Stereo—occupy the same area as standard mono optical prints and are capable of mono-compatible performance. The exact degree of mono-compatibility is mix-dependent.

Dolby Stereo on 70mm usually means four DISCRETE primary channels (left, center, right, surround), with the left-center and right-center tracks dedicated to "boom" information below 200 Hz. The four primary tracks are normally A-Type encoded, although selected films since 1987 have utilized SR encoding on 70mm prints.

The first Dolby Stereo film was *Lisztomania*. The first Dolby 70mm BABY BOOM film was *Star Wars* in 1977.

DOLBY SURROUND
The Dolby Laboratories trademark used for surround-encoded material on nonfilm uses such as videocassettes, videodiscs and television broadcasts. Also, for home surround decoding devices that do not have matrixed center-speaker output.

DOLBY SURROUND EX
The digital release format developed by Dolby Laboratories and THX for use in the upcoming *Star Wars Episode I: The Phantom Menace*. Three surround tracks are derived by matrix-encoding them into the two previously existing surround tracks. Should not be referred to as a 6.1-channel format.

"DOLBY WAS JUST HERE"
Standard answer by projectionists to the question, "When was the last time this theater was aligned?"

DOUBLE SYSTEM
Projecting a film with the picture, on 35mm film, in interlock with the soundtrack, most commonly on MAG FILM.

DOBLY
The system that would have saved Spinal Tap's *Smell the Glove* album from oblivion.

DOWNMIX
A mix derived from a multichannel (usually 5.1) source to create a compatible version of fewer channels. Common use today occurs in consumer Dolby Digital products to play back a 5.1-channel DVD either via Dolby Pro-Logic decoding or in standard two-channel stereo (for headphone listening). In those instances, an LT-RT or an LO-RO, respectively, are the result.

DS4 The name of the original Dolby Laboratories recording/monitoring unit used by re-recording stages during a DOLBY STEREO mix. Prior to the 2-track PRINT MASTER, the unit is used for 4:2:4 monitoring purposes, encoding a 4-channel composite mix into two tracks and decoding it back into four channels.

Later variations in the Dolby product line include the SEU4 and SDU4 units, which offer, respectively, the ability to encode and decode print masters, although without either the CONTAINER or the optical track simulation featured in the DS4. (A SPU4 unit is available to add those capabilities to studios that have SEU4/SDU4 units.) The DS10 contains a magneto-optical recorder for theatrical DOLBY DIGITAL mixes. It also records the LT-RT SR-encoded print master.

Neither the DS4, DS10 or SPU4 can be purchased, rented or leased; their use is free for use on films that have paid the appropriate license and trademark agreements.

DTS The 5.1-channel system developed by Digital Theater Systems of Westlake Village, Calif., that utilizes a CD-ROM interlocked to a 35mm or 70mm print with timecode. Audio on the CD-ROM utilizes apt-X 100 low-bit-rate coding. First used in 1993 for *Jurassic Park. See also* 70MM.

DTS STEREO The SVA encoding process developed by Digital Theater Systems.

DUB In the most general sense, to dub is to copy, although in film sound vernacular it has acquired many similar shadings. It can refer to the act of replacing dialog (usually via the ADR process), either in the original language or in a foreign language. "Dubbing" is also the common name for RE-RECORDING, at least insofar as Hollywood and New York are concerned.

DUB MASTERS *See* FINAL MIX.

DUBBER Film sound term for a playback-only MAG machine. *See* DIGITAL DUBBER.

DUBBING EDITOR The term for a SUPERVISING SOUND EDITOR in the U.K.

DUO-BILATERAL The technical term for the variable-area photographic soundtrack format used for almost all 35mm mono and stereo soundtracks.

EARWIG   Small earpiece used to give actors an audio reference (frequently a guide music track) so that their live audio, such as singing or music playing, can be recorded live. *See also* THUMPER.

EDGECODE   Inked numbers applied outside the sprocket holes on film prints and MAG FILM, used for synchronization reference. *See* ACMADE.

85   The sound pressure level when pink noise is sent through one speaker (left, center or right) at 0 VU bus level, which is the equivalent of –20 dBfs in digital recording. (Measurement is at the console, with an SPL meter set to C weighting and slow response.)

88   The sound pressure level for DOLBY STEREO SR films. If a film has been monitored at 85 during the final mix, the STEMS will be lowered 3 dB when making an SR LT-RT printmaster to accommodate for the increased monitor level.

EK NEG   Laboratory colloquialism for "original camera negative"; used in film vernacular to describe a release print made from the original negative. "EK" stands for "Eastman Kodak," although the term is used without regard to a film having been shot on Eastman stock. Also called "OCN."

11   The highest number that can be found silk-screened on electric guitars and guitar amplifiers.

ENCODING/DECODING   In audio, encoding refers to the altering of a signal prior to its being recorded or transmitted, with decoding during playback/reception resulting in the best possible reproduction of the original signal considering the limitations of the recording or transmission medium. In motion-picture sound this can have one of two meanings: Matrix encoding/decoding, used in 35mm DOLBY STEREO, encodes four channels into two in the studio, with the resulting optical print decoded from two tracks into four channels at the theater. For an explanation of encoding/decoding as they pertain to noise reduction, *see* NOISE REDUCTION.

EQUALIZATION, ROOM   The process in which a speaker system is aligned by playing PINK NOISE into a room and adjusting an equalizer to obtain the selected response when viewed by an RTA. Common room EQ utilizes 1/3-octave controls, with 31 knobs spaced across the audible frequency range, although parametric equalizers are also used. Most room equalizers also have an overall "bass" and "treble" adjustment.

50% LEVEL   The standard reference level for optical sound recordings that corresponds to the width of the track at 50% modulation, or 6 dB below clipping. In practice, there is about 2 dB of additional headroom available, assuming a perfectly aligned projector sound head.

FILL   The sound between words in a PRODUCTION TRACK that is used both to replace undesirable noises on the track and to create "handles" extending the track at the beginning and end. Handles enable the re-recording mixer to crossfade smoothly between shots with differing background tones. *See also* ROOM TONE.

FILL LEADER   The film that is inserted into UNITS of MAG FILM in order to keep synchronization during silent sections. Fill leader is usually made up of recycled RELEASE PRINTS.

FILM FOOTAGE   There are 16 frames per foot of a standard 35mm film image (running vertically through the camera and projector), each lasting four sprocket holes (perforations or "perfs"). At the standard rate of 24 frames per second, film runs at 90 feet per minute, or 18 inches per second.

FINAL MIX   The act of mixing the sound for a motion picture (or television show) into separate dialog, music and sound effects STEMS, which, combined and played at equal level through the monitor, represent the finished soundtrack. In a stereo film (or surround-encoded TV), it is most common to record the dialog, music and sound effects stems on three pieces of 4- or 6-track magnetic film, utilizing Dolby SR NOISE REDUCTION. (The choice of which noise reduction system is used at this stage—SR, A-TYPE, or even DBX—has no relation to what PRINT MASTERS might be made.) Final mixes are also frequently recorded on analog or digital MULTITRACK tape or on DIGITAL DUBBERS.

These stems, also known as "dub masters," are then used to create the PRINT MASTERS, the M&E, the mono mix and possibly even an AIRLINE VERSION.

The exact format and track layout of the stems is up to the post-production sound crew; if a multitrack or digital dubber is used, then additional tracks are opened up at no additional cost and little trouble. With these formats it is easier to record an additional set of stems, keeping, for example, the FOLEY, the background sound effects, a laugh or crowd track, or special creature voices separate, to allow for greater flexibility in the final mix, during print mastering and the M&E mix.

If the project is a non-surround-encoded stereo television show, then the stems might be in standard 2-track stereo format, although this is not recommended due to the use of 5.1-channel stereo in Digital Television. And, of course, mono films only require from three to six tracks, usually on the same piece of film or tape.

5.1 Stereo format utilizing three primary channels (left, center, right), two surround channels (left surround, right surround) and a subwoofer channel, which is the ".1" channel because it uses approximately one-tenth of the bandwidth of a full-frequency channel. Pronounced "five point one."

FLAT With respect to film projection, refers to non-ANAMORPHIC lenses. In the U.S. it's considered synonymous with 1.85:1 widescreen.

FM SYNC The 13.5kHz frequency-modulated sync pulse recorded on NAGRA IV-S recorders.

FOLEY Sound effects recorded in synchronization to edited picture in post-production. Named after Jack Foley, who was the head of the sound effects department at Universal Studios for many years. Contrary to popular myth, he did not invent the process. Foley is often expressed as "Foleys" in New York. Likewise, what is called the "cloth" track on the West Coast is referred to as "rustle" back East.

FOREIGN VERSION *See* M&E.

4+2 Four Plus Two. Film sound slang for a 6-track element (usually MAG FILM) that contains a 4-track M&E, one track of material which may or may not be needed in a foreign-language mix, and one track of the original dialog as a reference.

4:2:4   Four Two Four. Film sound slang for the act of monitoring a mix through matrix encoding (4:2) and decoding (2:4). This means that the effect of the matrix encoding will be heard (which they would not be when monitoring DISCRETE), and adjustments can be made accordingly.

FOX HOLES   Small perforations on 35mm release prints that allowed for the addition of MAG STRIPE for the CINEMASCOPE process, which was developed by Twentieth Century Fox. Whereas one had to be careful in the old days to ensure that sprockets that pulled the film through the projector could accommodate Fox holes (standard sprockets were too big and would tear them), all sprocket mechanisms today can handle Fox-hole prints with no problem. (This is ironic since the process has been used on less than a dozen films since the coming of DOLBY STEREO in 1975.)

FULLCOAT   *See* MAG FILM.

GAFFER   a) On a film set, the head electrician; since the early 1990s the term "Chief Lighting Technician" has been more common. b) In general film industry usage, the head of a crew, as in "gaffing mixer" to note the re-recording mixer in charge. Thus, "to gaff a mix." An older Hollywood phrase for the gaffing mixer was the "gunner."

GINK   Hollywood film sound vernacular for "to screw up."

GNAT'S NUT   Distaff mixer equivalent of RCH (*op cit*).

GRAPHIC EQ   Multiband equalizer utilizing slide pots for each band, with the resulting boost or cut forming a "graphic" representation of the sound. Generally considered to have been invented by Fred Wilson of the Samuel Goldwyn Studios sound department.

HANG   Film sound slang for the act of playing back a given element during a mix, as in, "We won't premix the FOLEY cloth but will hang it at the final mix instead."

HOT HOLE   Slang for the projector gate itself, where the picture start mark is threaded up at the beginning of a session.

HX   Headroom eXtension. The DOLBY LABORATORIES process used during recording only; it varies the bias current according to program needs. Now superseded by HX-Pro.

IN-BAND GAIN The standard for adjusting subwoofer response, such that the subwoofer sound pressure level, within its operating range, is louder than a full-range screen speaker in the same range. All of today's digital theatrical formats use 10 dB of in-band gain.

INTERNEGATIVE Laboratory film element that is made from an INTERPOSITIVE and is used to make RELEASE PRINTS not only at high speed (because the color is balanced and there are little or no splices to worry about), but more importantly because the EK NEG is protected.

INTERPOSITIVE Laboratory film elements made from the original camera negative in preparation either to make an INTERNEGATIVE or to be used in a TELECINE machine to transfer the film image to tape. (Unless they are the only extant elements of a film, standard RELEASE PRINTS are never used for video transfers.) Also known as an IP, an interpositive contains shot-to-shot color correction so that internegatives can be made with no further color adjustments, although further adjustment is always necessary when doing film-to-tape mastering. If the camera negative was cut in AB ROLLS, then the IP can incorporate first-generation fades and dissolves.

IRON Pejorative term for "equipment" in the context of its effect on sound quality: "He has so much iron in his CHAIN it's a wonder that we can distinguish between men and women on his dialog PREMIX."

ITC Intermittent Traffic Control. Film production term for the presence of traffic control during location shooting; very helpful for quality production sound recording.

KEY NUMBERS Numbers on the side of film stock created during film manufacture that are visible on the developed negative and positive prints made therefrom.

KIRSCH Film sound slang (popularized in Northern California) for when a director will request a change in the sound and will give his or her approval to what in fact was no change at all (either accidentally or deliberately) on the part of the mixers. Variants such as a "self-inflicted kirsch" in which the mixer will adjust a knob without it being in the signal path or will listen for a change while the PEC/DIRECT paddles are in playback (as opposed to input).

LAYBACK A transfer of a mix (usually a PRINT MASTER) to a video master.

LCRS Designates a recording in which four tracks are to be assigned, respectively, to the left-center-right-surround speaker channels. Thus, other variants such as LCRC, when the fourth track is to be assigned to the center, or even CCCC, as in a center-channel dialog PREMIX.

LEADER The head leader, at the beginning of each reel of a film, comprises a thread-up section that contains information about the reel's content (such as film title, reel number, etc.). The countdown section begins with the Picture Start frame, which is considered the "start mark," followed by a numbered rundown, totaling 12 feet or 8 seconds. The last number is two seconds (three feet) before the beginning of the active picture ("first frame of picture").

The Academy leader contains one number per foot following the Picture Start, with 11, 10, etc., leader to three. As projected, numbers are upside down. The SMPTE Universal leader is designed to be used primarily for video uses and features a sweep hand counting down from eight seconds.

LFE Low Frequency Effects. The low-frequency track assigned to the subwoofer in theatrical stereo formats. For home video formats, the subwoofer will frequently contain low-frequency information from the main channels in addition to the original LFE track.

LFOP Last Frame of Picture. Film industry acronym for the length of a given reel. In its standard meaning includes the head LEADER up to and including the last frame of the reel. Because it is standard to start counting with the "Picture Start" frame of the leader as 0000+00 (zero feet and zero frames), the actual running time of a reel can be calculated by subtracting 11 feet and 15 frames to account for the 12-foot, 8-second leader. The TWO-POP is at 0009+00 The first frame of picture of a reel is at 0012+00. Sometimes also referred to as LFOA, for "action."

LIGHTWORKS A nonlinear picture editing system.

LITTLE DIPPER Nickname of the popular DIP FILTER previously manufactured by UREI (Model 565).

LITTLE OLD LADIES WITH UMBRELLAS Colloquial expression in the film sound community for how loud a film can be before movie patrons will complain. Therefore, the top end of the dynamic range available to mixers is defined not necessarily with regard to a theater's ability to reproduce a mix. *See also* POPCORN NOISE.

LOOPING　The process of post-production dialog replacement using identical-length loops of picture, guide track and record track. The line to be replaced would thus repeat over and over, and the actor would go for a take when they were ready. Also referred to as "virgin looping," when recording onto a blank piece of mag film. When optical sound was used, the recordings were made sequentially on a roll and later manually synched to picture.

Although this process is not used these days (*see* ADR), the act of replacing dialog is still often referred to as "looping."

LO-RO　Left only-Right only. Indicates a standard left-right stereo signal that has been DOWNMIXED from a DISCRETE digital signal (such as a DOLBY DIGITAL 5.1). Because the surround information has been incorporated into the signal without matrix encoding, a Lo-Ro cannot be decoded back into the surround format.

LT-RT　Left total-Right total, *not* Left track-Right track. Indicates the presence of matrix encoding of four channels on a 2-track stereo master.

MAG FILM　Short for "sprocketed magnetic film." Can have either an acetate or polyester base, and from one to six tracks, depending upon the head stack used. Three-track head gaps are 200 mils wide, the equal of half-inch, 2-track tape; 35mm 4-track is 150 mils wide, and 6-track is 100 mils wide, the equivalent of 8-track, 1-inch or 16-track, 2-inch. The oxide coating is very thick, varying from 3 to 5 mils.

There is also "stripe," which has two magnetic stripes on a base of clear film. One stripe is large and contains a single track of audio (in the same size and location as track one of a 3-track), while the other stripe is smaller and exists only to make the film pack evenly when wound together, hence the term "balance stripe." The balance stripe is sometimes used to record timecode from 1/4-inch or DAT timecoded production masters.

Fullcoat is mag film that is covered edge-to-edge by the magnetic oxide.

MAG STRIPE PRINT　A 35mm or 70mm print with magnetic oxide stripes painted lengthwise down both sides of film on either side of the perforations. These formats are now obsolete.

M&E Music and Effects. Standard motion picture practice today entails creating a minus-original-dialog element that can be used to create a foreign-language mix by adding only the newly recorded foreign-language dialog. This requires that all sound effects that are otherwise included in the dialog stem be copied across to this element. If these production effects are not clear of dialog, then they must be replaced either by FOLEY or by CUT EFFECTS. Once the effects are "complete," the track is said to be "filled"; thus, contracts specify "music and filled effects." Also known as the "international" version.

MATRIX *See* DECODING/ENCODING.

MIL Short for one-thousandth of an inch. The width of standard 35mm single-stripe and 3-track head gaps are 200 mils, or 1/5-inch. Mils are a good increment to deal with for films since there are 999 of them between the sprockets.

MOS Scene shot silent, i.e., without sound rolling. Derives from "mit out sound," as in "ve vill shoot mit out sound," allegedly spoken by a director of Germanic descent to his Hollywood crew. Pronounced "m-o-s."

MOVIOLA The upright film editing machine that was the standard for picture editing until the '70s, when it was replaced (although not entirely) by flatbed editors. Remained the standard for sound editing until the early '90s, when it was gradually replaced by digital audio workstations.

M.P.S.E. Motion Picture Sound Editors. Los Angeles-based honorary organization of film and television sound editors; founded in 1965. Every spring the MPSE gives out its Golden Reel awards at its annual banquet.

MTS Multichannel Television Sound.

MUFEX *See* M&E.

MULTITRACK	A non-sprocketed tape recorder (analog or digital) that records and plays back eight or more tracks. The most common analog format is 24 tracks on 2-inch tape, frequently with some form of NOISE REDUCTION. The digital world is shared between the DASH (Digital Audio Stationary Head) format, with 1/2-inch tape recording either 24 or 48 tracks, and the PD (ProDigital) format, recording 32 tracks on 1-inch tape. Modular digital multitracks use video cassettes to store 8 to 12 tracks of audio. Locking together multiple transports can provide up to 128 tracks in a standard configuration.
MUSIC CUE SHEET	Not a standard CUE SHEET but instead a list of music used in a film, along with its type of usage (source, background instrumental, visual vocal, etc.).
MUT	MakeUp Table. The motor-driven BENCH designed to load and rewind film. In the acronym form usually refers to the setup that drives a large reel of MAG FILM during a DOUBLE SYSTEM preview screening.
NAGRA	The name of the line of professional 1/4-inch tape analog and digital recorders manufactured by Kudelski S.A. of Switzerland. Their battery-operated portable analog recorders, especially the 4.2 mono and IV-S stereo models, have been the standard of the motion picture industry for over 30 years. Nagra means "recorded" in Polish, founder Stefan Kudelski's native tongue. Use of a stereo Nagra on location is almost always to record two separate tracks simultaneously, and does *not* usually mean a stereophonic recording.
NAGRAMASTER	Equalization curve developed by Nagra which uses high-frequency boost during recording and de-emphasis during playback to increase the signal-to-noise ratio at 15 ips.
NEOPILOT	The sync pulse system used in Nagra mono recorders (such as the 4.2), recording the sync pulse (usually 50 or 60 Hz) twice, out of phase with each other. The sync signal will not be heard when played back on a full-track mono head.
NOISE REDUCTION	In audio, recording a signal onto tape or film utilizing a device that will modify the signal before recording it (encoding), and then perform the opposite modification (decoding) during playback, the purpose being to avoid the noise inherent in the transmission medium.

The best-known noise reduction processes are Dolby Laboratories' A-Type, B-Type, C-Type, S-Type and SPECTRAL RECORDING; DBX Type I and Type II; and telecom Cd4.

None of the above processes removes noise already present in a recording.

NORVALIZING Hollywood slang for the act of playing a sound effect at a lower level in a vain attempt to hide the fact that it is not in sync.

N.T. AUDIO Santa Monica, Calif.-based sound facility which is noted for its half-speed mastering of optical soundtracks.

1:1 One to one. In standard usage, a copy of the edited WORKTRACK onto another roll of STRIPE so that sound editors and mixers working on a film will have access to the worktrack. In general, though, it stands for any single-track-to-single-track identical copy, and thus has variants such as 3:3, 4:4, etc.

OPTICAL TRACK The analog sound recording medium on film which utilizes, in its classic form, an exciter lamp focused through a narrow slit onto a photocell. The track area on a 35mm print takes up a total width of 100 MILS, which being one-tenth the space between the sprocket holes, displaces the centerline of the image on the film 50 mils. Because the Academy of Motion Picture Arts and Sciences codified this standard back in the late '20s, this has become known as the Academy centerline.

ORC *See* CINEMA DIGITAL SOUND.

PADDLES *See* PEC/DIRECT.

PDL Projectionist Dummy Loader. Union terminology for person in a film re-recording facility who functions both as projectionist and as a machine room operator.

PEC/DIRECT In film re-recording, the act of switching between playback from the recorder (either off the play or record heads) and the console bus. "PEC" stands for photoelectric cell, and originates from when monitoring off optical photoelectric cell was as close as you could get to "playback."

PFX Production effects, i.e., sound effects from the PRODUCTION TRACK, kept separate during dialog editing and PREMIXING for ease of integration into the M&E.

PINK NOISE	Full-frequency noise, consisting of equal energy per logarithmic units of bandwidth (such as octave or 1/3-octave), used to align the frequency response of tape recorders and speaker systems. Pink noise can be thought of as (and indeed almost always is) filtered white noise, which contains equal energy per linear unit of bandwidth. The high end on white noise is "tipped up" because there are "more" frequencies between octave and third-octave divisions.
PIRATE SHIP	To make a copy of material for one's library. Commonly used to refer to making a copy of good sound effects recorded in production, thus the order to "pull up the pirate ship" and to make sure that those recordings will be available after the film is finished and the masters are sent away.
PLATTER PROJECTION	*See* PROJECTION.
"POP A TRACK"	The act of aligning a TWO-POP exactly nine feet from the START MARK, either on MAG FILM or a BENCH, or in a digital audio workstation.
POPCORN NOISE	Colloquial expression in the film sound community for the factors (such as popcorn chewing, air conditioning noise, and bleed from adjacent theaters) in a motion picture theater that influence the low end of the dynamic range, and how soft a sound will "read" in the real world. *See also* LITTLE OLD LADIES WITH UMBRELLAS.
POST-SYNCHRONIZATION	Term used on the Continent and in the UK for ADR, *op cit.*
PRE-LAY	Usually stands for the act of editing sound onto a multitrack. This writer, for one, finds this term stupid and meaningless (not to mention demeaning), as it seems to try to make something else out of what is simply "multitrack editing."
PREMIX	The act of mixing edited sound elements (either dialog, music or sound effects) so that the FINAL MIX can be accomplished with less work involving level, equalization, effects or panning. With sound effects and music, there will also be a substantial reduction in the number of tracks, as in premixing 24 tracks into a 4-track LCRS premix. Dialog premixing often does not actually reduce the number of tracks that will go to the final mix, but instead just copies a cut track across with careful equalization and fader moves.

PREVIEW CODES EDGECODING of edited WORKPRINT (or dupes made therefrom) and sound elements to create a new reference for a given version of the film. When the film is subsequently re-edited, the process of CONFORMING multiple tracks can be sped up greatly.

PRINT MASTER The final, composite (dialog, music and sound effects recorded together) mix of a film that can be transferred directly to a TRACK NEGATIVE or a MAG STRIPE print with no further changes in level or equalization. If noise reduction is used on a print master, it most often matches that of the final print format, and thus can be transferred STRETCHED to the MAG STRIPE PRINT or TRACK NEGATIVE. In the case of a stereo optical film, the print master contains two tracks, LT and RT, that are transferred directly to an optical sound negative.

The soundtrack of a DISCRETE 35mm 4-track or 70mm 6-track mag print will be recorded from a 4- or 6-track printing master in a real-time transfer.

PRODUCTION TRACK The track recorded synchronously during shooting. In film it's almost always on 1/4-inch tape or R-DAT digital cassette. *See also* WILD TRACK.

PROJECTION In most commercial movie theaters, all reels are joined together on a platter to form one continuous strip of film through one projector. In screening rooms equipped with two projectors, each reel is kept separate, and the projectionist will manually start the incoming projector when he sees "changeover" dots in the upper right corner of the screen. This first set of dots is the "motor cue," with a second set of dots (a second before the end of the outgoing reel) indicating to switch over the picture and sound to the next reel.

You can have DOUBLE SYSTEM or composite projection with both platter and changeover techniques. Movie previews are often conducted in commercial theaters, with the 35mm WORKPRINT "built up" on a platter, and the 35mm mag TEMP DUB on a MUT.

PULL Colloquial term for adding another recorder to a system. Also describes the act of deciding which sound effects from a library will be used in a scene. *See also* SPOT.

QUAD TRACK TRACK NEGATIVE, and release print made therefrom, which contains all three digital sound formats (DOLBY DIGITAL, DTS and SDDS) plus a standard SVA analog track.

RCH Smallest deflection visible in a standard VU meter; less than a needle-width. *See also* GNAT'S NUT.

REASSIGN Output bus designed for internal re-routing and combining within the console.

RECORDIST To some, a "sound recordist" is the person who records sound during shooting. This usage is more popular in the UK and on the Continent than in the U.S., where "production mixer" is more common. In U.S. re-recording parlance, the recordist is the person in the machine room who is in charge of aligning and loading the recorders and playback DUBBERS.

REEL For information on how reels of film are counted in motion pictures, *see* AB REEL and FILM FOOTAGE.

REGROUP The transfer procedure in which material is copied from one medium (most often multiple UNITs of MAG FILM) to another in order to facilitate RE-RECORDING. For example, a facility might have only five playback DUBBERs on a re-recording stage, and they might transfer 20 units of mag film to a piece of 24-track tape in four passes in order to be able to hear all 20 tracks simultaneously.

RELEASE PRINT A copy of a motion picture made from an INTERNEGATIVE and TRACK NEGATIVE.

RE-RECORDING Also known as DUBBING, the process in which dialog, music and sound effects are mixed to picture.

RESOLVER Device that governs the speed of audio machines with reference to either a given recording or a common, known reference, such as a crystal or AC line frequency. A resolved transfer ensures that material will always be transferred at the same speed, and in the case of motion pictures, will be in sync with picture.

ROOM TONE The sound present in any production recording between the words. Also known as "fill." Should not be confused (during post-production) with background sound effects.

RTA Real-time analyzer. Audio measuring equipment used to view the whole audio spectrum simultaneously, as opposed to the voltage of a specific frequency. Typically, the display resolution is 1/3-octave.

RUNNING MASTER   *See* PRINT MASTER.

'SCOPE   Film industry slang for ANAMORPHIC prints or lenses. Originally an abbreviation of CINEMASCOPE, *op cit.*

SDDS   Sony Dynamic Digital Sound. Digital film format that utilizes in its complete form five screen channels. The optical digital information is printed outside the sprocket holes on the print. First used in its final format in 1994 for *City Slickers II.*

SDU4   *See* DS4.

SENSURROUND   The now-obsolete low-frequency enhancement system for motion picture exhibition developed by Universal Studios in 1973 for *Earthquake.* The first film simply triggered a noise generator during the earthquake sequences, although later versions of Sensurround did record very low-frequency information on the print.

SEPMAG   "Separate mag": Laboratory terminology for a print whose track is on a separate roll of mag film to be run in interlock with the picture. Same as DOUBLE SYSTEM.

70MM   The motion picture exhibition format that contains 6-track magnetic sound. In use primarily from 1955 to 1971, 70mm films usually made use of camera equipment manufactured by TODD-AO and Panavision. The camera negative was 65mm wide, with the additional 5mm outside the sprocket holes used for the magnetic stripes on RELEASE PRINTS.

Almost all films released in 70mm from 1971-1992 were originally photographed in 35mm and then blown up primarily for the 6-track magnetic sound. With 6-track digital sound now available in 35mm, there is no need to do a blow-up for sound quality, and in fact almost all newly manufactured 70mm prints in the U.S. have no magnetic track, but instead use the DTS system in the form of two players (one as a backup) in conjunction with a wide timecode track outside of the perforations.

The image, in its widest and standard form, has an ASPECT RATIO of 2.20:1, which is *narrower* than the 2.40:1 ANAMORPHIC 35mm format that is the source of many 70mm prints. However, when FLAT 1.85:1 films are blown up to 70mm, they usually retain their original aspect ratio, with black borders on the side.

The IMAX/OMNIMAX special venue format also uses 70mm film, although it runs horizontally through the camera/projector, and each frame is 15 "perfs" long, as opposed to the standard five perfs. Sound is always double-system, utilizing mag film or custom digital formats.

"SHOOT"   Film sound slang for recording. Derives from the previous use of OPTICAL SOUND in all film sound recording.

SIMULDAT   A DAT recording made during TELECINE in which the production audio is transferred to a DAT whose timecode matches that of the videotape.

SINGLE SYSTEM   The act of shooting film or video in which the audio is recorded on the same medium as the image. (Video is by definition single-system, although it can also be DOUBLE SYSTEM if a separate recorder is used.)

SKYWALKER SOUND   The post-production sound company at George Lucas' Skywalker Ranch in Nicasio, Calif., approximately one hour north of San Francisco.

SMALL-ROOM X CURVE   *See* X CURVE.

SMART SLATE   Timecode slate that contains a timecode generator. A "dumb" slate must be fed timecode constantly, either hard-wired or via a wireless transmitter. It is a misnomer to refer to all timecode slates as "smart slates."

SMPTE CURVE   Reproduce equalization curve standard in the U.S. for 35mm mag film.

SMPTE LEADER   *See* LEADER.

SOUND DESIGNER   In its most common usage, the person who creates special sound effects for films. In its original and perhaps most proper usage, the person responsible for the overall sound of the film in much the same way the director of photography is responsible for picture. This person will usually supervise both sound editing and RE-RECORDING.

SOUNDING The act of recording sound on a mag release print.

SOUND STAGE Large warehouse-like room where sets are built and films are shot. Not to be confused with a re-recording stage.

SOUNDTRACK The sound for a film. Should be used to refer to the CD or other release of the music that is sold to the public but should not be used to refer to the music in the film.

SPECIAL EFFECTS Awkward term often given to sound effects. "Special sound effects" is a useful description, though, for out-of-the-ordinary effects that have to be created.

SPECTRAL RECORDING The recording process introduced by Dolby Laboratories in 1986 that offers up to 24 dB of noise reduction (16 dB below 800 Hz). SR is more similar to C-Type noise reduction than it is to their previous professional format, A-Type, in that it uses sliding-band circuits. S-Type is the consumer version of SR and was introduced in 1990.

"SPEED" Word yelled by the production sound mixer when the production recorder is up to speed (indicated by "flags" on a Nagra), indicating to the camera crew and the assistant director that he or she is recording. While both Nagras and digital machines get up to speed quite quickly, the term derives from Hollywood technology in which a common motor system drove cameras and film sound recorders (originally optical, and later either 17.5mm or 35mm mag) and sometimes even turntables for music playback.

"SPLICE" Incorrect word used by many journalists to describe what picture or sound editors do when they *edit*. In other words, it is bad usage, just as it is incorrect to refer to what journalists do as typing instead of writing.

SPLIT SURROUNDS Also known as "stereo surrounds." The nickname of the Dolby 70mm format that gives two surround channels (left-rear and right-rear) on a mono-surround-compatible print. Also stands for the use of separate surround speakers in any sound format, such as IMAX or Showscan, both of which have two completely discrete surround tracks.

SPO The optimum viewing spot in a theater: always in the center (unless there's an aisle there!), and usually about halfway between the projection booth and the screen (this depends on the length-to-width ratio of the room). Spo first came into usage during the mix of *Apocalypse Now*. Among the more common variants are "spo meter," usually the Radio Shack Sound Level Meter (Cat. No.33-2050) used to measure SPL.

SPOACH To arrive early at a movie theater and get the best seats for you and your yet-to-arrive friends.

SPOT In film sound, the act of listing the sound effects or music required for a scene. Also, the general act of reviewing the film with the director to determine work that will be needed on the soundtrack. For example, spots for a car chase scene would be tire skids, auto accelerating, auto suspension bumps, etc. The next step is to audition and PULL specific skids, bumps, etc. from the sound library.

SR *See* SPECTRAL RECORDING.

SR•D The 35mm digital sound print format developed by DOLBY LABORATORIES and first used in June 1992. It places five full-range digital tracks and one LFE track on a 35mm print in addition to an SR analog stereo optical track. The digital recording format—theatrical or home—is more properly referred to as DOLBY DIGITAL.

"THE STAGE" The RE-RECORDING room and the people contained therein: "The stage has broken for lunch," or "This is a stage rush" (and must be transferred now so the sound editor can cut it ASAP).

STAGE SYNC How close in (or out of) sync the FOLEY or ADR is when it is recorded.

STEMS The three or more final components of a stereo film mix, usually comprising three LCRS mixes, one each of dialog, music and sound effects that, combined, make up the final mix of a film. Minimal (hopefully no) additional level changes, equalization, etc., should be needed to create a PRINT MASTER, although of course a 6-track print master will have different requirements than a 2-track stereo optical print master.

The separation of elements afforded by stems allows domestic (English-language in the U.S.) mono and M&E stereo and mono mixes to be easily derived from the original stereo mix. The word "stem" should not be used for any other element prior to the final mix masters; it is a common mistake to refer to the various PREMIXes as stems.

STRETCHED   A recording that has been processed through noise reduction encoding. A stretched transfer involves making a new recording of a stretched recording without decoding and then re-encoding the material. In this manner, a stretched transfer retains the original noise reduction encoding level. As a rule, it is recommended to *not* transfer stretched because any response error is multiplied by the compression ratio, typically 2:1, of the noise reduction system.

STRIPE   Short for "single stripe"; *see* MAG FILM.

STRING OFF   Copying off a track from a multitrack master, usually to single-stripe 35mm MAG FILM, in order to facilitate editing. Can be either a noun or a verb. *See* REGROUP and LAYBACK.

SUBWOOFER   Speaker designed specifically to reproduce low-frequency information, usually between the range of 20 to 120 Hz.

SUPER 35   Widescreen film format that makes use of the full width of the 35mm film frame (including the area normally occupied by the OPTICAL SOUNDTRACK). Therefore, there can never be any 35mm EK NEG prints from a Super 35 negative. An INTERPOSITIVE from the full-aperture original negative is enlarged to an ANAMORPHIC internegative when the aspect ratio is 2.40:1.

SUPERVISING SOUND EDITOR   The person in charge of the sound editorial process, including dialog, FOLEY and sound effects editing.

SURROUND CHANNEL   The single track that feeds multiple speakers usually placed on the walls of a theater. In standard practice it is used for ambient information only.

SVA   Stereo Variable Area. The technical term for the recording format of Dolby Stereo in optical 35mm prints. The term is not used much anymore.

SWEETEN To add a sound to other, previously existing (i.e., cut or mixed) sounds. ("We sweetened the car crash with some dumpster hits.") Should never be used in reference to mixing, although this usage is indeed common, especially in reference to television shows.

SWELLTONE The dubbing theater speaker system first used in 1991 for the film *Kafka*.

SYNC POP A single film frame of 1 kHz used as a guide to synchronize sound and picture. The pop on the resulting TRACK NEGATIVE creates a visual guide to the negative cutter, who uses it to make a printing start mark. The pop occurs two seconds before the first frame of picture, and thus corresponds to the "2" frame on the sweep-hand SMPTE Universal Leader, which counts down in seconds. On standard film leaders, the number at the pop is "3," because they count down in film footages.

TAP Theater Alignment Program. Beginning in 1983, Lucasfilm Ltd. began an organized process of inspecting selected (mostly 70mm in the early days) prints and theaters for their films and anyone who contracts their services.

TELECINE The process in which film is transferred to video. Telecine occurs at three points in the filmmaking process: 1) When film is transferred to video in preparation for editing on a nonlinear system. 2) When an edited WORKPRINT is transferred to video to give sound editors a guide with which to edit sound. 3) When an INTERPOSITIVE is transferred to a videotape to create a master for home video release.

TEMP DUB Quick mix of a film made during the post-production process, allowing the movie to be screened and evaluated in DOUBLE SYSTEM.

THUMPER A pure, low-frequency tone (around 30 Hz), triggered by a noise gate keyed to a click track. Used to give dancers the beat of a song while recording synchronous production sound, which can be used once the "thumper" track is filtered out.

THX Specifications for motion picture sound systems and home theater systems licensed by Lucasfilm Ltd. The only part of the theatrical system manufactured by Lucasfilm is the speaker crossover network; other parts, such as amplifiers and speakers, must be on the "approved" THX list. Installation procedures in a THX theater also must follow rigorous Lucasfilm specifications.

The name is a *double entendre,* partly being derived from the name of George Lucas' first feature film, *THX-1138,* and partly as an acronym standing for Tomlinson Holman's eXperiment, as he was the person responsible for the system design and philosophy.

To clear up a few misconceptions: THX has nothing to do with the recording of sound on a print, and therefore is not a competitor to DOLBY STEREO or any of the digital release formats. Films do not "play in THX," and there is no such thing as a "THX film." Also, it has nothing to do with whether or not the soundtrack has been edited or mixed by the staff of Lucasfilm Ltd. and its SKYWALKER SOUND facility.

TODD-AO a) The 70MM widescreen process developed by the promoter Mike Todd in association with the American Optical Company. b) The Hollywood-based film sound company.

TOP SHEET *See* BINKY.

TRACK NEGATIVE Standard laboratory terminology for the soundtrack negative. "Photographic sound" might be more by the book, though.

TROMBONE GOBBLE Classic sound effect used when Warner Bros. cartoon characters are hit in the head.

TURD POLISHING Colloquial film sound term for the futility of the work undertaken by mixers in trying to make bad tracks sound good.

TWO-POP *See* SYNC POP.

TYPE C PRINTER Industry-standard printer, originally manufactured by Bell & Howell, for the slow-speed (up to 180 feet per minute) manufacture of film prints.

ULTRA STEREO The stereo optical process designed to be compatible with standard A-TYPE DOLBY STEREO prints.

UNADVERTISED SPECIALS Sounds that appear on a track but whose presence is not noted by the CUE SHEET.

UNIT A single reel of edited MAG FILM, corresponding to a given picture reel. The unit can be made up of either single-stripe or fullcoat MAG FILM, and will almost always contain FILL LEADER in certain sections in order to maintain sync.

VOICE OF THE THEATER The theater speaker system developed in the 1940s by Altec Lansing Corp. for motion picture theaters, and the industry standard for 40 years until the introduction of direct-radiator speakers such as the JBL 4675 in the early '80s. (The basic horn-loaded design dates back to the '30s and speakers manufactured at MGM and The Bell Laboratories.) The product line included the single-cabinet A-7 and A-4, and the dual-cabinet A-2 for larger theaters. These speakers are no longer made.

VOICING *See* EQUALIZATION, 1/3-OCTAVE ROOM.

WALLA Film sound slang for the sound of a group of people talking. "Group walla" is when a number of actors will create background crowd sounds in a studio against edited picture.

WESTREX The sound company that, along with RCA, ruled over film sound for the first 40 years. Its equipment—which encompassed the whole chain from microphones, production recorders, re-recording consoles and machines to optical cameras—was leased to studios in exchange for royalty fees. By the mid-'70s most licenses were not being renewed with the coming of manufacturers of specialized gear: consoles (Quad-Eight), mag machines (Magna-Tech) and stereo processes (DOLBY LABORATORIES).

Licensees to Westrex equipment included Paramount Pictures, Twentieth Century-Fox, MGM, TODD-AO, and Universal Studios. RCA's domain included Republic, Warner Bros. and Walt Disney Pictures.

WIDE-RANGE CURVE/ WIDE-RANGE MONITORING *See* X CURVE.

WIG-WAG Hollywood slang for the lights outside SOUND STAGES to indicate when shooting is taking place.

WILD TRACK   A recording of dialog or sound effects on the set of a film but without the camera running. Wild tracks are frequently used to get a clean recording of dialog that was otherwise unobtainable because of the noise-production devices (e.g., wind machines) that have to be on during filming.

WORLDIZE   To re-record a track (usually music) in the space where it would naturally occur. This "worldized" track (or two) is then mixed together with the dry original.

WORKPRINT/WORKTRACK   Respectively, the edited sound and picture elements that the picture editor cuts together during editing. They both are invaluable because of the ACMADE edge numbers (placed by the editorial department on both sound and picture to guide in synchronization) and KEY NUMBERS (placed on the film negative by the manufacturer).

X-COPY   An exact copy of material. *See* 1:1.

X CURVE   Stands for "extended," as opposed to the "N" (normal) curve, which is the same as the ACADEMY CURVE. The "X" curve is also known as the "wide-range curve," and is codified in ISO Bulletin 2969. Specifications call for pink noise, at listening position in a re-recording situation or two-thirds of the way back in a theater, to be flat to 2 kHz, rolling off 3 dB per octave after that.

The "small-room X curve" is designed to be used in rooms with less than 150 cubic meters, or 5,300 cubic feet. This standard specifies flat response to 2 kHz, rolling off 1.5 dB per octave after that. Some people use a modified small-room curve, starting the roll-off at 4 kHz, with the response down 3 dB per octave thereafter.

X-TRACK   Portions of PRODUCTION TRACK that are split off into a separate UNIT (or separate track on a workstation) because they will be replaced by ADR.

ZIEGFELD   Large first-run movie theater in midtown Manhattan. This is the proper spelling; it is *not* the "Ziegfield."

Academy Award® Winners

Note: From the 1929/30 Awards through the 1957 Awards this category was called Sound Recording. From the 1929/30 Awards through the 1968 Awards, the award was given to the studio sound department and not to any individual(s). Beginning with the 1969 Awards, the award was given to the person(s) who actually recorded the sound. Nominees are included; winners are denoted by an asterisk.

1998

* SAVING PRIVATE RYAN: Ronald Judkins, Andy Nelson, Gary Rydstrom, Gary Summers
ARMAGEDDON: Kevin O'Connell, Greg P. Russell, Keith A. Wester
THE MASK OF ZORRO: Pud Cusack, Kevin O'Connell, Greg P. Russell
SHAKESPEARE IN LOVE: Peter Glossop, Dominic Lester, Robin O'Donoghue
THE THIN RED LINE: Anna Behlmer, Paul Brincat, Andy Nelson

1997

* TITANIC: Tom Johnson, Gary Rydstrom, Gary Summers, Mark Ulano
AIR FORCE ONE: D. M. Hemphill, Rick Kline, Paul Massey, Keith A. Wester
CON AIR: Kevin O'Connell, Arthur Rochester, Greg P. Russell
CONTACT- Tom Johnson, William B. Kaplan, Dennis Sands, Randy Thom
L.A. CONFIDENTIAL: Anna Behlmer, Kirk Francis, Andy Nelson

1996

* THE ENGLISH PATIENT: Mark Berger, Walter Murch, Chris Newman, David Parker
EVITA: Anna Behlmer, Andy Nelson, Ken Weston
INDEPENDENCE DAY: Bob Beemer, Bill W. Benton, Chris Carpenter, Jeff Wexler
THE ROCK: Kevin O'Connell, Greg P. Russell, Keith A. Wester
TWISTER: Gregg Landaker, Steve Maslow, Kevin O'Connell, Geoffrey Patterson

1995

* APOLLO 13: Rick Dior, David MacMillan, Scott Millan, Steve Pederson
BATMAN FOREVER: Michael Herbick, Petur Hliddal, Donald O. Mitchell, Frank A. Montaño
BRAVEHEART: Anna Behlmer, Scott Millan, Andy Nelson, Brian Simmons

CRIMSON TIDE: William B. Kaplan, Rick Kline, Kevin O'Connell,
Gregory H. Watkins

WATERWORLD: Gregg Landaker, Steve Maslow, Keith A. Wester

1994

* SPEED: Bob Beemer, Gregg Landaker, David R. B. MacMillan, Steve Maslow

CLEAR AND PRESENT DANGER: Michael Herbick, Donald O. Mitchell,
Frank A. Montaño, Arthur Rochester

FORREST GUMP: Tom Johnson, William B. Kaplan, Dennis Sands, Randy Thom

LEGENDS OF THE FALL: David Campbell, Christopher David, Douglas Ganton,
Paul Massey

THE SHAWSHANK REDEMPTION: Willie Burton, Michael Herbick, Robert J. Litt,
Elliot Tyson

1993

* JURASSIC PARK: Ron Judkins, Shawn Murphy, Gary Rydstrom, Gary Summers

CLIFFHANGER: Bob Beemer, Tim Cooney, Michael Minkler

THE FUGITIVE: Michael Herbick, Donald O. Mitchell, Frank A. Montaño,
Scott D. Smith

GERONIMO: AN AMERICAN LEGEND: Bill W. Benton, Chris Carpenter,
D. M. Hemphill, Lee Orloff

SCHINDLER'S LIST: Ron Judkins, Scott Millan, Andy Nelson, Steve Pederson

1992

* THE LAST OF THE MOHICANS: Doug Hemphill, Chris Jenkins, Simon Kaye, Mark
Smith

ALADDIN: David J. Hudson, Doc Kane, Mel Metcalfe, Terry Porter

A FEW GOOD MEN: Bob Eber, Rick Kline, Kevin O'Connell

UNDER SIEGE: Rick Hart, Don Mitchell, Frank A. Montaño, Scott Smith

UNFORGIVEN: Dick Alexander, Les Fresholtz, Vern Poore, Rob Young

1991

* TERMINATOR 2: JUDGMENT DAY: Tom Johnson, Lee Orloff, Gary Rydstrom,
Gary Summers

BACKDRAFT: Gary Rydstrom, Gary Summers, Randy Thom, Glenn Williams

BEAUTY AND THE BEAST: David J. Hudson, Doc Kane, Mel Metcalfe, Terry Porter

JFK: Gregg Landaker, Tod A. Maitland, Michael Minkler

THE SILENCE OF THE LAMBS: Tom Fleischman, Christopher Newman

1990

* DANCES WITH WOLVES: Bill W. Benton, Jeffrey Perkins, Greg Watkins,
    Russell Williams II
DAYS OF THUNDER: Rick Kline, Donald O. Mitchell, Kevin O'Connell,
    Charles Wilborn
DICK TRACY: David E. Campbell, Thomas Causey, D. M. Hemphill, Chris Jenkins
THE HUNT FOR RED OCTOBER: Don Bassman, Kevin F. Cleary,
    Richard Bryce Goodman, Richard Overton
TOTAL RECALL: Carlos de Larios, Michael J. Kohut, Aaron Rochin, Nelson Stoll

1989

* GLORY: Donald O. Mitchell, Gregg C. Rudloff, Elliot Tyson, Russell Williams II
THE ABYSS: Don Bassman, Kevin F. Cleary, Lee Orloff, Richard Overton
BLACK RAIN: Donald O. Mitchell, Kevin O'Connell, Greg P. Russell,
    Keith A. Wester
BORN ON THE FOURTH OF JULY: Tod A. Maitland, Michael Minkler,
    Wylie Stateman, Gregory H. Watkins
INDIANA JONES AND THE LAST CRUSADE: Ben Burtt, Tony Dawe,
    Shawn Murphy, Gary Summers

1988

* BIRD: Dick Alexander, Willie D. Burton, Les Fresholtz, Vern Poore
DIE HARD: Don Bassman, Kevin F. Cleary, Al Overton, Richard Overton
GORILLAS IN THE MIST: Peter Handford, Andy Nelson, Brian Saunders
MISSISSIPPI BURNING: Rick Kline, Robert Litt, Danny Michael, Elliot Tyson
WHO FRAMED ROGER RABBIT: John Boyd, Tony Dawe, Don Digirolamo,
    Robert Knudson

1987

* THE LAST EMPEROR: Bill Rowe, Ivan Sharrock
EMPIRE OF THE SUN: John Boyd, Tony Dawe, Don Digirolamo, Robert Knudson
LETHAL WEAPON: Dick Alexander, Les Fresholtz, Bill Nelson, Vern Poore
ROBOCOP: Carlos de Larios, Michael J. Kohut, Aaron Rochin, Robert Wald
THE WITCHES OF EASTWICK: Wayne Artman, Tom Beckert, Tom Dahl,
    Art Rochester

1986

* PLATOON: Charles "Bud" Grenzbach, Simon Kaye, Richard Rogers,
   John K. Wilkinson
ALIENS: Michael A. Carter, Roy Charman, Graham V. Hartstone,
   Nicolas Le Messurier
HEARTBREAK RIDGE: Dick Alexander, Les Fresholtz, William Nelson, Vern Poore
STAR TREK IV: THE VOYAGE HOME: Gene S. Cantamessa, Dave Hudson
TOP GUN: William B. Kaplan, Rick Kline, Donald O. Mitchell, Kevin O'Connell

1985

* OUT OF AFRICA: Gary Alexander, Peter Handford, Chris Jenkins, Larry
   Stensvold
BACK TO THE FUTURE: William B. Kaplan, B. Tennyson Sebastian II,
   Robert Thirlwell, Bill Varney
A CHORUS LINE: Gerry Humphreys, Michael Minkler, Donald O. Mitchell,
   Chris Newman
LADYHAWKE: Dick Alexander, Bud Alper, Les Fresholtz, Vern Poore
SILVERADO: Rick Kline, Donald O. Mitchell, Kevin O'Connell, David Ronne

1984

* AMADEUS: Mark Berger, Todd Boekelheide, Chris Newman, Tom Scott
2010: Gene S. Cantamessa, Carlos De Larios, Michael J. Kohut, Aaron Rochin
DUNE: Steve Maslow, Kevin O'Connell, Nelson Stoll, Bill Varney
A PASSAGE TO INDIA: Michael A. Carter, Graham V. Hartstone,
   Nicolas Le Messurier, John Mitchell
THE RIVER: Nick Alphin, Richard Portman, David Ronne, Robert Thirlwell

1983

* THE RIGHT STUFF: Mark Berger, David MacMillan, Tom Scott, Randy Thom
NEVER CRY WOLF: Todd Boekelheide, David Parker, Alan R. Splet, Randy Thom
RETURN OF THE JEDI: Ben Burtt, Tony Dawe, Gary Summers, Randy Thom
TERMS OF ENDEARMENT: Jim Alexander, Rick Kline, Donald O. Mitchell,
   Kevin O'Connell
WARGAMES: Willie D. Burton, Carlos de Larios, Michael J. Kohut, Aaron Rochin

1982

* E.T. THE EXTRA-TERRESTRIAL: Gene Cantamessa, Don Digirolamo,
   Robert Glass, Robert Knudson
DAS BOOT: Milan Bor, Mike Le-Mare, Trevor Pyke
GANDHI: Jonathan Bates, Gerry Humphreys, Simon Kaye, Robin O'Donoghue
TOOTSIE: Dick Alexander, Les Fresholtz, Les Lazarowitz, Arthur Piantadosi
TRON: Jim La Rue, Bob Minkler, Lee Minkler, Michael Minkler

1981

* RAIDERS OF THE LOST ARK: Roy Charman, Gregg Landaker, Steve Maslow,
Bill Varney

ON GOLDEN POND: Richard Portman, David Ronne

OUTLAND: Robert W. Glass, Jr., Robin Gregory, Robert M. Thirlwell,
John K. Wilkinson

PENNIES FROM HEAVEN: Jay M. Harding, Michael J. Kohut, Al Overton,
Richard Tyler

REDS: Tom Fleischman, Simon Kaye, Dick Vorisek

1980

* THE EMPIRE STRIKES BACK: Gregg Landaker, Steve Maslow, Peter Sutton,
Bill Varney

ALTERED STATES: Willie D. Burton, Les Fresholtz, Michael Minkler,
Arthur Piantadosi

COAL MINER'S DAUGHTER: Jim Alexander, Roger Heman, Richard Portman

FAME: Jay M. Harding, Michael J. Kohut, Chris Newman, Aaron Rochin

RAGING BULL: David J. Kimball, Les Lazarowitz, Donald O. Mitchell,
Bill Nicholson

1979

* APOCALYPSE NOW: Richard Beggs, Mark Berger, Nat Boxer, Walter Murch

1941: Gene S. Cantamessa, Robert J. Glass, Robert Knudson, Don MacDougall

THE ELECTRIC HORSEMAN: Les Fresholtz, Michael Minkler, Al Overton,
Arthur Piantadosi

METEOR: Michael J. Kohut, William McCaughey, Aaron Rochin, Jack Solomon

THE ROSE: Theodore Soderberg, Jim Webb, Paul Wells, Douglas Williams

1978

* THE DEER HUNTER: Darin Knight, William McCaughey, Richard Portman,
Aaron Rochin

THE BUDDY HOLLY STORY: Willie Burton, Joel Fein, Tex Rudloff, Curly Thirlwell

DAYS OF HEAVEN: Robert W. Glass, Jr., John T. Reitz, Barry Thomas,
John K. Wilkinson

HOOPER: Robert J. Glass, Robert Knudson, Don MacDougall, Jack Solomon

SUPERMAN: Roy Charman, Graham Hartstone, Nicolas Le Messurier, Gordon K.
McCallum

1977

* STAR WARS: Derek Ball, Don MacDougall, Bob Minkler, Ray West
CLOSE ENCOUNTERS OF THE THIRD KIND: Gene S. Cantamessa, Robert J. Glass,
        Robert Knudson, Don MacDougall
THE DEEP: Dick Alexander, Tom Beckert, Walter Goss, Robin Gregory
SORCERER: Jean-Louis Ducarme, Robert J. Glass, Robert Knudson, Richard Tyler
THE TURNING POINT: Jerry Jost, Theodore Soderberg, Paul Wells,
        Douglas O. Williams

1976

* ALL THE PRESIDENT'S MEN: Dick Alexander, Les Fresholtz, Arthur Piantadosi,
        Jim Webb
KING KONG: William McCaughey, Aaron Rochin, Jack Solomon,
        Harry Warren Tetrick
ROCKY: Bud Alper, Lyle Burbridge, William McCaughey, Harry Warren Tetrick
SILVER STREAK: Hal Etherington, Donald Mitchell, Richard Tyler,
        Douglas Williams
A STAR IS BORN: Robert Glass, Robert Knudson, Tom Overton, Dan Wallin

1975

* JAWS: John Carter, Roger Heman, Robert L. Hoyt, Earl Madery
BITE THE BULLET: Les Fresholtz, Al Overton, Jr., Arthur Piantadosi, Richard Tyler
FUNNY LADY: Don MacDougall, Richard Portman, Jack Solomon, Curly Thirlwell
THE HINDENBURG: John A. Bolger, Jr., John Mack, Leonard Peterson,
        Don K. Sharpless
THE WIND AND THE LION: Roy Charman, William McCaughey, Aaron Rochin,
        Harry W. Tetrick

1974

* EARTHQUAKE: Melvin Metcalfe, Sr., Ronald Pierce
CHINATOWN: Bud Grenzbach, Larry Jost
THE CONVERSATION: Walter Murch, Arthur Rochester
THE TOWERING INFERNO: Herman Lewis, Theodore Soderberg
YOUNG FRANKENSTEIN: Gene Cantamessa, Richard Portman

1973

* THE EXORCIST: Robert Knudson, Chris Newman
THE DAY OF THE DOLPHIN: Lawrence O. Jost, Richard Portman
THE PAPER CHASE: Lawrence O. Jost, Donald O. Mitchell
PAPER MOON: Les Fresholtz, Richard Portman
THE STING: Robert Bertrand, Ronald K. Pierce

1972

* CABARET: David Hildyard, Robert Knudson
BUTTERFLIES ARE FREE: Charles Knight, Arthur Piantadosi
THE CANDIDATE: Gene Cantamessa, Richard Portman
THE GODFATHER: Bud Grenzbach, Christopher Newman, Richard Portman
THE POSEIDON ADVENTURE: Herman Lewis, Theodore Soderberg

1971

* FIDDLER ON THE ROOF: David Hildyard, Gordon K. McCallum
DIAMONDS ARE FOREVER: Gordon K. McCallum, John Mitchell,
    Alfred J. Overton [Sr.]
THE FRENCH CONNECTION: Christopher Newman, Theodore Soderberg
KOTCH: Richard Portman, Jack Solomon
MARY, QUEEN OF SCOTS: John Aldred, Bob Jones

1970

* PATTON: Don Bassman, Douglas Williams
AIRPORT: David Moriarty, Ronald Pierce
RYAN'S DAUGHTER: John Bramall, Gordon K. McCallum
TORA! TORA! TORA!: Herman Lewis, Murray Spivack
WOODSTOCK: Larry Johnson, Dan Wallin

1969

* HELLO, DOLLY!: Jack Solomon, Murray Spivack
ANNE OF THE THOUSAND DAYS: John Aldred
BUTCH CASSIDY AND THE SUNDANCE KID: David Dockendorf,
    William Edmundson
GAILY, GAILY: Robert Martin, Clem Portman
MAROONED: Les Fresholtz, Arthur Piantadosi

1968

* OLIVER!: Shepperton Studio Sound Department
BULLITT: Warner Bros.-Seven Arts Studio Sound Department
FINIAN'S RAINBOW: Warner Bros.-Seven Arts Studio Sound Department
FUNNY GIRL: Columbia Studio Sound Department
STAR!: 20th Century-Fox Studio Sound Department

1967

* IN THE HEAT OF THE NIGHT: Samuel Goldwyn Studio Sound Department
CAMELOT: Seven Arts Studio Sound Department
THE DIRTY DOZEN: Metro-Goldwyn-Mayer Studio Sound Department

DOCTOR DOLITTLE: 20th Century-Fox Studio Sound Department
THOROUGHLY MODERN MILLIE: Universal City Studio Sound Department

1966

* GRAND PRIX: Metro-Goldwyn-Mayer Studio Sound Department,
    Franklin E. Milton, Sound Director
GAMBIT: Universal City Studio Sound Department, Waldon O. Watson,
    Sound Director
HAWAII: Samuel Goldwyn Studio Sound Department, Gordon E. Sawyer,
    Sound Director
THE SAND PEBBLES: 20th Century-Fox Studio Sound Department,
    James P. Corcoran, Sound Director
WHO'S AFRAID OF VIRGINIA WOOLF?: Warner Bros. Studio Sound Department,
    George R. Groves, Sound Director

1965

* THE SOUND OF MUSIC: Todd-AO Sound Department, Fred Hynes,
    Sound Director, 20th Century-Fox Studio Sound Department,
    James P. Corcoran, Sound Director
THE AGONY AND THE ECSTASY: 20th Century-Fox Studio Sound Department,
    James P. Corcoran, Sound Director
DOCTOR ZHIVAGO: Metro-Goldwyn-Mayer British Studio Sound Department,
    A. W. Watkins, Sound Director, Metro-Goldwyn-Mayer Studio Sound
    Department, Franklin E. Milton, Sound Director
THE GREAT RACE: Warner Bros. Studio Sound Department, George R. Groves,
    Sound Director
SHENANDOAH: Universal City Studio Sound Department, Waldon O. Watson,
    Sound Director

1964

* MY FAIR LADY: Warner Bros. Studio Sound Department, George R. Groves,
    Sound Director
BECKET: Shepperton Studio Sound Department, John Cox, Sound Director
FATHER GOOSE: Universal City Studio Sound Department, Waldon O. Watson,
    Sound Director
MARY POPPINS: Walt Disney Studio Sound Department, Robert O. Cook,
    Sound Director
THE UNSINKABLE MOLLY BROWN: Metro-Goldwyn-Mayer Studio Sound
    Department, Franklin E. Milton, Sound Director

1963

* HOW THE WEST WAS WON: Metro-Goldwyn-Mayer Studio Sound Department,
    Franklin E. Milton, Sound Director
BYE BYE BIRDIE: Columbia Studio Sound Department, Charles Rice,
    Sound Director
CAPTAIN NEWMAN, M.D.: Universal City Studio Sound Department,
    Waldon O. Watson, Sound Director
CLEOPATRA (1963): Todd-AO Sound Department, Fred Hynes, Sound Director,
    20th Century-Fox Studio Sound Department, James P. Corcoran,
    Sound Director
IT'S A MAD, MAD, MAD, MAD WORLD: Samuel Goldwyn Studio Sound
Department, Gordon E. Sawyer, Sound Director

1962

* LAWRENCE OF ARABIA: Shepperton Studio Sound Department,
    John Cox, Sound Director
BON VOYAGE!: Walt Disney Studio Sound Department, Robert O. Cook,
    Sound Director
MEREDITH WILLSON'S THE MUSIC MAN: Warner Bros. Studio Sound
    Department, George R. Groves, Sound Director
THAT TOUCH OF MINK: Universal City Studio Sound Department,
    Waldon O. Watson, Sound Director
WHAT EVER HAPPENED TO BABY JANE?: Glen Glenn Sound Department, Joseph
    Kelly, Sound Director

1961

* WEST SIDE STORY: Samuel Goldwyn Studio Sound Department,
    Gordon E. Sawyer, Sound Director, Todd-AO Sound Department,
    Fred Hynes, Sound Director
THE CHILDREN'S HOUR: Samuel Goldwyn Studio Sound Department,
    Gordon E. Sawyer, Sound Director
FLOWER DRUM SONG: Revue Studio Sound Department, Waldon O. Watson,
    Sound Director
THE GUNS OF NAVARONE: Shepperton Studio Sound Department, John Cox,
    Sound Director
THE PARENT TRAP: Walt Disney Studio Sound Department, Robert O. Cook,
    Sound Director

1960

* THE ALAMO: Samuel Goldwyn Studio Sound Department, Gordon E. Sawyer,
    Sound Director, Todd-AO Sound Department, Fred Hynes, Sound Director
THE APARTMENT: Samuel Goldwyn Studio Sound Department,
    Gordon E. Sawyer, Sound Director

CIMARRON (1960): Metro-Goldwyn-Mayer Studio Sound Department,
   Franklin E. Milton, Sound Director
PEPE: Columbia Studio Sound Department, Charles Rice, Sound Director
SUNRISE AT CAMPOBELLO: Warner Bros. Studio Sound Department,
   George R. Groves, Sound Director

1959

* BEN-HUR: Metro-Goldwyn-Mayer Studio Sound Department, Franklin E. Milton,
   Sound Director
JOURNEY TO THE CENTER OF THE EARTH: 20th Century-Fox Studio Sound
   Department, Carl Faulkner, Sound Director
LIBEL!: Metro-Goldwyn-Mayer London Studio Sound Department, A. W. Watkins,
   Sound Director
THE NUN'S STORY: Warner Bros. Studio Sound Department, George R. Groves,
   Sound Director
PORGY AND BESS: Samuel Goldwyn Studio Sound Department,
   Gordon E. Sawyer, Sound Director, Todd-AO Sound Department,
   Fred Hynes, Sound Director

1958

* SOUTH PACIFIC: Todd-AO Sound Department, Fred Hynes, Sound Director
I WANT TO LIVE!: Samuel Goldwyn Studio Sound Department,
   Gordon E. Sawyer, Sound Director
A TIME TO LOVE AND A TIME TO DIE: Universal-International Studio Sound
   Department, Leslie I. Carey, Sound Director
VERTIGO: Paramount Studio Sound Department, George Dutton, Sound Director
THE YOUNG LIONS: 20th Century-Fox Studio Sound Department, Carl Faulkner,
   Sound Director

1957

* SAYONARA: Warner Bros. Studio Sound Department, George Groves,
   Sound Director
GUNFIGHT AT THE O.K. CORRAL: Paramount Studio Sound Department,
   George Dutton, Sound Director
LES GIRLS: Metro-Goldwyn-Mayer Studio Sound Department,
   Dr. Wesley C. Miller, Sound Director
PAL JOEY: Columbia Studio Sound Department, John P. Livadary, Sound Director
WITNESS FOR THE PROSECUTION: Samuel Goldwyn Studio Sound Department,
   Gordon E. Sawyer, Sound Director

1956

* THE KING AND I: 20th Century-Fox Studio Sound Department, Carl Faulkner, Sound Director

THE BRAVE ONE: King Bros. Productions, Inc., Sound Department, John Myers, Sound Director

THE EDDY DUCHIN STORY: Columbia Studio Sound Department, John Livadary, Sound Director

FRIENDLY PERSUASION: Samuel Goldwyn Studio Sound Department, Gordon Sawyer, Sound Director, Westrex Sound Services, Inc., Gordon R. Glennan, Sound Director

THE TEN COMMANDMENTS: Paramount Studio Sound Department, Loren L. Ryder, Sound Director

1955

* OKLAHOMA!: Todd-AO Sound Department, Fred Hynes, Sound Director

LOVE IS A MANY-SPLENDORED THING: 20th Century-Fox Studio Sound Department, Carl W. Faulkner, Sound Director

LOVE ME OR LEAVE ME: Metro-Goldwyn-Mayer Studio Sound Department, Wesley C. Miller, Sound Director

MISTER ROBERTS: Warner Bros. Studio Sound Department, William A. Mueller, Sound Director

NOT AS A STRANGER: Radio Corporation of America Sound Department, Watson Jones, Sound Director

1954

* THE GLENN MILLER STORY: Universal-International Studio Sound Department, Leslie I. Carey, Sound Director

BRIGADOON: Metro-Goldwyn-Mayer Studio Sound Department, Wesley C. Miller, Sound Director

THE CAINE MUTINY: Columbia Studio Sound Department, John P. Livadary, Sound Director

REAR WINDOW: Paramount Studio Sound Department, Loren L. Ryder, Sound Director

SUSAN SLEPT HERE: RKO Radio Studio Sound Department, John O. Aalberg, Sound Director

1953

* FROM HERE TO ETERNITY: Columbia Studio Sound Department,
    John P. Livadary, Sound Director
CALAMITY JANE: Warner Bros. Studio Sound Department, William A. Mueller,
    Sound Director
KNIGHTS OF THE ROUND TABLE: Metro-Goldwyn-Mayer Studio Sound
    Department, A. W. Watkins, Sound Director
THE MISSISSIPPI GAMBLER: Universal-International Studio Sound Department,
    Leslie I. Carey, Sound Director
THE WAR OF THE WORLDS: Paramount Studio Sound Department,
    Loren L. Ryder, Sound Director

1952

* BREAKING THE SOUND BARRIER: London Film Sound Department
HANS CHRISTIAN ANDERSEN: Samuel Goldwyn Studio Sound Department,
    Gordon Sawyer, Sound Director
THE PROMOTER: Pinewood Studios Sound Department
THE QUIET MAN: Republic Studio Sound Department, Daniel J. Bloomberg,
    Sound Director
WITH A SONG IN MY HEART: 20th Century-Fox Studio Sound Department,
    Thomas T. Moulton, Sound Director

1951

* THE GREAT CARUSO: Metro-Goldwyn-Mayer Studio Sound Department,
    Douglas Shearer, Sound Director
BRIGHT VICTORY: Universal-International Studio Sound Department,
    Leslie I. Carey, Sound Director
I WANT YOU: Samuel Goldwyn Studio Sound Department, Gordon Sawyer, Sound
    Director
A STREETCAR NAMED DESIRE: Warner Bros. Studio Sound Department,
    Col. Nathan Levinson, Sound Director
TWO TICKETS TO BROADWAY: RKO Radio Studio Sound Department,
    John O. Aalberg, Sound Director

1950

* ALL ABOUT EVE: 20th Century-Fox Studio Sound Department,
    Thomas T. Moulton, Sound Director

CINDERELLA: Walt Disney Studio Sound Department, C. O. Slyfield,
    Sound Director

LOUISA: Universal-International Studio Sound Department, Leslie I. Carey,
    Sound Director

OUR VERY OWN: Samuel Goldwyn Studio Sound Department, Gordon Sawyer,
    Sound Director

TRIO: Pinewood Studio Sound Department, Cyril Crowhurst, Sound Director

1949

* TWELVE O'CLOCK HIGH: 20th Century-Fox Studio Sound Department,
    Thomas T. Moulton, Sound Director

ONCE MORE, MY DARLING: Universal-International Studio Sound Department,
    Leslie I. Carey, Sound Director

SANDS OF IWO JIMA: Republic Studio Sound Department, Daniel J. Bloomberg,
    Sound Director

1948

* THE SNAKE PIT: 20th Century-Fox Studio Sound Department,
    Thomas T. Moulton, Sound Director

JOHNNY BELINDA: Warner Bros. Studio Sound Department,
    Col. Nathan O. Levinson, Sound Director

MOONRISE: Republic Studio Sound Department, Daniel J. Bloomberg,
    Sound Director

1947

* THE BISHOP'S WIFE: Samuel Goldwyn Studio Sound Department,
    Gordon Sawyer, Sound Director

GREEN DOLPHIN STREET: Metro-Goldwyn-Mayer Studio Sound Department,
    Douglas Shearer, Sound Director

T-MEN: Sound Service, Inc., Jack R. Whitney, Sound Director

1946

* JOLSON STORY: Columbia Studio Sound Department, John Livadary,
    Sound Director

THE BEST YEARS OF OUR LIVES: Samuel Goldwyn Studio Sound Department,
    Gordon Sawyer, Sound Director

IT'S A WONDERFUL LIFE: RKO Radio Studio Sound Department, John Aalberg,
    Sound Director

1945

* THE BELLS OF ST. MARY'S: RKO Radio Studio Sound Department, Stephen Dunn, Sound Director

FLAME OF BARBARY COAST: Republic Studio Sound Department, Daniel J. Bloomberg, Sound Director

LADY ON A TRAIN: Universal Studio Sound Department, Bernard B. Brown, Sound Director

LEAVE HER TO HEAVEN: 20th Century-Fox Studio Sound Department, Thomas T. Moulton, Sound Director

RHAPSODY IN BLUE: Warner Bros. Studio Sound Department, Nathan Levinson, Sound Director

A SONG TO REMEMBER: Columbia Studio Sound Department, John P. Livadary, Sound Director

THE SOUTHERNER: General Service, Jack Whitney, Sound Director

THEY WERE EXPENDABLE: Metro-Goldwyn-Mayer Studio Sound Department, Douglas Shearer, Sound Director

THE THREE CABALLEROS: Walt Disney Studio Sound Department, C. O. Slyfield, Sound Director

THREE IS A FAMILY: RCA Sound, W. V. Wolfe, Sound Director

THE UNSEEN: Paramount Studio Sound Department, Loren L. Ryder, Sound Director

WONDER MAN: Samuel Goldwyn Studio Sound Department, Gordon Sawyer, Sound Director

1944

* WILSON: 20th Century-Fox Studio Sound Department, E. H. Hansen, Sound Director

BRAZIL (1944): Republic Studio Sound Department, Daniel J. Bloomberg, Sound Director

CASANOVA BROWN: Samuel Goldwyn Studio Sound Department, Thomas T. Moulton, Sound Director

COVER GIRL: Columbia Studio Sound Department, John Livadary, Sound Director

DOUBLE INDEMNITY: Paramount Studio Sound Department, Loren L. Ryder, Sound Director

HIS BUTLER'S SISTER: Universal Studio Sound Department, Bernard B. Brown, Sound Director

HOLLYWOOD CANTEEN: Warner Bros. Studio Sound Department, Nathan Levinson, Sound Director

IT HAPPENED TOMORROW: Sound Service, Inc., Jack Whitney, Sound Director

KISMET: Metro-Goldwyn-Mayer Studio Sound Department, Douglas Shearer, Sound Director

MUSIC IN MANHATTAN: RKO Radio Studio Sound Department, Stephen Dunn, Sound Director

VOICE IN THE WIND: RCA Sound, W. M. Dalgleish, Sound Director

1943

*THIS LAND IS MINE: RKO Radio Studio Sound Department, Stephen Dunn, Sound Director

HANGMEN ALSO DIE: Sound Service, Inc., Jack Whitney, Sound Director

IN OLD OKLAHOMA: Republic Studio Sound Department, Daniel J. Bloomberg, Sound Director

MADAME CURIE: Metro-Goldwyn-Mayer Studio Sound Department, Douglas Shearer, Sound Director

THE NORTH STAR: Samuel Goldwyn Studio Sound Department, Thomas T. Moulton, Sound Director

PHANTOM OF THE OPERA: Universal Studio Sound Department, Bernard B. Brown, Sound Director

RIDING HIGH: Paramount Studio Sound Department, Loren L. Ryder, Sound Director

SAHARA: Columbia Studio Sound Department, John Livadary, Sound Director

SALUDOS AMIGOS: Walt Disney Studio Sound Department, C. O. Slyfield, Sound Director

SO THIS IS WASHINGTON: RCA Sound, J. L. Fields, Sound Director

THE SONG OF BERNADETTE: 20th Century-Fox Studio Sound Department, E. H. Hansen, Sound Director

THIS IS THE ARMY: Warner Bros. Studio Sound Department, Nathan Levinson, Sound Director

1942

*YANKEE DOODLE DANDY: Warner Bros. Studio Sound Department, Nathan Levinson, Sound Director

ARABIAN NIGHTS: Universal Studio Sound Department, Bernard B. Brown, Sound Director

BAMBI: Walt Disney Studio Sound Department, Sam Slyfield, Sound Director

FLYING TIGERS: Republic Studio Sound Department, Daniel Bloomberg, Sound Director

FRIENDLY ENEMIES: Sound Service, Inc., Jack Whitney, Sound Director

THE GOLD RUSH: RCA Sound, James Fields, Sound Director

MRS. MINIVER: Metro-Goldwyn-Mayer Studio Sound Department, Douglas Shearer, Sound Director

ONCE UPON A HONEYMOON: RKO Radio Studio Sound Department, Steve Dunn, Sound Director

THE PRIDE OF THE YANKEES: Samuel Goldwyn Studio Sound Department, Thomas T. Moulton, Sound Director

ROAD TO MOROCCO: Paramount Studio Sound Department, Loren Ryder, Sound Director

THIS ABOVE ALL: 20th Century-Fox Studio Sound Department, E. H. Hansen, Sound Director

YOU WERE NEVER LOVELIER: Columbia Studio Sound Department, John Livadary, Sound Director

1941

* THAT HAMILTON WOMAN: General Service Sound Department, Jack Whitney, Sound Director

APPOINTMENT FOR LOVE: Universal Studio Sound Department, Bernard B. Brown, Sound Director

BALL OF FIRE: Samuel Goldwyn Studio Sound Department, Thomas T. Moulton, Sound Director

THE CHOCOLATE SOLDIER: Metro-Goldwyn-Mayer Studio Sound Department, Douglas Shearer, Sound Director

CITIZEN KANE: RKO Radio Studio Sound Department, John Aalberg, Sound Director

THE DEVIL PAYS OFF: Republic Studio Sound Department, Charles Lootens, Sound Director

HOW GREEN WAS MY VALLEY: 20th Century-Fox Studio Sound Department, E. H. Hansen, Sound Director

THE MEN IN HER LIFE: Columbia Studio Sound Department, John Livadary, Sound Director

SERGEANT YORK: Warner Bros. Studio Sound Department, Nathan Levinson, Sound Director

SKYLARK: Paramount Studio Sound Department, Loren Ryder, Sound Director

TOPPER RETURNS: Hal Roach Studio Sound Department, Elmer Raguse, Sound Director

1940

* STRIKE UP THE BAND: Metro-Goldwyn-Mayer Studio Sound Department, Douglas Shearer, Sound Director

BEHIND THE NEWS: Republic Studio Sound Department, Charles L. Lootens, Sound Director

CAPTAIN CAUTION: Hal Roach Studio Sound Department, Elmer A. Raguse, Sound Director

THE GRAPES OF WRATH: 20th Century-Fox Studio Sound Department, E. H. Hansen, Sound Director

THE HOWARDS OF VIRGINIA: General Service Sound Department, Jack Whitney, Sound Director

KITTY FOYLE: RKO Radio Studio Sound Department, John Aalberg, Sound Director

NORTH WEST MOUNTED POLICE: Paramount Studio Sound Department, Loren L. Ryder, Sound Director

OUR TOWN: Samuel Goldwyn Studio Sound Department, Thomas T. Moulton, Sound Director

THE SEA HAWK: Warner Bros. Studio Sound Department, Nathan Levinson, Sound Director

SPRING PARADE: Universal Studio Sound Department, Bernard B. Brown, Sound Director

TOO MANY HUSBANDS: Columbia Studio Sound Department, John Livadary, Sound Director

1939

* WHEN TOMORROW COMES: Universal Studio Sound Department,
    Bernard B. Brown, Sound Director

BALALAIKA: Metro-Goldwyn-Mayer Studio Sound Department, Douglas Shearer,
    Sound Director

GONE WITH THE WIND: Samuel Goldwyn Studio Sound Department,
    Thomas T. Moulton, Sound Director

GOODBYE, MR. CHIPS (1939): Denham Studio Sound Department,
    A. W. Watkins, Sound Director

THE GREAT VICTOR HERBERT: Paramount Studio Sound Department,
    Loren L. Ryder, Sound Director

THE HUNCHBACK OF NOTRE DAME (1939): RKO Radio Studio Sound
    Department, John Aalberg, Sound Director

MAN OF CONQUEST: Republic Studio Sound Department, Charles L. Lootens,
    Sound Director

MR. SMITH GOES TO WASHINGTON: Columbia Studio Sound Department,
    John Livadary, Sound Director

OF MICE AND MEN: Hal Roach Studio Sound Department, Elmer A. Raguse,
    Sound Director

THE PRIVATE LIVES OF ELIZABETH AND ESSEX: Warner Bros. Studio Sound
    Department, Nathan Levinson, Sound Director

THE RAINS CAME: 20th Century-Fox Studio Sound Department, E. H. Hansen,
    Sound Director

1938

* THE COWBOY AND THE LADY: United Artists Studio Sound Department, Thomas
    T. Moulton, Sound Director

ARMY GIRL: Republic Studio Sound Department, Charles L. Lootens,
    Sound Director

FOUR DAUGHTERS: Warner Bros. Studio Sound Department, Nathan Levinson,
    Sound Director

IF I WERE KING: Paramount Studio Sound Department, Loren L. Ryder,
    Sound Director

MERRILY WE LIVE: Hal Roach Studio Sound Department, Elmer A. Raguse,
    Sound Director

SUEZ: 20th Century-Fox Studio Sound Department, Edmund H. Hansen,
    Sound Director

SWEETHEARTS: Metro-Goldwyn-Mayer Studio Sound Department,
    Douglas Shearer, Sound Director

THAT CERTAIN AGE: Universal Studio Sound Department, Bernard B. Brown,
    Sound Director

VIVACIOUS LADY: RKO Radio Studio Sound Department, John Aalberg,
    Sound Director

YOU CAN'T TAKE IT WITH YOU: Columbia Studio Sound Department,
    John Livadary, Sound Director

1937

* THE HURRICANE: United Artists Studio Sound Department, Thomas T. Moulton,
    Sound Director

THE GIRL SAID NO: Grand National Studio Sound Department, A. E. Kaye,
    Sound Director

HITTING A NEW HIGH: RKO Radio Studio Sound Department, John Aalberg,
    Sound Director

IN OLD CHICAGO: 20th Century-Fox Studio Sound Department, E. H. Hansen,
    Sound Director

THE LIFE OF EMILE ZOLA: Warner Bros. Studio Sound Department,
    Nathan Levinson, Sound Director

LOST HORIZON: Columbia Studio Sound Department, John Livadary,
    Sound Director

MAYTIME: Metro-Goldwyn-Mayer Studio Sound Department, Douglas Shearer,
    Sound Director

ONE HUNDRED MEN AND A GIRL: Universal Studio Sound Department,
    Homer G. Tasker, Sound Director

TOPPER: Hal Roach Studio Sound Department, Elmer A. Raguse, Sound Director

WELLS FARGO: Paramount Studio Sound Department, Loren L. Ryder,
    Sound Director

1936

* SAN FRANCISCO: Metro-Goldwyn-Mayer Studio Sound Department,
    Douglas Shearer, Sound Director

BANJO ON MY KNEE: 20th Century-Fox Studio Sound Department, E. H. Hansen,
    Sound Director

THE CHARGE OF THE LIGHT BRIGADE: Warner Bros. Studio Sound Department,
    Nathan Levinson, Sound Director

DODSWORTH: United Artists Studio Sound Department, Thomas T. Moulton,
    Sound Director

GENERAL SPANKY: Hal Roach Studio Sound Department, Elmer A. Raguse,
    Sound Director

MR. DEEDS GOES TO TOWN: Columbia Studio Sound Department,
    John Livadary, Sound Director

THE TEXAS RANGERS: Paramount Studio Sound Department,
    Franklin B. Hansen, Sound Director

THAT GIRL FROM PARIS: RKO Radio Studio Sound Department, J. O. Aalberg,
    Sound Director

THREE SMART GIRLS: Universal Studio Sound Department, Homer G. Tasker,
    Sound Director

1935

* NAUGHTY MARIETTA: Metro-Goldwyn-Mayer Studio Sound Department,
Douglas Shearer, Sound Director

$1,000 A MINUTE: Republic Studio Sound Department

BRIDE OF FRANKENSTEIN: Universal Studio Sound Department, Gilbert Kurland,
Sound Director

CAPTAIN BLOOD: Warner Bros.-First National Studio Sound Department,
Nathan Levinson, Sound Director

THE DARK ANGEL: United Artists Studio Sound Department, Thomas T. Moulton,
Sound Director

I DREAM TOO MUCH: RKO Radio Studio Sound Department, Carl Dreher,
Sound Director

THE LIVES OF A BENGAL LANCER: Paramount Studio Sound Department,
Franklin B. Hansen, Sound Director

LOVE ME FOREVER: Columbia Studio Sound Department, John Livadary,
Sound Director

THANKS A MILLION: 20th Century-Fox Studio Sound Department, E. H. Hansen,
Sound Director

1934

* ONE NIGHT OF LOVE: Columbia Studio Sound Department, John Livadary,
Sound Director

THE AFFAIRS OF CELLINI: United Artists Studio Sound Department,
Thomas T. Moulton, Sound Director

CLEOPATRA (1934): Paramount Studio Sound Department, Franklin B. Hansen,
Sound Director

FLIRTATION WALK: Warner Bros.-First National Studio Sound Department, Nathan
Levinson, Sound Director

THE GAY DIVORCEE: RKO Radio Studio Sound Department, Carl Dreher,
Sound Director

IMITATION OF LIFE (1934): Universal Studio Sound Department,
Theodore Soderberg, Sound Director

VIVA VILLA!: Metro-Goldwyn-Mayer Studio Sound Department, Douglas Shearer,
Sound Director

THE WHITE PARADE: Fox Studio Sound Department, E. H. Hansen,
Sound Director

1932/33

* A FAREWELL TO ARMS: Paramount Studio Sound Department,
    Franklin B. Hansen, Sound Director

42ND STREET: Warner Bros. Studio Sound Department, Nathan Levinson,
    Sound Director

GOLD DIGGERS OF 1933: Warner Bros. Studio Sound Department,
    Nathan Levinson, Sound Director

I AM A FUGITIVE FROM A CHAIN GANG: Warner Bros. Studio Sound Department,
    Nathan Levinson, Sound Director

1931/32

Metro-Goldwyn-Mayer Studio Sound Department, Paramount Publix Studio
    Sound Department, RKO Radio Studio Sound Department, Warner Bros.-
    First National Studio Sound Department

1930/31

Samuel Goldwyn: United Artists Studio Sound Department, Metro-Goldwyn-
    Mayer Studio Sound Department, Paramount Publix Studio Sound
    Department, RKO Radio Studio Sound Department

1929/30

* THE BIG HOUSE: Metro-Goldwyn-Mayer Studio Sound Department,
    Douglas Shearer, Sound Director

THE CASE OF SERGEANT GRISCHA: RKO Radio Studio Sound Department,
    John Tribby, Sound Director

THE LOVE PARADE: Paramount Famous Lasky Studio Sound Department, Franklin
    Hansen, Sound Director

RAFFLES: United Artists Studio Sound Department, Oscar Lagerstrom,
    Sound Director

SONG OF THE FLAME: First National Studio Sound Department, George Groves,
    Sound Director

Note: From the 1963 Awards to the 1975 Awards, this category was known as "Sound Effects." For the 1979 Awards, the category was known as "Sound Editing." For the 1964 Awards through the 1967 Awards, this category was listed as an "Other" Award, and not necessarily given each year. From the 1975 Awards to the present, this category could also be given as a "Special Achievement Award" or not necessarily given in a particular year.

1998
* SAVING PRIVATE RYAN: Richard Hymns, Gary Rydstrom
ARMAGEDDON: George Watters II
THE MASK OF ZORRO: David McMoyler

1997
* TITANIC: Tom Bellfort, Christopher Boyes
FACE/OFF: Per Hallberg, Mark P. Stoeckinger
THE FIFTH ELEMENT: Mark Mangini

1996
* THE GHOST AND THE DARKNESS: Bruce Stambler
DAYLIGHT: Richard L. Anderson, David A. Whittaker
ERASER: Bub Asman, Alan Robert Murray

1995
* BRAVEHEART: Lon Bender, Per Hallberg
BATMAN FOREVER: John Leveque, Bruce Stambler
CRIMSON TIDE: George Watters II

1994
*SPEED: Stephen Hunter Flick
CLEAR AND PRESENT DANGER: John Leveque, Bruce Stambler
FORREST GUMP: Gloria S. Borders, Randy Thom

1993
* JURASSIC PARK: Richard Hymns, Gary Rydstrom
CLIFFHANGER: Gregg Baxter, Wylie Stateman
THE FUGITIVE: John Leveque, Bruce Stambler

1992

* BRAM STOKER'S DRACULA: Tom C. McCarthy, David E. Stone
ALADDIN: Mark Mangini
UNDER SIEGE: John Leveque, Bruce Stambler

1991

* TERMINATOR 2: JUDGMENT DAY: Gloria S. Borders, Gary Rydstrom
BACKDRAFT: Richard Hymns, Gary Rydstrom
STAR TREK VI THE UNDISCOVERED COUNTRY: F. Hudson Miller, George Watters II

1990

* THE HUNT FOR RED OCTOBER: Cecelia Hall, George Watters II
FLATLINERS: Charles L. Campbell, Richard Franklin
TOTAL RECALL: Stephen H. Flick

1989

* INDIANA JONES AND THE LAST CRUSADE: Ben Burtt, Richard Hymns
BLACK RAIN: Milton C. Burrow, William L. Manger
LETHAL WEAPON 2: Robert Henderson, Alan Robert Murray

1988

* WHO FRAMED ROGER RABBIT: Charles L. Campbell, Louis L. Edemann
DIE HARD: Stephen H. Flick, Richard Shorr
WILLOW: Ben Burtt, Richard Hymns

1987

(SPECIAL ACHIEVEMENT AWARD, Sound Effects Editing)
ROBOCOP: Stephen Flick, John Pospisil

1986

* ALIENS: Don Sharpe
STAR TREK IV: THE VOYAGE HOME: Mark Mangini
TOP GUN: Cecelia Hall, George Watters II

1985

* BACK TO THE FUTURE: Charles L. Campbell, Robert Rutledge
LADYHAWKE: Bob Henderson, Alan Murray
RAMBO: FIRST BLOOD PART II: Frederick J. Brown

1984
(SPECIAL ACHIEVEMENT AWARD, Sound Effects Editing)
THE RIVER: Kay Rose

1983
* THE RIGHT STUFF: Jay Boekelheide
RETURN OF THE JEDI: Ben Burtt

1982
* E.T. THE EXTRA-TERRESTRIAL: Ben Burtt, Charles L. Campbell
DAS BOOT: Mike Le-Mare
POLTERGEIST: Richard L. Anderson, Stephen Hunter Flick

1981
(SPECIAL ACHIEVEMENT AWARD, Sound Effects Editing)
RAIDERS OF THE LOST ARK: Richard L. Anderson, Ben Burtt

1979
(SPECIAL ACHIEVEMENT AWARD, Sound Editing)
THE BLACK STALLION: Alan Splet

1977
(SPECIAL ACHIEVEMENT AWARD, Sound Effects Editing)
CLOSE ENCOUNTERS OF THE THIRD KIND: Frank E. Warner

1975
(SPECIAL ACHIEVEMENT AWARD, Sound Effects)
THE HINDENBURG: Peter Berkos

1967
(SOUND EFFECTS)
* THE DIRTY DOZEN: John Poyner
IN THE HEAT OF THE NIGHT: James A. Richard

1966
(SOUND EFFECTS)
* GRAND PRIX: Gordon Daniel
FANTASTIC VOYAGE: Walter Rossi

1965

(SOUND EFFECTS)

* THE GREAT RACE: Tregoweth Brown

VON RYAN'S EXPRESS: Walter A. Rossi

1964

(SOUND EFFECTS)

* GOLDFINGER: Norman Wanstall

THE LIVELY SET: Robert L. Bratton

1963

(SOUND EFFECTS)

* IT'S A MAD, MAD, MAD, MAD WORLD: Walter G. Elliott

A GATHERING OF EAGLES: Robert L. Bratton

Lists courtesy of the Academy of Motion Picture Arts and Sciences.®